A Potful

of Recipes

ALSO BY JOANNA M. LUND

The Arthritis Healthy Exchanges Cookbook
The Best of Healthy Exchanges Food Newsletter '92 Cookbook
The Cancer Recovery Healthy Exchanges Cookbook
Cooking Healthy Across America
Cooking Healthy with a Man in Mind
Cooking Healthy with the Kids in Mind
Dessert Every Night!
The Diabetic's Healthy Exchanges Cookbook
The Heart Smart Healthy Exchanges Cookbook
The Healthy Exchanges Cookbook
HELP: The Healthy Exchanges Lifetime Plan
It's Not a Diet, It's a Way of Life (audiotape)
Letters from the Heart
Make a Joyful Table
Notes of Encouragement
String of Pearls
The Strong Bones Healthy Exchanges Cookbook

A Potful

of Recipes

A HEALTHY EXCHANGES® COOKBOOK

JoAnna M. Lund
with Barbara Alpert

A Perigee Book

A Perigee Book
Published by The Berkley Publishing Group
A division of Penguin Putnam Inc.
375 Hudson Street
New York, New York 10014

For more information about Healthy Exchanges products, contact:
Healthy Exchanges, Inc.
P.O. Box 80
DeWitt, Iowa 52742-0080
(563) 659-8234

First edition: January 2001

Published simultaneously in Canada.

Visit our website at
www.penguinputnam.com

Library of Congress Cataloging-in-Publication Data
Lund, JoAnna M.
    A potful of recipes / JoAnna M. Lund, with Barbara Alpert.
        p. cm.
    ISBN 0-399-52650-1
        1. Electric cookery, Slow. I. Alpert, Barbara. II. Title.

TX827 .L86 2001
641.5'884—dc21   00-049206

Printed in the United States of America
20   19   18   17   16   15   14   13   12

This book is dedicated in loving memory to my parents, Jerome and Agnes McAndrews. If I hadn't inherited their earthly talents, I wouldn't have been able to create my "common folk" healthy recipes—after all, it's a blending of my father's analytical talents and my mother's creative abilities that allows my mind to taste the dish before my mouth ever does!

From the very first cookbook I ever wrote back in 1992 to this one, I've always shared one of my mother's beautiful poems in my dedication. Many people have told me that this makes my books that much more special for them. I know that pleases my parents in Heaven every bit as much as it pleases me here on Earth.

As the slow cooker truly saves us time in the kitchen, it's wise for us to put that savings to good use. This poem of my mother's speaks to that very subject.

The Clock of Life

Life
    is like one fleeting hour—
    here for sixty precious minutes.
Each second fills the heart
    with sunshine, joy and even bitter pain
    which we cherish unto the end.
When the clock strikes,
    the hour at last has come and with strained ears
So like our lives
    then all is silent—
    as only the Master can determine the time.

—Agnes Carrington McAndrews

Contents

Acknowledgments

Just as it takes many ingredients stirred in the pot to ensure a good stew, many people helped me create this cookbook. For helping "flavor the project just right," I want to thank:

Cliff Lund—my husband, my business partner, and my "official" taste tester

Barbara Alpert—my writing partner and my friend

Shirley Morrow, Rita Ahlers, and Connie Schultz—my helpers with typing, testing, and dish washing

Angela Miller and Coleen O'Shea—my agents and my private cheerleaders

John Duff—my editor and my visionary facilitator

God—my creator and my savior.

Living in the Fast Lane—and Deciding to Slow Down

This particular cookbook has come along at an interesting time in my life and, I hope, in yours as well. Like so many Americans, I spent most of the 1990s moving through my days at top speed. I kept looking for new ways to grow my business and to share my message about healthy living.

For most of our marriage, it had been my husband, Cliff, who put in thousands of miles a year as he drove his big rig from one end of the country to the other for his job. But over the past few years, I began accumulating an astonishing number of miles myself, touring to promote my cookbooks, appearing on QVC regularly, and speaking to groups in just about every state in the union except Alaska and Hawaii!

I loved what I was doing, but I was exhausted by it. I had chosen to be that busy, and I was proud of what I had accomplished. But I began to realize the price I was paying for zipping down life's highway at breakneck speed. And I decided that I wasn't willing to pay it anymore.

So I made some changes in my life that surprised many people who knew me. Instead of trying to do everything I could think of, I chose what was really important to me, and I focused my energy only in those directions. In some ways it was a scary step to take, but I felt with every ounce of my being that it was the right one. Now, as we're more than a year into the new century, I've learned that my impulse to put my

1

foot on the brake has been good for my family, my marriage, and yes, even my work.

I want you to know that I planned quite a few years ago to write a cookbook devoted to delicious healthy recipes for the slow cooker, and I planned to do it in the year 2000, after I'd completed so many others. Now I understand better than I did before that while we may outline the way we expect our lives to unfold, God's hand is everywhere in how those plans come to pass. I've never been more ready to share this message than I am now—that even those of us who have been deeply committed to living in the fast lane have the capacity, and even the mission, to decide to slow down and take stock of our lives.

I want this cookbook to help you pause in your headlong pursuit of success and fulfillment. For me, it goes so much deeper than just offering you helpful hints for cooking healthy. This book also carries a kind of soft-spoken message—that time is precious, that we can't satisfy every demand on us, and that life is enriched by choosing to do what matters most.

Your Slow Cooker As a Way to Nurture Yourself

Is there an aging slow cooker gathering dust in the garage or basement of your house? This handy household timesaver was hailed years ago as the appliance that would get women out of the kitchen and into the world, where they could follow their dreams of professional accomplishment instead of being stuck for hours preparing family meals. Most of us bought them, and some of us used them for a while.

But after a few months or perhaps years, they were pushed aside by the next new thing. People worried that they didn't heat food thoroughly enough to prevent food poisoning, or they feared that leaving a pot cooking even on a low flame while they were out could be a fire hazard. I suspect a lot of people couldn't figure out what to cook in them or how to adapt favorite recipes for slow cooking.

In any case, slow cooker cookery soon went from being hot-hot-hot to being considered old-hat and out-of-date!

Well, don't they say that everything that goes around comes around again? It certainly seems to be true in fashion, where designers have recently been doing their best to revive some styles from the 1960s and 1970s (ugh!).

The good news on the slow cooker front is that there are terrific new models of this appliance that respond to all those early concerns— they are safer, heat their contents more thoroughly, retain their heat for longer periods, and offer some new options for cooking more than one recipe at a time.

So, there's no better time to start cooking long and slow than right now!

Why Slow Down?

The food-related reasons for using a slow cooker are pretty simple:

- Dinner cooks while you're at work or school.

- Instead of having to watch the pot, you're free to do something else.

- Low-fat cooking is easier than ever, since long, slow cooking tenderizes meats and allows flavors to develop fully.

- Slow cookers save money on fuel, they don't heat up the kitchen in summer, and they're great for keeping food warm at a buffet.

There. I hope I've convinced you of the culinary reasons for changing the way you prepare meals, at least some of the time.

Now, let's talk about the other reasons I've discovered for slowing down. While we were testing recipes for this book, so many ideas came to me that I wanted to share them with you, too.

It's rare in our lives that someone else says, "Go and do whatever your heart desires for the next six hours." It's extremely unusual for us to be handed a chunk of time that has no schedule attached to it.

Oh, we take vacations, but they're often scheduled quite fully—10 A.M., breakfast with family; 11 A.M., pack the car for the beach; 12 noon, put up the umbrella, lay out the towels, put sunblock on the kids, locate everyone's boogie board and flippers. . . . You get the picture, right?

What I'm talking about is time for YOU. Maybe some of it isn't available because you've got work and errands and projects you need to work on. But I hope that while using these slow cooker recipes, you'll find a way to carve out a piece of time that you can use any way you wish.

De-Stress, Slow Down, Simplify

One of the most common causes of stress is the feeling that you don't have enough time to do what you need to do *and* what you want to do. You know the sensation—your chest tightens, your forehead wrinkles, your muscles tense—and if it happens often enough, your good health is likely to be compromised.

So let's start there, first with the recognition that wanting and needing more time is a legitimate concern, and second, that even when we sometimes get it, we don't put it to good use. I'm not suggesting that you trade one overcrowded schedule for another full of "things to do with your spare time"—well, not exactly. It's the pressure I want to alleviate, the "ought-to's" I want to help you banish where you can.

There was a Broadway show years ago called *Stop the World, I Want to Get Off.* Do you ever feel that way, that you're trapped in a house or office that just keeps spinning out of control? I know I've felt that way, and I'm certain most of my readers have at one time or another, too. But the title of the show implies an "either-or" proposition—much like dieting. You're either *on* or you're *off*—the world or the diet. That's a pretty extreme view, and not exactly a healthy or helpful one. Instead of jumping off the world or the nearest cliff (or out a window!) when stress becomes too difficult to handle, it makes more sense to analyze what's gotten you to that point—and what you can do about it.

Slow Down.
Think about the pace at which you live your life. Are you always racing from one appointment to another, always late, always breathless and furious because you're so rushed? Are there ways you can put on the brakes a bit—by allowing more time to get somewhere, by not scheduling yourself so tightly, by not being the most helpful person on your block when it comes to carpooling, PTA bake sales, or organizing the company softball team? I know, I know, you like the feeling of being the hero who steps in whenever needed, but living with what a friend of mine called "an overabundance of the helpful gene" can be exhausting.

It can also steal precious time from activities and interests that could be more satisfying. So perhaps one inspiration you might take from your slow cooker is the option to make some small changes to create a less frenetic existence.

Simplify.
This suggestion is so timely that there are whole magazines currently devoted to leading a simpler life. Books and articles urge us to divest our homes of too much stuff, liberate our lives from too many commitments, empty our closets and cabinets of what we no longer use. But that's a project in itself, and perhaps one you feel you don't have time for. Well, why not simplify your simplifying by choosing the tiniest segment of a project you can imagine? This afternoon, clean *one* shelf of the refrigerator or *one* shelf of a kitchen cabinet. Or decide to fill *one* plastic garbage bag with broken and useless toys from your child's room. Just one bag, now, and then you have to stop and sip some lemonade. The trick with simplifying is not to complicate the process by feeling you must complete it all in one weekend. The truth is, simplifying is a lifelong process, because what you value—what you choose to keep while eliminating other items—is likely to change over time.

Let Go.
Again, this is related to the first two ideas, with the end result being fewer commitments that overstuff your free time. Grab your handy calendar (or Filofax or PalmPilot, if you are so inclined) and try to take an objective look at the past two weeks of your life. Each day is likely crammed with a "To Do" list that bulges at the seams (not unlike those size 28 slacks did when I finally decided to commit to living healthy once and for all!). Think over what you did in that fourteen day period. What did you enjoy most? What gave you the most satisfaction? What (if anything) was relaxing or soothing? And what was incredibly frustrating? What felt like a waste of energy and time? What did you wish while you were doing it that you didn't have to?

Now, what can you learn from this examination? Let's take the energy drainers first: is there some way to ensure you never have to do them again? Maybe it's time to surrender the presidency of your block association to someone else, even if no one can do it as well as you do. Maybe you're ready to accept that your long-term friendship with a high school classmate has pretty much petered out and should be limited to five-year class reunions. And maybe, just maybe, you need to relinquish some chores to your spouse or kids for a change.

Say No.

It's one of the hardest words we ever say, and most of us find it easier to agree to something we don't really want to do than defend our right not to do it! But saying no (and meaning it) is a survival technique worth learning, and now is a great time to practice. Start with something small—a colleague invites you to have lunch with the gang, but you really want to go for a walk during lunch. Say no, but leave the door open for another time so she knows you're not rejecting her, just this single invitation. You can also practice saying "no" to yourself. When that little voice inside you says, "The bathroom floor looks a little grungy. Maybe I should mop it before leaving for work," look at yourself in the mirror (slightly grungy or not) and say, "No, not now. Maybe later." Practice may not make perfect, as the old adage suggested, but it definitely makes it easier to say what you really feel. Then when bigger issues arise, your lips will have an easier time forming the word.

Okay, so now we've cleared your schedule and worked on silencing the guilty conscience that prods you into thinking that all "free" time isn't really free and never will be! What can and will you do with those liberated minutes, hours, even days? I've got a few ideas and maybe one or more will be just right for you.

Communicate.

Letter writing may be a lost art now that e-mail has become the favorite form of communication for everyone from age 5 to 95. I have a sort of love-hate relationship with it myself. When I love it, it's because someone has used this electronic mailbox to share feelings and experiences with me, touched me in some way from across the miles. So even when I'm feeling tense about having to read through piles of mail after a trip, I try to remember how the best e-mail make me feel—and I hope to feel that again. Is there someone—a friend from long ago, an older relative you rarely get a chance to visit with—who would be pleased to hear from you, by letter, e-mail, or phone? By choosing to spend some of your newly free time on this, instead of "squeezing" it into a rushed note or call as usual, you may be delighted at how good "making the connection" can make you feel.

Keep a Journal.

Not the weight-loss kind, though that is certainly a useful tool for many of us. Instead, many people truly enjoy the journey of self-discovery that begins when they start to confide their thoughts on paper, for no one's eyes but their own. Expressing feelings too long bottled up can be wonderfully energizing; allowing yourself the time to explore how you feel about aspects of your life or friendships is an opportunity for real personal growth. Spend some time choosing the notebook and even the pen you're going to use to write your deepest thoughts and feelings, so that the time you choose to spend on this is even happier.

Learn Something New.

Have you always dreamed of going to Italy but young children and a tight budget make it seem as if "someday" might just as well be never? Why not carve out a piece of that fantasy and enjoy a taste of it—in this case, by borrowing language tapes from the library, by making one evening a week "Italian Night" at your supper table, by renting every Fellini movie you can find at your local video store—or even ordering one over the Internet? If you feel that you're in a rut of some kind, learning something new is the best medicine. It makes you feel young, it opens doors and windows to new worlds, it stimulates your brain and your senses, and it invites a world of possibilities into your life. I know that some adults worry about their ability to acquire knowledge as easily as they did when they were young, but here's the great thing: because you are choosing to educate yourself, you can learn at your own pace. In most cases, you aren't being graded and there are no exams to pass (unless, of course, you choose to take a college course for credit—which requires a bit of courage but pays terrific rewards if you dare!). If you can't travel the world, bring it home a piece at a time by reading, studying, exploring, and expanding your limitations.

Get Fit.

I heard that groan, but the fact remains that moderate exercise is good for us, and making time for fitness activities you enjoy is a wonderful way to use your newly liberated time out of the kitchen. One woman said to me, "Oh, but I hate exercise, I always have." I said to her, "Did you ever like any of it—swimming or dancing or jumping rope as a kid?" She admitted that she'd loved to swim as a child, but for most of her adult years she'd had long hair that took forever to dry. "But I recently cut it shorter," she added. "And there's a community pool only two blocks from my house. Maybe it's time to get back in the water."

Psychologists tell us that our brains hear the negative comments we make and then "program" us to make them true. So when you say, "I hate exercise," your brain will do its best to squelch any effort on your part to incorporate exercise into your life. But if you say, "I like how I feel when I work out—I just don't do it often enough," you leave the door open. The brain hears a positive message, that fitness feels good, and so when you hear a tiny voice saying, "There's time for a walk while dinner is cooking," you're more likely to listen to it.

Give exercising a real chance, and devote some time to finding something you truly enjoy: Walking with a friend. Bicycling with your kids. Putting on a pair of Rollerblades, skating around the neighborhood, and not acting your age at all. Swimming the breast stroke. Learning how to do the mambo (just like in *Dirty Dancing!*). And, one of my personal favorites, gardening to your heart's content. Fitness activities you're more inclined to do regularly and throughout your life are a powerful prescription for good health. But unlike orders from your doctors, you get to select what you want to "take."

Create.

When we were in school, art and music classes were loads of fun for the talented, but frustrating and even humiliating for anyone who couldn't draw well or figure out the fingering on the piano. Most of us recognized that our talents lay elsewhere and put away the paints and the instruments forever.

But the desire to create—and the pleasure it brings—has nothing to do with talent as teachers and critics judge. Creativity is about expression, and we all can benefit from experiencing the freedom of allowing yourself to play with art, music, writing, and other creative pursuits. If you liked what Demi Moore was doing at the potter's wheel in *Ghost*, go for it. There's probably a pottery-making class at your high school or YWCA. If you never really got over giving up your finger paints, why not buy some inexpensive tubes of paint, a brush or two, and a pad, and just explore what you can do? No one needs to see what you paint or sculpt. You can pick up a secondhand guitar and hide out in the basement trying to make like the Dixie Chicks if you like. The important thing is how free and fun making music and art can feel!

I've always expressed my creativity in my cooking and my writing, but I also used to sew and design clothes for myself and others. I gave it up for years when working on Healthy Exchanges took up so much time, but recently I've made a little time for sewing again—and I love how it makes me feel.

Be a Friend and Volunteer.

It may be hard to believe that you can feel less stressed and overburdened by taking on someone else's needs, but it's often true that helping others makes you feel better about your own life. If you don't have children of your own, perhaps offering to baby-sit regularly for a neighbor's kids will benefit you *and* their mother—you'll develop a relationship with young people and share in their lives, while at the same time, you'll be offering an escape valve to someone with twenty-four-hour-a-day responsibilities for children that can be overwhelming much of the time.

Perhaps your own parents have passed away and you miss the presence of elders in your life. By making regular calls or visits to someone you know, or by asking to be "hooked up" with a senior who needs people contact in his or her life, you will realize wonderful rewards while providing much-needed emotional support. I saw a poster recently that reminded us that loneliness can be just as devastating as an illness like cancer or AIDS. By reaching out, you both give and receive comfort, more than you ever expected.

Commune with Nature.

Take your binoculars to the park and listen for bird calls. Plant a Victorian-style garden that you learned about in a favorite book. Put on your sneakers and hike up a nearby hill. Feed the fish with a group of preschoolers at the town pond. Breathe the air, feast your eyes and ears, enjoy the beauties of the world that God created. And leave your watch at home (if you can, of course)!

Express Your Faith.

Religious observance is a personal choice, but some people, if given the time, would choose to devote themselves more completely to their relationship with the Lord. For a devout Catholic, that might mean deciding to attend daily mass instead of only on Sundays. Or it might be assisting the priest by bringing Communion to homebound members of the parish. Others might want to focus on faith by teaching Sunday school, or by giving time to social action projects of your church or synagogue that benefit the homeless or new immigrants. If you would like to participate more fully in your faith through self-education or by doing good works, this is your time!

Preserve Your Memories.

One of the most beautiful and satisfying ways to use your free time is by sharing and saving your family's heritage for your children and grandchildren. For some of us, this might mean organizing boxes of old photos and labeling and captioning them to identify friends and family members. For others, it might be creating a family genealogy or writing the story of how your ancestors got here and built new lives. One of my readers told me about setting out to interview all four of her great-aunts so that their memories of their lives could be passed down to their many grandnieces and nephews. Scrapbooking has become so popular that there are now magazines devoted to this craft. If you have envied the family albums of friends and relatives, there's no better way to spend some time than by getting to know the juicy details of a really good story: YOURS.

Finally, I hope you'll use your time to **Dream.** We need to focus our energies and discover what we'd most want to do *if only we had the time.* Well, I've tried to give you back some of the time in this collection of slow cooker recipes. But it's up to you to decide how that time will be spent. Let yourself fantasize as wildly and fully as you like, and I believe that a wonderful clarity will come. It's only by giving voice to your dreams that you can make them come true, and only by being willing to look deep inside yourself can you discover what matters most.

Dear Friends,

People often ask me why I include the same general information at the beginning of all my cookbooks. If you've seen any of my other books you'll know that my "common folk" recipes are just one part of the Healthy Exchanges picture. You know that I firmly believe—and say so whenever and wherever I can—that *Healthy Exchanges is not a diet, it's a way of life!* That's why I include the story of Healthy Exchanges in every book, because I know that the tale of my struggle to lose weight and regain my health is one that speaks to the hearts of many thousands of people. And because Healthy Exchanges is not just a collection of recipes, I always include the wisdom that I've learned from my own experiences and the knowledge of the health and cooking professionals I meet. Whether it's learning about nutrition or making shopping and cooking easier, no Healthy Exchanges book would be complete without features like "A Peek into My Pantry" or "JoAnna's Ten Commandments of Successful Cooking."

Even if you've read my other books, you might still want to skim the following chapters—you never know when I'll slip in a new bit of wisdom or suggest a new product that will make your journey to health an easier and tastier one. If you're sharing this book with a friend or family member, you'll want to make sure they read the following pages before they start stirring up the recipes.

If this is the first book of mine that you've read, I want to welcome you with all my heart to the Healthy Exchanges Family. (And, of course, I'd love to hear your comments or questions. See the back of the book for my mailing address.)

JoAnna

JoAnna M. Lund

and Healthy

Exchanges

ood is the first invited guest to every special occasion in every family's memory scrapbook. From baptism to graduation, from bar mitzvahs to anniversaries, and from weddings to wakes, food brings us together.

It wasn't always that way at our house. I used to eat alone, even when my family was there, because while they were dining on real food, I was nibbling at whatever my newest diet called for. In fact, for twenty-eight years, I called myself the diet queen of DeWitt, Iowa.

I tried every diet I ever came across, every one I could afford, and every one that found its way to my small town in eastern Iowa. I was willing to try anything that promised to "melt off the pounds," determined to deprive my body in every possible way in order to become thin at last.

I sent away for expensive "miracle" diet pills. I starved myself on the Cambridge Diet and the Bahama Diet. I gobbled diet candies, took thyroid pills, fiber pills, prescription and over-the-counter diet pills. I went to endless weight-loss support group meetings—but I somehow managed to turn healthy programs such as Overeaters Anonymous, Weight Watchers, and TOPS into unhealthy diets . . . diets I could never follow for more than a few months.

I was determined to discover something that worked long-term, but each new failure increased my desperation that I'd never find it.

I ate strange concoctions and rubbed on even stranger potions. I tried liquid diets. I agreed to be hypnotized. I tried reflexology and even had an acupressure device stuck in my ear!

Does my story sound a lot like yours? I'm not surprised. No wonder the weight-loss business is a billion-dollar industry!

Every new thing I tried seemed to work—at least at first. And losing that first five or ten pounds would get me so excited, I'd believe that this new miracle diet would, finally, get my weight off for keeps.

Inevitably, though, the initial excitement wore off. The diet's routine and boredom set in, and I quit. I shoved the pills to the back of the medicine chest; pushed the cans of powdered shake mix to the rear of the kitchen cabinets; slid all the program materials out of sight under my bed; and once more I felt like a failure.

Like most dieters, I quickly gained back the weight I'd lost each time, along with a few extra "souvenir" pounds that seemed always to settle around my hips. I'd done the diet-lose-weight-gain-it-all-back "yo-yo" on the average of once a year. It's no exaggeration to say that over the years I've lost 1,000 pounds—and gained back 1,150 pounds.

Finally, at the age of forty-six, I weighed more than I'd ever imagined possible. I'd stopped believing that any diet could work for me. I drowned my sorrows in sacks of cake donuts and wondered if I'd live long enough to watch my grandchildren grow up.

Something had to change.

I had to change.

Finally, I did.

I'm over fifty now—and I weigh 130 pounds less than my all-time high of close to 300 pounds. I've kept the weight off for more than seven years. I'd like to lose another ten pounds, but I'm not obsessed about it. If it takes me two or three years to accomplish it, that's okay.

What I *do* care about is never saying hello again to any of those unwanted pounds I said good-bye to!

How did I jump off the roller coaster I was on? For one thing, I finally stopped looking to food to solve my emotional problems. But what really shook me up—and got me started on the path that changed my life—was Operation Desert Storm in early 1991. I sent three children off to the Persian Gulf War—my son-in-law Matt, a medic in Special Forces; my daughter Becky, a full-time college student and member of a medical unit in the Army Reserve; and my son James, a member of the Inactive Army Reserve reactivated as a chemicals expert.

Somehow, knowing that my children were putting their lives on the line got me thinking about my own mortality—and I knew in my heart the last thing they needed while they were overseas was to get a letter from home saying that their mother was ill because of a food-related problem.

The day I drove the third child to the airport to leave for Saudi Arabia, something happened to me that would change my life for the better—and forever. I stopped praying my constant prayer as a professional dieter, which was simply "Please, God, let me lose ten pounds by Friday." Instead, I began praying, "God, please help me not to be a burden to my kids and my family." I quit praying for what I wanted and started praying for what I needed—and in the process my prayers were answered. I couldn't keep the kids safe—that was out of my hands—but I could try to get healthier to better handle the stress. It was the least I could do on the homefront.

That quiet prayer was the beginning of the new JoAnna Lund. My initial goal was not to lose weight or create healthy recipes. I only wanted to become healthier for my kids, my husband, and myself.

Each of my children returned safely from the Persian Gulf War. But something didn't come back—the 130 extra pounds I'd been lugging around for far too long. I'd finally accepted the truth after all those agonizing years of suffering through on-again, off-again dieting.

There are no "magic" cures in life.

No "miracle" potion, pill, or diet will make unwanted pounds disappear.

I found something better than magic, if you can believe it. When I turned my weight and health dilemma over to God for guidance, a new JoAnna Lund and Healthy Exchanges were born.

I discovered a new way to live my life and uncovered an unexpected talent for creating easy "common folk" healthy recipes and sharing my commonsense approach to healthy living. I learned that I could motivate others to change their lives and adopt a positive outlook. I began publishing cookbooks and a monthly food newsletter and speaking to groups all over the country.

I like to say, *"When life handed me a lemon, not only did I make healthy, tasty lemonade, I wrote the recipe down!"*

What I finally found was not a quick fix or a short-term diet, but a great way to live well for a lifetime.

I want to share it with you.

Food Exchanges and Weight Loss Choices™

If you've ever been on one of the national weight-loss programs like Weight Watchers or Diet Center, you've already been introduced to the concept of measured portions of the different food groups that make up your daily food plan. If you are not familiar with such a system of weight-loss choices or exchanges, here's a brief explanation. (If you want or need more detailed information, you can write to the American Dietetic Association or the American Diabetes Association for comprehensive explanations.)

The idea of food exchanges is to divide foods into basic food groups. The foods in each group are measured in servings that have comparable values. These groups include Proteins/Meats, Breads/Starches, Vegetables, Fats, Fruits, Skim Milk, Free Foods, and Optional Calories.

Each choice or exchange included in a particular group has about the same number of calories and a similar carbohydrate, protein, and fat content as the other foods in that group. Because any food on a particular list can be "exchanged" for any other food in that group, it makes sense to call the food groups *exchanges* or *choices*.

I like to think we are also "exchanging" bad habits and food choices for good ones!

By using Weight Loss Choices or exchanges you can choose from a variety of foods without having to calculate the nutrient value of each one. This makes it easier to include a wide variety of foods in your daily menus and gives you the opportunity to tailor your choices to your unique appetite.

If you want to lose weight, you should consult your physician or other weight-control expert regarding the number of servings that would be best for you from each food group. Since men generally require more calories than women, and since the requirements for growing children and teenagers differ from those of adults, the right number of exchanges for any one person is a personal decision.

I have included a suggested plan of weight-loss choices in the pages following the exchange lists. It's a program I used to lose 130 pounds, and it's the one I still follow today.

(If you are a diabetic or have been diagnosed with heart problems, it is best to meet with your physician before using this or any other food program or recipe collection.)

Food Group Weight Loss Choices/ Exchanges

Not all food group exchanges are alike. The ones that follow are for anyone who's interested in weight loss or maintenance. If you are a diabetic, you should check with your health-care provider or dietitian to get the information you need to help you plan your diet. Diabetic exchanges are calculated by the American Diabetic Association, and information about them is provided in *The Diabetic's Healthy Exchanges Cookbook* (Perigee Books).

Every Healthy Exchanges recipe provides calculations in three ways:

- Weight Loss Choices/Exchanges

- Calories, Fat, Protein, Carbohydrates, and Fiber in grams, and Sodium and Calcium in milligrams

- Diabetic Exchanges calculated for me by a registered dietitian

Healthy Exchanges recipes can help you eat well and recover your health, whatever your health concerns may be. Please take a few minutes to review the exchange lists and the suggestions that follow on how to count them. You have lots of great eating in store for you!

Proteins

Meat, poultry, seafood, eggs, cheese, and legumes. One exchange of Protein is approximately 60 calories. Examples of one Protein choice or exchange:

> 1 ounce cooked weight of lean meat, poultry, or seafood
> 2 ounces white fish
> 1½ ounces 97% fat-free ham
> 1 egg (limit to no more than 4 per week)
> ¼ cup egg substitute
> 3 egg whites
> ¾ ounce reduced-fat cheese
> ½ cup fat-free cottage cheese
> 2 ounces cooked or ¾ ounce uncooked dry beans
> 1 tablespoon peanut butter (also count 1 fat exchange)

Breads

Breads, crackers, cereals, grains, and starchy vegetables. One exchange of Bread is approximately 80 calories. Examples of one Bread choice or exchange:

> 1 slice bread or 2 slices reduced-calorie bread (40 calories or less)
> 1 roll, any type (1 ounce)
> ½ cup cooked pasta or ¾ ounce uncooked (scant ½ cup)
> ½ cup cooked rice or 1 ounce uncooked (⅓ cup)
> 3 tablespoons flour
> ¾ ounce cold cereal
> ½ cup cooked hot cereal or ¾ ounce uncooked (2 tablespoons)
> ½ cup corn (kernels or cream-style) or peas
> 4 ounces white potato, cooked, or 5 ounces uncooked
> 3 ounces sweet potato, cooked, or 4 ounces uncooked

3 cups air-popped popcorn
7 fat-free crackers (¾ ounce)
3 (2½-inch squares) graham crackers
2 (¾-ounce) rice cakes or 6 mini
1 tortilla, any type (6-inch diameter)

Fruits

All fruits and fruit juices. One exchange of Fruit is approximately 60 calories. Examples of one Fruit choice or exchange:

1 small apple or ½ cup slices
1 small orange
½ medium banana
¾ cup berries (except strawberries and cranberries)
1 cup strawberries or cranberries
½ cup canned fruit, packed in fruit juice or rinsed well
2 tablespoons raisins
1 tablespoon spreadable fruit spread
½ cup apple juice (4 fluid ounces)
½ cup orange juice (4 fluid ounces)
½ cup applesauce

Skim Milk

Milk, buttermilk, and yogurt. One exchange of Skim Milk is approximately 90 calories. Examples of one Skim Milk choice or exchange:

1 cup skim milk
½ cup evaporated skim milk
1 cup low-fat buttermilk
¾ cup plain fat-free yogurt
⅓ cup nonfat dry milk powder

Vegetables

All fresh, canned, or frozen vegetables other than the starchy vegetables. One exchange of Vegetable is approximately 30 calories. Examples of one Vegetable choice or exchange:

>*½ cup vegetable*
>*¼ cup tomato sauce*
>*1 medium fresh tomato*
>*½ cup vegetable juice*
>*1 cup shredded lettuce or cabbage*

Fats

Margarine, mayonnaise, vegetable oils, salad dressings, olives, and nuts. One exchange of Fat is approximately 40 calories. Examples of one Fat choice or exchange:

>*1 teaspoon margarine or 2 teaspoons reduced-calorie margarine*
>*1 teaspoon butter*
>*1 teaspoon vegetable oil*
>*1 teaspoon mayonnaise or 2 teaspoons reduced-calorie mayonnaise*
>*1 teaspoon peanut butter*
>*1 ounce olives*
>*¼ ounce pecans or walnuts*

Free Foods

Foods that do not provide nutritional value but are used to enhance the taste of foods are included in the Free Foods group. Examples of these are spices, herbs, extracts, vinegar, lemon juice, mustard, Worcestershire sauce, and soy sauce. Cooking sprays and artificial sweeteners used in moderation are also included in this group. However, you'll see that I include the caloric value of artificial sweeteners in the Optional Calories of the recipes.

You may occasionally see a recipe that lists "free food" as part of the portion. According to the published exchange lists, a free food contains fewer than 20 calories per serving. Two or three servings per day of free foods/drinks are usually allowed in a meal plan.

Optional Calories

Foods that do not fit into any other group but are used in moderation in recipes are included in Optional Calories. Foods that are counted in this way include sugar-free gelatin and puddings, fat-free mayonnaise and dressings, reduced-calorie whipped toppings, reduced-calorie syrups and jams, chocolate chips, coconut, and canned broth.

Sliders™

These are 80 Optional Calorie increments that do not fit into any particular category. You can choose which food group to *slide* these into. It is wise to limit this selection to approximately three to four per day to ensure the best possible nutrition for your body while still enjoying an occasional treat.

Sliders may be used in either of the following ways:

1. If you have consumed all your Protein, Bread, Fruit, or Skim Milk Weight Loss Choices for the day and you want to eat additional foods from those food groups, you simply use a Slider. It's what I call "healthy horse trading." Remember that Sliders may not be traded for choices in the Vegetables or Fats food groups.

2. Sliders may also be deducted from your Optional Calories for the day or week. One-quarter Slider equals 20 Optional Calories; ½ Slider equals 40 Optional Calories; ¾ Slider equals 60 Optional Calories; and 1 Slider equals 80 Optional Calories.

Healthy Exchanges Weight Loss Choices

My original Healthy Exchanges program of Weight Loss Choices was based on an average daily total of 1,400 to 1,600 calories per day. That was what I determined was right for my needs, and for those of most women. Because men require additional calories (about 1,600 to 1,900), here are my suggested plans for women and men. *(If you require more or fewer calories, please revise this plan to meet your individual needs.)*

Each day, women should plan to eat:

2 Skim Milk choices, 90 calories each
2 Fat choices, 40 calories each
3 Fruit choices, 60 calories each
4 or more Vegetable choices, 30 calories each
5 Protein choices, 60 calories each
5 Bread choices, 80 calories each

Each day, men should plan to eat:

2 Skim Milk choices, 90 calories each
4 Fat choices, 40 calories each
3 Fruit choices, 60 calories each
4 or more Vegetable choices, 30 calories each
6 Protein choices, 60 calories each
7 Bread choices, 80 calories each

Young people should follow the program for men but add 1 Skim Milk choice for a total of 3 servings.

You may also choose to add up to 100 Optional Calories per day, and up to 21 to 28 Sliders per week at 80 calories each. If you choose to include more Sliders in your daily or weekly totals, deduct those 80 calories from your Optional Calorie "bank."

A word about **Sliders**: These are to be counted toward your totals after you have used your allotment of choices of Skim Milk, Protein,

Bread, and Fruit for the day. By "sliding" an additional choice into one of these groups, you can meet your individual needs for that day. Sliders are especially helpful when traveling, stressed-out, eating out, or for special events. I often use mine so I can enjoy my favorite Healthy Exchanges desserts. Vegetables are not to be counted as Sliders. Enjoy as many Vegetable choices as you need to feel satisfied. Because we want to limit our fat intake to moderate amounts, additional Fat choices should not be counted as Sliders. If you choose to include more fat on an *occasional* basis, count the extra choices as Optional Calories.

Keep a daily food diary of your Weight Loss Choices, checking off what you eat as you go. If, at the end of the day, your required selections are not 100 percent accounted for, but you have done the best you can, go to bed with a clear conscience. There will be days when you have ¼ Fruit or ½ Bread left over. What are you going to do—eat two slices of an orange or half a slice of bread and throw the rest out? I always say, "Nothing in life comes out exact." Just do the best you can . . . *the best you can.*

Try to drink at least eight 8-ounce glasses of water a day. Water truly is the "nectar" of good health.

As a little added insurance, I take a multivitamin each day. It's not essential, but if my day's worth of well-planned meals "bites the dust" when unexpected events intrude on my regular routine, my body still gets its vital nutrients.

The calories listed in each group of Choices are averages. Some choices within each group may be higher or lower, so it's important to select a variety of different foods instead of eating the same three or four all the time.

Use your Optional Calories! They are what I call "life's little extras." They make all the difference in how you enjoy your food and appreciate the variety available to you. Yes, we can get by without them, but do you really want to? Keep in mind that you should be using all your daily Weight Loss Choices first to ensure you are getting the basics of good nutrition. But I guarantee that Optional Calories will keep you from feeling deprived and help you reach your weight-loss goals.

Sodium, Fat, Cholesterol, and Processed Foods

A *re Healthy Exchanges ingredients really healthy?*
When I first created Healthy Exchanges, many people asked about sodium, about whether it was necessary to calculate the percentage of fat, saturated fat, and cholesterol in a healthy diet, and about my use of processed foods in many recipes. I researched these questions as I was developing my program, so you can feel confident about using the recipes and food plan.

Sodium

Most people consume more sodium than their bodies need. The American Heart Association and the American Diabetes Association recommend limiting daily sodium intake to no more than 3,000 milligrams per day. If your doctor suggests you limit your sodium even further, then *you really must read labels.*

Sodium is an essential nutrient and should not be completely eliminated. It helps to regulate blood volume and is needed for normal daily muscle and nerve functions. Most of us, however, have no trouble getting all we need and then some.

As with everything else, moderation is my approach. I rarely ever have salt on my list as an added ingredient. But if you're especially sodium-sensitive, make the right choice for yourself and save high-sodium foods such as sauerkraut for an occasional treat.

I use lots of spices to enhance flavors, so you won't notice the absence of salt. In the few cases where it is used, salt is vital for the success of the recipe, so please don't omit it.

When I do use an ingredient high in sodium, I try to compensate by using low-sodium products in the remainder of the recipe. Many fat-free products are a little higher in sodium to make up for any loss of flavor that disappeared along with the fat. But when I take advantage of these fat-free, higher-sodium products, I stretch that ingredient within the recipe, lowering the amount of sodium per serving. A good example is my use of fat-free and reduced-sodium canned soups. While the suggested number of servings per can is two, I make sure my final creation serves at least four and sometimes six. So the soup's sodium has been "watered down" from one-third to one-half of the original amount.

Even if you don't have to watch your sodium intake for medical reasons, using moderation is another "healthy exchange" to make on your own journey to good health.

Fat Percentages

We've been told that 30 percent is the magic number—that we should limit fat intake to 30 percent or less of our total calories. It's good advice, and I try to have a weekly average of 15 percent to 25 percent myself. I believe any less than 15 percent is really just another restrictive diet that won't last. And more than 25 percent on a regular basis is too much of a good thing.

When I started listing fat grams along with calories in my recipes, I was tempted to include the percentage of calories from fat. After all, in the vast majority of my recipes, that percentage is well below 30 percent. This even includes my pie recipes that allow you a realistic serving instead of many "diet" recipes that tell you a serving is 1/12 of a pie.

Figuring fat grams is easy enough. Each gram of fat equals 9 calories. Multiply fat grams by 9, then divide that number by the total calories to get the percentage of calories from fat.

So why don't I do it? After consulting four registered dietitians for advice, I decided to omit this information. They felt that it's too easy for people to become obsessed by that 30 percent figure, which is after all supposed to be a percentage of total calories over the course of a day or a week. We mustn't feel we can't include a healthy ingredient such as pecans or olives in one recipe just because, on its own, it has more than 30 percent of its calories from fat.

An example of this would be a casserole made with 90 percent lean red meat. Most of us benefit from eating red meat in moderation, as it provides iron and niacin in our diets, and it also makes life more enjoyable for us and those who eat with us. If we *only* look at the percentage of calories from fat in a serving of this one dish, which might be as high as 40 to 45 percent, we might choose not to include this recipe in our weekly food plan.

The dietitians suggested that it's important to consider the total picture when making such decisions. As long as your overall food plan keeps fat calories to 30 percent, it's all right to enjoy an occasional dish that is somewhat higher in fat content. Healthy foods I include in **MODERATION** include 90 percent lean red meat, olives, and nuts. I don't eat these foods every day, and you may not either. But occasionally, in a good recipe, they make all the difference in the world between just getting by (deprivation) and truly enjoying your food.

Remember, the goal is eating in a healthy way so you can enjoy and live well the rest of your life.

Saturated Fats and Cholesterol

You'll see that I don't provide calculations for saturated fats or cholesterol amounts in my recipes. It's for the simple and yet not-so-simple reason that accurate, up-to-date, brand-specific information can be difficult to obtain from food manufacturers, especially since the way in which they produce food keeps changing rapidly. But once more I've consulted with registered dietitians and other professionals and found that, because I use only a few products that are high in saturated fat, and use them in such limited quantities, my recipes are suitable for patients concerned about controlling or lowering cholesterol. You'll also find that whenever I do use one of these ingredients *in moderation*, everything else in the recipe, and in the meals my family and I enjoy, is low in fat.

Processed Foods

Just what *is* processed food, anyway? What do I mean by the term "processed foods," and why do I use them, when the "purest" recipe developers in Recipe Land consider them "pedestrian" and won't ever use something from a box, container, or can? A letter I received and a passing statement from a stranger made me reflect on what I mean when I refer to processed foods and helped me reaffirm why I use them in my "common folk" healthy recipes.

If you are like the vast millions who agree with me, then I'm not sharing anything new with you. And if you happen to disagree, that's okay, too.

A while back, a woman sent me several articles from various "whole food" publications and wrote that she was wary of processed foods and wondered why I used them in my recipes. She then scribbled on the bottom of her note, "Just how healthy *is* Healthy Exchanges?" Then, a few weeks later, during a chance visit at a public food event with a very pleasant woman, I was struck by how we all have our own definitions of what processed foods are. She shared with me, in a some-what self-righteous manner, that she *never* uses processed foods. She only cooked with fresh fruits and vegetables, she told me. Then later she said that she used canned reduced-fat soups all the time! Was her definition different than mine, I wondered? Soup in a can, whether it's reduced in fat or not, still meets my definition of a processed food.

So I got out a copy of my book *HELP: Healthy Exchanges Lifetime Plan* and reread what I had written back then about processed foods. Nothing in my definition had changed since I wrote that section. I still believe that healthy processed foods, such as canned soups, prepared piecrusts, sugar-free instant puddings, fat-free sour cream, and frozen whipped topping, when used properly, all have a place as ingredients in healthy recipes.

I never use an ingredient that hasn't been approved by either the American Diabetic Association, the American Dietetic Association, or the American Heart Association. Whenever I'm in doubt, I send for their position papers then ask knowledgeable registered dietitians to explain those papers to me in layman's language. I've been assured by all of them that the sugar- and fat-free products I use in my recipes are indeed safe.

If you don't agree, nothing I can say or write will convince you otherwise. But, if you've been using healthy processed foods and have been concerned about the almost daily hoopla you hear about yet another product that's going to be the doom of all of us, then just stick with reason. For every product on the grocery shelves, there are those who want you to buy it and there are those who don't, *because they want you to buy their products instead.* So we have to learn to sift the fact from the fiction. Let's take sugar substitutes, for example. In making your own evaluations, you should be skeptical about any information provided by the sugar substitute manufacturers, because they have a vested interest in our buying their products. Likewise, ignore any information provided by the sugar industry, because they have a vested interest in our *not* buying sugar substitutes. Then, if you aren't sure if you can really trust the government or any of its agencies, toss out their data, too. That leaves the three associations I mentioned earlier. Do you think any of them would say a product is safe if it isn't? Or say a product isn't safe when it is? They have nothing to gain or lose, *other than their integrity*, if they intentionally try to mislead us. That's why I only go to these associations for information concerning healthy processed foods.

I certainly don't recommend that everything we eat should come from a can, box, or jar. I think the best of all possible worlds is to start with the basics: grains such as rice, pasta, or corn. Then, for example, add some raw vegetables and extra-lean meat such as poultry, fish, beef, or pork. Stir in some healthy canned soup or tomato sauce, and you'll end up with something that is not only healthy but tastes so good, everyone from toddlers to great-grandparents will want to eat it!

I've never been in favor of spraying everything we eat with chemicals, and I don't believe that all our foods should come out of packages. But I do think we should use the best available healthy processed foods to make cooking easier and food taste better. I take advantage of the good-tasting low-fat and low-sugar products found in any grocery store. My recipes are created for busy people like me, people who want to eat healthily and economically but who still want their food to satisfy their tastebuds. I don't expect anyone to visit out-of-the-way health food stores or find the time to cook beans from scratch—*because I don't!* Most of you can't grow fresh food in the backyard and many of you may not have access to farmers' markets or large supermarkets. I want to help you figure out realistic ways to make healthy eating a reality *wherever you live*, or you will not stick to a healthy lifestyle for long.

So if you've been swayed (by individuals or companies with vested interests or hidden agendas) into thinking that all processed foods are bad for you, you may want to reconsider your position. Or if you've been fooling yourself into believing that you *never* use processed foods but regularly reach for that healthy canned soup, stop playing games with yourself—you are using processed foods in a healthy way. And, if you're like me and use healthy processed foods in *moderation*, don't let anyone make you feel ashamed about including these products in your healthy lifestyle. Only *you* can decide what's best for *you* and your family's needs.

Part of living a healthy lifestyle is making those decisions and then getting on with life. Congratulations on choosing to live a healthy lifestyle, and let's celebrate together by sharing a piece of Healthy Exchanges pie that I've garnished with Cool Whip Lite!

JoAnna's Ten Commandments of Successful Cooking

A very important part of any journey is knowing where you are going and the best way to get there. If you plan and prepare before you start to cook, you should reach mealtime with foods to write home about!

1. **Read the entire recipe from start to finish** and be sure you understand the process. Check that you have all the equipment you will need *before* you begin.

2. **Check the ingredient list** and be sure you have *everything* and in the amounts required. Keep cooking sprays handy—while they're not listed as ingredients, I use them all the time (just a quick squirt!).

3. **Set out *all* the ingredients and equipment needed** to prepare the recipe on the counter near you *before* you start. Remember that old saying "A stitch in time saves nine"? It applies in the kitchen, too.

4. **Do as much advance preparation as possible** before actually cooking. Chop, cut, grate, or do whatever is needed to prepare the ingredients and have them ready before you start to mix. Turn the oven on at least ten minutes before putting food in to bake, to allow the oven to preheat to the proper temperature.

5. **Use a kitchen timer** to tell you when the cooking or baking time is up. Because stove temperatures vary slightly by manu-

facturer, you may want to set your timer for five minutes less than the suggested time just to prevent overcooking. Check the progress of your dish at that time, then decide if you need the additional minutes or not.

6. **Measure carefully.** Use glass measures for liquids and metal or plastic cups for dry ingredients. My recipes are based on standard measurements. Unless I tell you it's a scant or full cup, measure the cup level.

7. **For best results, follow the recipe instructions exactly**. Feel free to substitute ingredients that *don't tamper* with the basic chemistry of the recipe, but be sure to leave key ingredients alone. For example, you could substitute sugar-free instant chocolate pudding for sugar-free instant butterscotch pudding, but if you used a six-serving package when a four-serving package was listed in the ingredients, or you used instant when cook-and-serve is required, you won't get the right result.

8. **Clean up as you go.** It is much easier to wash a few items at a time than to face a whole counter of dirty dishes later. The same is true for spills on the counter or floor.

9. **Be careful about doubling or halving a recipe.** Though many recipes can be altered successfully to serve more or fewer people, *many cannot.* This is especially true when it comes to spices and liquids. If you try to double a recipe that calls for 1 teaspoon pumpkin-pie spice, for example, and you double the spice, you may end up with a too-spicy taste. I usually suggest increasing spices or liquid by 1½ times when doubling a recipe. If it tastes a little bland to you, you can increase the spice to 1¾ times the original amount the next time you prepare the dish. Remember: You can always add more, but you can't take it out after it's stirred in.

The same is true with liquid ingredients. If you wanted to **triple** a main dish recipe because you were planning to serve a crowd, you might think you should use three times as much of every ingredient. Don't, or you could end up with soup instead! If the original recipe calls for 1¾ cup tomato sauce, I'd suggest using 3½ cups when you **triple** the recipe (or 2¾ cups if you **double** it). You'll still have a good-tasting dish that won't run all over the plate.

10. **Write your reactions next to each recipe once you've served it.** Yes, that's right, I'm giving you permission to write in this book. It's yours, after all. Ask yourself: Did everyone like it? Did you have to add another half teaspoon of chili seasoning to please your family, who like to live on the spicier side of the street? You may even want to rate the recipe on a scale of 1★ to 4★, depending on what you thought of it. (Four stars would be the top rating—and I hope you'll feel that way about many of my recipes.) Jotting down your comments while they are fresh in your mind will help you personalize the recipe to your own taste the next time you prepare it.

Secrets for Slow Cooker Success: What I've Learned Along the Way

Creating and testing recipes is a terrific time to discover what works for the home cook—and what definitely doesn't! Because each dish is tested and retested to get it just right, I learn firsthand about possible pitfalls; and because I'm preparing so many different recipes over the course of several months, I find the best and easiest methods to streamline healthy food preparation—so I can pass them along to you.

All of my cookbooks to date and most of the recipes I've shared in my newsletter emphasize stovetop, microwave, and oven cooking, for which very little "equipment" instruction is required. But each slow cooker may be slightly different from others on the market, so I encourage you to begin your new adventure into slow cooking by carefully reading all the materials that came with your particular model. The manufacturers use their appliances in test kitchens before offering them to consumers, and they may have some good ideas that will help you get the most out of the one you purchase.

(If your slow cooker is ten years old or older, treat yourself to a new one, and make sure that it has a removable liner. While we were testing the recipes for this book, we tried using some older cookers from the 1970s and 1980s that we borrowed from friends and found that the results weren't as reliable. The older appliances didn't keep an even temperature, and some never even got warm enough to cook the food thoroughly. If you believe in the possibilities and convenience of slow cooking enough to invest in this cookbook, then I hope you will spend a few dollars more and get a new cooker too!)

Some Great Reasons to Use a Slow Cooker

Slow cooker recipes work *with* your schedule, not the other way around. If you like, you can prepare your meal in advance, store the liner container in your refrigerator and then put it on to cook all the way while you are out for the day. What could be more perfect for today's busy lifestyles? Depending on your schedule, you can prepare the recipe the night before or first thing in the morning, turn the cooker on before you leave the house for work or play, and your meal will be waiting for you when you return home hours later.

More **nutrients are retained** in the food you prepare in a slow cooker because of the lower temperature used. Extra lean meats cook up tender because of the slow and long cooking, so you get both good taste and the health benefits of eating food with lower fat. And slow cooker meals **cut way down on cleanup**—you're only using one pot!

Did you know that **slow cookers are excellent energy savers**? When you cook on LOW, you use less energy than you would with a 100-watt lightbulb.

Even so, **slow cookers still provide a safe cooking environment for foods**. According to the USDA, bacteria in foods is killed at a temperature of 165 degrees Fahrenheit if maintained for 2 hours or more. Since the LOW setting on slow cookers cooks at 185 to 200 degrees, it is well above the safety limit.

Less counter space is needed for cooking, so slow cookers are ideal for RV cooking as well as on boats, in cabins, and in efficiency kitchens.

When cooking on LOW, **you can leave your home** without any worries about having to "watch the pot boil." Low heat will not dry out or burn foods.

Slow cookers don't heat up the kitchen, so they are perfect for summer cooking.

Exact cooking times are not critical, so if you are delayed and don't get home exactly when you planned, your food won't be too overdone.

Slow cookers are **great for buffets and informal dining** because you can serve directly from the pot. You can actually use your slow cooker as a chafing dish to keep the food warm.

The Basics

All of my recipes were created and cooked in either 3½, 4 or 5 quart slow cookers, and **most of the recipes were designed to serve 4 to 6 people**. If that's the right number for your family or household, your main meal is covered; for smaller families, you've got planned leftovers for the coming week's work lunches.

Most **vegetables cook better when cut into small pieces or quartered**. Also, I recommend placing vegetables on the sides or bottom of the container. Root vegetables, such as carrots, potatoes, turnips, and parsnips, will take longer to cook than other vegetables, and will cook best when covered by liquid.

(Some vegetables, such as **onions or carrots**, can also develop a more intense flavor during the slow cooking process, so you may want to decrease the amount called for. In my recipes, try it my way first and note if the finished dish is too strongly flavored for you. I just wanted you to be aware of this possibility.)

Meats usually cook faster than vegetables.

I suggest **browning ground meats for better flavor and texture** in the finished dish. Except for ground meats, however, you *don't* need to brown your meat before adding it to the recipes. Even though I ask you to use extra lean cuts of meat, the slow cooker will tenderize it nicely during the long cooking process.

Whole herbs and spices are usually more intense when cooked in a slow cooker, so a little generally goes a long way. But very fine ground spices may lose some flavor as the hours pass. I've adjusted for this in my recipes, but if you are planning to use your slow cooker for other dishes, keep this in mind—and remember that it's probably best to do most of your seasoning shortly before serving.

If cooked longer than 3 or 4 hours, pasta has a tendency to fall apart or become gummy. So, **if you are using pasta in a recipe that calls for longer cooking times, it is better to add it only for the last**

2 or 3 hours OR cook it conventionally on the stove and stir it in just before serving.

Skim milk has a tendency to curdle, and **natural cheese** will break down during extended cooking. Evaporated skim milk, condensed soups, processed cheeses, and nonfat dry milk powder work much better.

For **best results**, fill the pot at least half full of ingredients.

Since the **liquid content** of meats and vegetables will vary, sometimes a recipe will have more liquid than desired. The extra can be drained off or reduced by taking the cover off and cooking on HIGH for 30 to 45 minutes. Most if not all recipes cooked on LOW will be juicier, since the lower heat keeps the liquid from boiling away. That's the main reason we need to begin with less liquid when cooking on LOW than you would need if simmering in a pot on the stove.

If you use frozen foods, you will need to add an extra 2 to 3 hours cooking time. That's why I suggest throughout this book that you "thaw" frozen veggies by placing them in a colander and running hot water over them for a couple of minutes, then draining them carefully. By spending a few extra minutes at the start, you'll save hours later on!

All ingredients in most recipes can be added at the same time. Try, though, to add liquids and sauces last. Be sure to mix well before closing the lid and then again when lifting the lid off the finished product.

To make for **easier cleanup**, spray the inside of your pot with a nonstick cooking spray before using it each time.

To **protect the slow cooker** liner, try not to subject it to sudden temperature changes. For example, don't preheat the cooker and then add food.

Cooking Temperatures

Remember that the **cooking temperature in a slow cooker** is about 200 degrees (or just below boiling) when it's set on LOW and about 300 degrees when it's set on HIGH. Slow cooking is what gives the dish such a moist and tender taste. One hour on HIGH is usually equal to two hours on LOW. LOW is the best choice most of the time, but read the instructions carefully. Some dishes do better when cooked on HIGH. Consider what I've chosen for my recipes and evaluate your results, so you can start to experiment with your own family favorites. One important note: *Never* leave the slow cooker unattended if you are cooking on HIGH, as occasional stirring may be necessary.

When **cooking on the LOW setting**, don't be tempted to "lift the lid" just to stir or check on the progress of your meal. By doing that, you release the all-important heat and steam that are necessary for success, and so you will likely have to add to the cooking time called for in the recipe. Your best bet is only to take the lid off your slow cooker close to the first suggested cooking time, to test for doneness (for example, at 6 hours if the recipe suggests 6 to 8 hours), OR if the recipe explicitly tells you to!

However, when **cooking on HIGH** for short periods, an occasional stirring of the pot helps to distribute the flavors and generally doesn't affect the called-for cooking time.

Troubleshooting—What If the Dish Isn't Done?

If a recipe isn't done after the 6 to 8 hours suggested, one of the following reasons could be causing the problem:

1. **House voltage variations**. This is more commonplace than you might expect. The slight fluctuations in power do not have a noticeable effect on most appliances, but due to the extended cooking times a slow cooker demands, these variations in power can require longer cooking times for some ingredients.

2. **Higher altitudes**. If you live at an altitude above 3,500 feet, you may need to add 1 to 2 hours to the suggested cooking times. Not every recipe may need more time, so you'll have to experiment and decide what works best for you.

3. **Extreme humidity**. It may surprise you to learn that very high humidity can cause ingredients to cook more slowly than expected. If you are using a new slow cooker with a reliable temperature, it's almost impossible to "overcook" most dishes. If you suspect your environment may require additional cooking time, allow for it the first few times. You'll soon learn

through experience what works best for your cooker, your kitchen, and you.

Preparing Just About Anything in Your Slow Cooker

Here's a quick guideline to **convert your own favorite recipes to the slow cooker method**: a recipe that bakes for one hour at 350 degrees should be cooked on LOW for 6 to 8 hours; a recipe that bakes for 30 minutes at 325 degrees should be cooked on LOW for 3 to 4 hours. Remember to cut the liquid considerably when converting a non–slow-cooker recipe—about half of what's originally called for is a good place to start. The only exception to this rule are soups and any recipes that contain long grain converted rice.

Now, let me end as I started—no matter which model of slow cooker you buy, **be sure to read the manufacturer's specific instructions** for proper settings, safety, and cleaning of your particular brand.

Let the cooking—and your liberation from the kitchen—begin!

Help Me Cook Healthy: My Best Healthy Exchanges Cooking Tips

Not all of these tips are appropriate for this particular cookbook, which uses a slow cooker in every recipe. But I wanted you to have it as a handy reference guide to making your kitchen a truly healthy place to prepare the foods you love!

Measurements, General Cooking Tips, and Basic Ingredients

The word **moderation** best describes **my use of fats, sugar substitutes,** and **sodium** in these recipes. Wherever possible, I've used cooking spray for sautéing and for browning meats and vegetables. I also use reduced-calorie margarine and fat-free mayonnaise and salad dressings. Lean ground turkey *or* ground beef can be used in the recipes. Just be sure whatever you choose is at least *90 percent lean.*

Sugar Substitutes

I've also included **small amounts of sugar substitutes as the sweetening agent** in many of the recipes. I don't drink a hundred cans of soda a day or eat enough artificially sweetened foods in a 24-hour time period to be troubled by sugar substitutes. But if this is a concern of yours and you *do not* need to watch your sugar intake, you can always replace the sugar substitutes with processed sugar and the sugar-free products with regular ones.

I created my recipes knowing they would also be used by hypoglycemics, diabetics, and those concerned about triglycerides. If you choose to use sugar instead, be sure to count the additional calories.

A word of caution when cooking with **sugar substitutes**: Use **sucralose-** or **saccharin**-based sweeteners when **heating or baking**. In recipes that **don't require heat, aspartame** (known as NutraSweet) works well in uncooked dishes but leaves an aftertaste in baked products.

Splenda and **Sugar Twin** are my best choices for sugar substitutes. They measure like sugar, you can cook and bake with them, they're inexpensive, and they are easily poured from their boxes. (If you can't find **Splenda** in your store yet, try their website: http://www.splenda.com to order directly.)

Many of my recipes for quick breads, muffins, and cakes include a package of sugar-free instant pudding mix, which is sweetened with NutraSweet. Yet we've been told that NutraSweet breaks down under heat. I've tested my recipes again and again, and here's what I've found: baking with a NutraSweet product sold for home sweetening doesn't work, but baking with NutraSweet-sweetened instant pudding mixes turns out great. I choose not to question why this is but continue to use these products in creating my Healthy Exchanges recipes.

How much sweetener is the right amount? I use pourable Splenda, Sugar Twin, Brown Sugar Twin, and Sprinkle Sweet in my recipes because they measure just like sugar. What could be easier? I also use them because they work wonderfully in cooked and baked products.

If you are using a brand other than these, you will need to check the package to figure out how much of your sweetener will equal what's called for in the recipe.

If you choose to use real sugar or brown sugar, then you would use the same amount the recipe lists for pourable Splenda, Sugar Twin, or Brown Sugar Twin.

You'll see that I list only the specific brands when the recipe preparation involves heat. In a salad or other recipe that doesn't require cooking, I will list the ingredient as "sugar substitute to equal 2 tablespoons sugar." You can then use any sweetener you choose—Equal, Sweet 'n Low, Sweet Ten, or any other aspartame-based sugar substitute. Just check the label so you'll be using the right amount to equal those 2 tablespoons of sugar. Or, if you choose, you can use regular sugar.

With Healthy Exchanges recipes, the "sweet life" is the only life for me!

Pan Sizes

I'm often asked why I use an **8-by-8-inch baking dish** in my recipes. It's for portion control. If the recipe says it serves 4, just cut down the center, turn the dish, and cut again. Like magic, there's your serving. Also, if this is the only recipe you are preparing requiring an oven, the square dish fits into a tabletop toaster oven easily so energy can be conserved.

While many of my recipes call for an 8-by-8-inch baking dish, others ask for a 9-by-9-inch cake pan. If you don't have a 9-inch-square pan, is it all right to use your 8-inch dish instead? In most cases, the small difference in the size of these two pans won't significantly affect the finished product, so until you can get your hands on the right size pan, go ahead and use your baking dish.

However, since the 8-inch dish is usually made of glass, and the 9-inch cake pan is made of metal, you will want to adjust the baking temperature. If you're using a glass baking dish in a recipe that calls for a 9-inch pan, be sure to lower your baking temperature by 15 degrees *or* check your finished product at least 6 to 8 minutes before the specified baking time is over.

But it really is worthwhile to add a 9-by-9-inch pan to your collection, and if you're going to be baking lots of my Healthy Exchanges cakes, you'll definitely use it frequently. A cake baked in this pan will have a better texture, and the servings will be a little larger. Just think of it—an 8-by-8-inch pan produces 64 square inches of dessert, while a 9-by-9-inch pan delivers 81 square inches. Those 17 extra inches are too tasty to lose!

To make life even easier, **whenever a recipe calls for ounce measurements** (other than raw meats) I've included the closest cup equivalent. I need to use my scale daily when creating recipes, so I've measured for you at the same time.

Freezing Leftovers

Most of the recipes are for **4 to 6 servings.** If you don't have that many to feed, do what I do: freeze individual portions. Then all you have to do is choose something from the freezer and take it to work for lunch or have your evening meals prepared in advance for the week. In this way, I always have something on hand that is both good to eat and good for me.

Unless a recipe includes hard-boiled eggs, cream cheese, mayonnaise, or a raw vegetable or fruit, **the leftovers should freeze well.** (I've marked recipes that freeze well with the symbol of a **snowflake** ❄.) This includes most of the cream pies. Divide any recipe into individual servings and freeze for your own "TV" dinners.

Another good idea is **cutting leftover pie into individual pieces and freezing each one separately** in a small Ziploc freezer bag. Once you've cut the pie into portions, place them on a cookie sheet and put it in the freezer for 15 minutes. That way, the creamy topping won't get smashed and your pie will keep its shape.

When you want to thaw a piece of pie for yourself, you don't have to thaw the whole pie. You can practice portion control at the same time, and it works really well for brown-bag lunches. Just pull a piece out of the freezer on your way to work and by lunchtime you will have a wonderful dessert waiting for you.

Why do I so often recommend freezing leftover desserts? One reason is that if you leave baked goods made with sugar substitutes out on the counter for more than a day or two, they get moldy. Sugar is a preservative and retards the molding process. It's actually what's called an antimicrobial agent, meaning it works against microbes such as molds, bacteria, fungi, and yeasts that grow in foods and can cause food poisoning. Both sugar and salt work as antimicrobial agents to withdraw water from food. Since microbes can't grow without water, food protected in this way doesn't spoil.

So what do we do if we don't want our muffins to turn moldy but we also don't want to use sugar because of the excess carbohydrates and calories? Freeze them! Just place each muffin or individually sliced bread serving into a Ziploc sandwich bag, seal, and toss them into your freezer. Then, whenever you want one for a snack or a meal, you can choose to let it thaw naturally or "zap" it in the microwave. If you know that baked goods will be eaten within a day or two, packaging them in a sealed plastic container and storing in the refrigerator will do the trick.

Unless I specify **"covered" for simmering or baking,** prepare my recipes **uncovered.** Occasionally you will read a recipe that asks you to cover a dish for a time, then to uncover, so read the directions carefully to avoid confusion—and to get the best results.

Cooking Spray

Low-fat cooking spray is another blessing in a Healthy Exchanges kitchen. It's currently available in three flavors:

- **OLIVE OIL or GARLIC FLAVORED** when cooking Mexican, Italian, or Greek dishes

- **BUTTER or LEMON FLAVORED** when a hint of butter or lemon is desired

- **REGULAR** for everything else.

A quick spray of butter flavored makes air-popped popcorn a low-fat taste treat, or try it as a butter substitute on steaming-hot corn on the cob. One light spray of the skillet when browning meat will convince you that you're using "old-fashioned fat," and a quick coating of the casserole dish before you add the ingredients will make serving easier and cleanup quicker.

Baking Times

Sometimes I give you a range as a **baking time,** such as 22 to 28 minutes. Why? Because every kitchen, every stove, and every chef's cooking technique is slightly different. On a hot and humid day in Iowa, the optimum cooking time won't be the same as on a cold, dry day. Some stoves bake hotter than the temperature setting indicates; other stoves bake cooler. Electric ovens usually are more temperamental than gas ovens. If you place your baking pan on a lower shelf, the temperature is warmer than if you place it on a higher shelf. If you stir the mixture more vigorously than I do, you could affect the required baking time by a minute or more.

The best way to gauge the heat of your particular oven is to purchase an oven temperature gauge that hangs in the oven. These can be found in any discount store or kitchen equipment store, and if you're going to be cooking and baking regularly, it's a good idea to own one. Set the oven to 350 degrees, and when the oven indicates that it has reached that temperature, check the reading on the gauge. If it's less than 350 degrees, you know your oven cooks cooler, and you need to add a few minutes to the cooking time *or* set your oven at a higher temperature. If it's more than 350 degrees, then your oven is warmer and you need to subtract a few minutes from the cooking time. In any event, always treat the suggested baking time as approximate. Check on your baked product at the earliest suggested time. You can always continue baking a few minutes more if needed, but you can't unbake it once you've cooked it too long.

Miscellaneous Ingredients and Tips

I use reduced-sodium **canned chicken broth** in place of dry bouillon to lower the sodium content. The intended flavor is still present in the prepared dish. As a reduced-sodium beef broth is not currently available (at least not in DeWitt, Iowa), I use the canned regular beef broth. The sodium content is still lower than regular dry bouillon.

Whenever **cooked rice or pasta** is an ingredient, follow the package directions but eliminate the salt and/or margarine called for. This helps lower the sodium and fat content. It tastes just fine; trust me on this.

Here's another tip: When **cooking rice or noodles**, why not cook extra "for the pot"? After you use what you need, store leftover rice in a covered container (where it will keep for a couple of days). With noodles like spaghetti or macaroni, first rinse and drain as usual, then measure out what you need. Put the leftovers in a bowl covered with water, then store them in the refrigerator, covered, until they're needed. Then, measure out what you need, rinse and drain them, and they're ready to go.

Does your **pita bread** often tear before you can make a sandwich? Here's my tip to make them open easily: cut the bread in half, put the halves in the microwave for about 15 seconds, and they will open up by themselves. *Voilà!*

When **chunky salsa** is listed as an ingredient, I leave the degree of "heat" up to your personal taste. In our house, I'm considered a wimp. I go for the "mild" while Cliff prefers "extra-hot." How do we compromise? I prepare the recipe with mild salsa because he can always add a spoonful or two of the hotter version to his serving, but I can't enjoy the dish if it's too spicy for me.

You can make purchased **fat-free salad dressings** taste **more like the "real thing"** by adding a small amount of fat-free mayonnaise and a pinch of sugar substitute to the diet dressing. Start with 2 tablespoons of salad dressing (such as Ranch), add 1 teaspoon fat-free mayo and sugar substitute to equal ½ teaspoon sugar. Mix well and spoon over your salad. Unless you remind yourself you're eating the fat-free version, you may just fool yourself into thinking you reached for the high-fat counterpart instead!

Milk, Yogurt, and More

Take it from me—nonfat dry milk powder is great! I *do not* use it for drinking, but I *do* use it for cooking. Three good reasons why:

1. It is very **inexpensive**.

2. It does not **sour** because you use it only as needed. Store the box in your refrigerator or freezer and it will keep almost forever.

3. You can easily **add extra calcium** to just about any recipe without added liquid.

I consider nonfat dry milk powder one of Mother Nature's modern-day miracles of convenience. But do purchase a good national name brand (I like Carnation), and keep it fresh by proper storage.

I've said many times, "Give me my mixing bowl, my wire whisk, and a box of nonfat dry milk powder, and I can conquer the world!" Here are some of my favorite ways to use dry milk powder:

1. You can make a **pudding** with the nutrients of 2 cups skim milk, but the liquid of only 1¼ to 1½ cups by using ⅔ cup nonfat dry milk powder, a 4-serving package of sugar-free instant pudding, and the lesser amount of water. This makes the pudding taste much creamier and more like homemade. Also, pie filling made my way will set up in minutes. If company is knocking at your door, you can prepare a pie for them almost as fast as you can open the door and invite them in. And if by chance you have leftovers, the filling will not separate the way it does when you use the 2 cups skim milk suggested on the package. (If you absolutely refuse to use this handy powdered milk, you can substitute skim milk in the amount of water I call for. Your pie won't be as creamy, and will likely get runny if you have leftovers.)

2. You can make your own "**sour cream**" by combining ¾ cup plain fat-free yogurt with ⅓ cup nonfat dry milk powder. What you did by doing this is fourfold: (1) The dry milk stabilizes the yogurt and keeps the whey from separating. (2) The dry milk slightly helps to cut the tartness of the yogurt. (3) It's still virtually fat-free. (4) The calcium has been increased by 100 percent. Isn't it great how we can make that distant relative of sour cream a first kissin' cousin by adding the nonfat dry milk powder? Or, if you place 1 cup plain fat-free yogurt in a sieve lined with a coffee filter, and place the sieve over a small bowl and refrigerate for about 6 hours, you will end up with a very good alternative for sour cream. To **stabilize yogurt** when cooking or baking with it, just add 1 teaspoon cornstarch to every ¾ cup yogurt.

3. You can make **evaporated skim milk** by using ⅓ cup nonfat dry milk powder and ½ cup water for every ½ cup evaporated skim milk you need. This is handy to know when you want to prepare a recipe calling for evaporated skim milk and you don't have any in the cupboard. And if you are using a recipe that requires only 1 cup evaporated skim milk, you don't have to worry about what to do with the leftover milk in the can.

4. You can make **sugar-free and fat-free sweetened condensed milk** by using 1⅓ cups nonfat dry milk powder mixed with ½

cup cold water, microwaved on HIGH until the mixture is hot but not boiling. Then stir in ½ cup Splenda or pourable Sugar Twin. Cover and chill at least 4 hours.

5. For any recipe that calls for **buttermilk**, you might want to try **JO's Buttermilk**: Blend 1 cup water and ⅔ cup nonfat dry milk powder (the nutrients of 2 cups of skim milk). It'll be thicker than this mixed-up milk usually is, because it's doubled. Add 1 teaspoon white vinegar and stir, then let it sit for at least 10 minutes.

What else? Nonfat dry milk powder adds calcium without fuss to many recipes, and it can be stored for months in your refrigerator or freezer.

And for **a different taste when preparing sugar-free instant pudding mixes**, use ¾ cup plain fat-free yogurt for one of the required cups of milk. Blend as usual. It will be thicker and creamier—and no, it doesn't taste like yogurt.

Another **variation for the sugar-free instant vanilla pudding** is to use 1 cup skim milk and 1 cup crushed pineapple with juice. Mix as usual.

Soup Substitutes

One of my subscribers was looking for a way to further restrict salt intake and needed a substitute for **cream of mushroom soup**. For many of my recipes, I use Healthy Request Cream of Mushroom Soup, as it is a reduced-sodium product. The label suggests two servings per can, but I usually incorporate the soup into a recipe serving at least four. By doing this, I've reduced the sodium in the soup by half again.

But if you must restrict your sodium even more, try making my Healthy Exchanges **Creamy Mushroom Sauce.** Place 1½ cups evaporated skim milk and 3 tablespoons flour in a covered jar. Shake well and pour the mixture into a medium saucepan sprayed with butter-flavored cooking spray. Add ½ cup canned sliced mushrooms, rinsed and drained. Cook over medium heat, stirring often, until the mixture thickens. Add any seasonings of your choice. You can use this sauce in any recipe that calls for one 10¾-ounce can of cream of mushroom soup.

Why did I choose these proportions and ingredients?

- 1½ cups evaporated skim milk is the amount in one can.

- It's equal to three Skim Milk choices or exchanges.

- It's the perfect amount of liquid and flour for a medium cream sauce.

- 3 tablespoons flour is equal to one bread/starch choice or exchange.

- Any leftovers will reheat beautifully with a flour-based sauce, but not with a cornstarch base.

- The mushrooms are one Vegetable choice or exchange.

- This sauce is virtually fat-free, sugar-free, and sodium-free.

Proteins

Eggs

I use eggs in moderation. I enjoy the real thing on an average of three to four times a week. So, my recipes are calculated on using whole eggs. However, if you choose to use egg substitute in place of eggs, the finished product will turn out just fine and the fat grams per serving will be even lower than those listed.

If you like the look, taste, and feel of **hard-boiled eggs** in salads but haven't been using them because of the cholesterol in the yolk, I have a couple of alternatives for you. (1) Pour an 8-ounce carton of egg substitute into a medium skillet sprayed with cooking spray. Cover the skillet tightly and cook over low heat until substitute is just set, about 10 minutes. Remove from heat and let set, still covered, for 10 minutes more. Uncover and cool completely. Chop the set mixture. This will make about 1 cup of chopped egg. (2) Even easier is to hard-boil "real eggs," toss the yolk away, and chop the white. Either way, you don't deprive yourself of the pleasure of egg in your salad.

In most recipes calling for **egg substitutes**, you can use 2 egg whites in place of the equivalent of 1 egg substitute. Just break the eggs open and toss the yolks away. I can hear some of you already saying, "But that's wasteful!" Well, take a look at the price on the egg substitute package (which usually has the equivalent of 4 eggs in it), then look at the price of a dozen eggs, from which you'd get the equivalent of 6 egg substitutes. Now, what's wasteful about that?

Meats

Whenever I include **cooked chicken** in a recipe, I use roasted white meat without skin. Whenever I include **roast beef or pork** in a recipe, I use the loin cuts because they are much leaner. However, most of the time, I do my roasting of all these meats at the local deli. I just ask for a chunk of their lean roasted meat, 6 or 8 ounces, and ask them not to slice it. When I get home, I cube or dice the meat and am ready to use it in my recipe. The reason I do this is threefold: (1) I'm getting just the amount I need without leftovers; (2) I don't have the expense of heating the oven; and (3) I'm not throwing away the bone, gristle, and fat I'd be cutting off the meat. Overall, it is probably cheaper to "roast" it the way I do.

Did you know that you can make an acceptable meat loaf without using egg for the binding? Just replace every egg with ¼ cup of liquid. You could use beef broth, tomato sauce, even applesauce, to name just a few alternatives. For a meat loaf to serve 6, I always use 1 pound of extra-lean ground beef or turkey, 6 tablespoons of dried fine bread crumbs, and ¼ cup of the liquid, plus anything else healthy that strikes my fancy at the time. I mix well and place the mixture in an 8-by-8-inch baking dish or 9-by-5-inch loaf pan sprayed with cooking spray. Bake uncovered at 350 degrees for 35 to 50 minutes (depending on the added ingredients). You will never miss the egg.

Any time you are **browning ground meat** for a casserole and want to get rid of almost all the excess fat, just place the uncooked meat loosely in a plastic colander. Set the colander in a glass pie plate. Place in the microwave and cook on HIGH for 3 to 6 minutes (depending on the amount being browned), stirring often. Use as you would for any casserole. You can also chop up onions and brown them with the meat if you want.

To **brown meat for any Italian dish** (and to add some extra "zip"), simply pour a couple of tablespoons of fat-free Italian dressing into a skillet and add your ingredients to be browned. The dressing acts almost like olive oil in the process and adds a touch of flavor as well.

And to make an **Italian Sloppy Joe**, brown 16 ounces of extra lean ground meat and 1 cup chopped onion in ¼ cup fat-free Italian dressing, then add 1 cup tomato sauce, lower heat, and simmer for 10 minutes. *Bravo!*

Remember, always opt for the leanest ground beef or turkey you can find. Here in DeWitt, we can buy 95% extra lean ground sirloin, which provides about 8 to 10 grams fat in a 2 to 3 ounce serving. Lean ground turkey provides about 5 to 7 grams of fat. But cheaper cuts can "cost" you up to 20 grams of fat per serving. It's standard practice to grind the skin into inexpensive ground turkey found in most one-pound frozen packages, so beware.

Gravy and Mashed Potatoes

For **gravy** with all the "old-time" flavor but without the extra fat, try this almost effortless way to prepare it. First, pour your pan drippings (from roasted turkey, roast beef, or roast pork) into a large cake pan and set the pan in your freezer for at least 15 to 20 minutes so that the fat can congeal on the top and be skimmed off. Use a large pan even if you only have a small amount of drippings so that you get maximum air exposure for quick congealing. (If you prefer, you can purchase one of those fat separator pitchers that separates the fat from the juice.)

Pour your defatted juice into a large skillet. This recipe begins with about one cup of "stock." Now, pour either one cup of potato water (water that potatoes were boiled in before mashing) or regular water into a large jar. Potato water is my first choice because it's loaded with nutrients so I use it whenever I'm making fresh mashed potatoes to go with my homemade gravy. Add 3 tablespoons of all-purpose flour, screw the lid on, and shake until the mixture is well-blended. This easy step assures that you won't get lumps in your gravy!

Pour the mixture into the skillet with defatted stock and add any seasonings you like. Cook over medium heat, stirring constantly with a wire whisk, until the mixture thickens and starts to boil. (The whisk is another secret for lump-free gravy.) Now pour the gravy into your prettiest gravy bowl and serve with pride!

Why did I use flour instead of cornstarch? Because any leftovers will reheat nicely with the flour base and would not with a cornstarch base. Also, 3 tablespoons of flour works out to 1 Bread/Starch exchange.

This virtually fat-free gravy makes about 2 cups, so you could spoon about ½ cup gravy on your low-fat mashed potatoes and only have to count your gravy as ¼ Bread/Starch exchange.

Here's how to make the **best mashed potatoes**: For a 6-serving batch, quarter 6 medium potatoes and boil until they are tender in just enough water to cover them. Drain the potatoes, but *do not* throw the water away. Return the potatoes to the saucepan, whip them gently with an electric mixer, then add about ½ cup of the reserved potato water, ⅓ cup Carnation nonfat dry milk powder, and 2 tablespoons fat-free sour cream. Continue whipping with the mixer until smooth. You're sure to be begged to share the "secret" of your creamy mashed potatoes!

Fruits and Vegetables

If you want to enjoy a **"fruit shake"** with some pizzazz, just combine soda water and unsweetened fruit juice in a blender. Add crushed ice. Blend on HIGH until thick. Refreshment without guilt.

You'll see that many recipes use ordinary **canned vegetables.** They're much cheaper than reduced-sodium versions, and once you rinse and drain them, the sodium is reduced anyway. I believe in saving money wherever possible so we can afford the best fat-free and sugar-free products as they come onto the market.

All three kinds of **vegetables—fresh, frozen, and canned**—have their place in a healthy diet. My husband, Cliff, hates the taste of frozen or fresh green beans, thinks the texture is all wrong, so I use canned green beans instead. In this case, canned vegetables have their proper place when I'm feeding my husband. If someone in your family has a similar concern, it's important to respond to it so everyone can be happy and enjoy the meal.

When I use **fruits or vegetables** like apples, cucumbers, and zucchini, I wash them really well and **leave the skin on.** It provides added color, fiber, and attractiveness to any dish. And because I use processed flour in my cooking, I like to increase the fiber in my diet by eating my fruits and vegetables in their closest-to-natural state.

To help **keep fresh fruits and veggies fresh**, just give them a quick "shower" with lemon juice. The easiest way to do this is to pour purchased lemon juice into a kitchen spray bottle and store it in the refrigerator. Then, every time you use fresh fruits or vegetables in a salad or dessert, simply give them a quick spray with your "lemon spritzer." You just might be amazed by how this little trick keeps your produce from turning brown so fast.

Another great way to **keep fruits from turning brown**: try dipping them in Diet Mountain Dew!

Here's a way to enjoy **cranberries** all year round: buy a few extra bags while they are in season and freeze them for future use. By the way, cranberries chop better when frozen!

The next time you warm canned vegetables such as carrots or green beans, drain and heat the vegetables in ¼ cup beef or chicken broth. It gives a nice variation to an old standby. Here's a simple **white sauce** for vegetables and casseroles without using added fat that can be made by spraying a medium saucepan with butter-flavored cooking spray. Place 1½ cups evaporated skim milk and 3 tablespoons flour in a covered jar. Shake well. Pour into the sprayed saucepan and cook over medium heat until thick, stirring constantly. Add salt and pepper to taste. You can also add ½ cup canned drained mushrooms and/or 3 ounces (¾ cup) shredded reduced-fat cheese. Continue cooking until the cheese melts.

Zip up canned or frozen green beans with **chunky salsa**: ½ cup to 2 cups beans. Heat thoroughly. Chunky salsa also makes a wonderful dressing on lettuce salads. It only counts as a vegetable, so enjoy.

Another wonderful **South of the Border dressing** can be stirred up by using ½ cup of chunky salsa and ¼ cup fat-free ranch dressing. Cover and store in your refrigerator. Use as a dressing for salads or as a topping for baked potatoes.

To **"roast" green or red peppers**, pierce a whole pepper in four or six places with the tines of a fork, then place the pepper in a glass pie plate and microwave on HIGH for 10 to 12 minutes, turning after every four minutes. Cover and let set for 5 minutes. Then, remove the seeds and peel the skin off and cut into strips. Use right away or freeze for future use.

Delightful Dessert Ideas

For a special treat that tastes anything but "diet," try placing **spreadable fruit** in a container and microwave it for about 15 seconds. Then pour the melted fruit spread over a serving of nonfat ice cream or frozen yogurt. One tablespoon of spreadable fruit is equal to 1 Fruit choice or exchange. Some combinations to get you started are apricot over chocolate ice cream, strawberry over strawberry ice cream, or any flavor over vanilla.

Another way I use spreadable fruit is to make a delicious **topping for a cheesecake or angel food cake**. I take ½ cup fruit and ½ cup Cool Whip Lite and blend the two together with a teaspoon of coconut extract.

Here's a really **good topping** for the fall of the year. Place 1½ cups unsweetened applesauce in a medium saucepan or 4-cup glass measure. Stir in 2 tablespoons raisins, 1 teaspoon apple pie spice, and 2 tablespoons Cary's Sugar Free Maple Syrup. Cook over medium heat on the stovetop or microwave on HIGH until warm. Then spoon about ½ cup of the warm mixture over pancakes, French toast, or sugar- and fat-free vanilla ice cream. It's as close as you will get to guilt-free apple pie!

Do you love hot fudge sundaes as much as I do? Here's my secret for making **Almost Sinless Hot Fudge Sauce**. Just combine the contents of a 4-serving package of JELL-O sugar-free chocolate cook-and-serve pudding with ⅔ cup Carnation Nonfat Dry Milk Powder in a medium saucepan. Add 1¼ cups water. Cook over medium heat, stirring constantly with a wire whisk, until the mixture thickens and starts to boil. Remove from heat and stir in 1 teaspoon vanilla extract, 2 teaspoons reduced-calorie margarine, and ½ cup miniature marshmallows. This makes six ¼ cup servings. Any leftovers can be refrigerated and reheated later in the microwave. Yes, you can buy fat-free chocolate syrup nowadays, but have you checked the sugar content? For a ¼-cup serving of store-bought syrup (and you show me any true hot fudge sundae lover who would settle for less than ¼ cup) it clocks in at over 150 calories with 39 grams of sugar! Hershey's Lite Syrup, while better, still has 100 calories and 10 grams of sugar. But this "homemade" version costs you only 60 calories, less than ½ gram of fat, and just 6 grams of sugar for the same ¼-cup serving. For an occasional squirt on something where 1 teaspoon is enough, I'll use Hershey's Lite Syrup. But when I crave a hot fudge sundae, I scoop out some sugar- and fat-free ice cream, then spoon my Almost Sinless Hot Fudge Sauce over the top and smile with pleasure.

A quick yet tasty way to prepare **strawberries for shortcake** is to place about ¾ cup sliced strawberries, 2 tablespoons Diet Mountain

Dew, and sugar substitute to equal $\frac{1}{4}$ cup sugar in a blender container. Process on BLEND until mixture is smooth. Pour the mixture into a bowl. Add $1\frac{1}{4}$ cups sliced strawberries and mix well. Cover and refrigerate until ready to serve with shortcakes. This tastes just like the strawberry sauce I remember my mother making when I was a child.

Here's a wonderful secret for **making shortcakes**: just follow the recipe for shortcakes on the Bisquick Reduced-Fat Baking Mix box, but substitute Splenda or pourable Sugar Twin for the sugar, skim milk for the regular milk, and fat-free sour cream for the margarine. When you serve these light and tasty shortcakes to your loved ones, I defy any of them to notice the difference between your version and the original!

Have you tried **thawing Cool Whip Lite** by stirring it? Don't! You'll get a runny mess and ruin the look and taste of your dessert. You can *never* treat Cool Whip Lite the same way you did regular Cool Whip because the "lite" version just doesn't contain enough fat. Thaw your Cool Whip Lite by placing it in your refrigerator at least two hours before you need to use it. When they took the excess fat out of Cool Whip to make it "lite," they replaced it with air. When you stir the living daylights out of it to hurry up the thawing, you also stir out the air. You also can't thaw your Cool Whip Lite in the microwave, or you'll end up with Cool Whip Soup!

Always have a thawed container of Cool Whip Lite in your refrigerator, as it keeps well for up to two weeks. It actually freezes and thaws and freezes and thaws again quite well, so if you won't be using it soon, you could refreeze your leftovers. Just remember to take it out a few hours before you need it, so it'll be creamy and soft and ready to use.

Remember, anytime you see the words "fat-free" or "reduced-fat" on the labels of cream cheese, sour cream, or whipped topping, handle it gently. The fat has been replaced by air or water, and the product has to be treated with special care.

How can you **frost an entire pie with just $\frac{1}{2}$ cup of whipped topping?** First, don't use an inexpensive brand. I use Cool Whip Lite or La Creme Lite. Make sure the topping is fully thawed. Always spread from the center to the sides using a rubber spatula. This way, $\frac{1}{2}$ cup topping will cover an entire pie. Remember, the operative word is *frost*, not pile the entire container on top of the pie!

Here's my vote for the easiest **crumb topping** ever! Simply combine 3 tablespoons of purchased graham cracker crumbs (or three $2\frac{1}{2}$-inch squares made into fine crumbs) with 2 teaspoons reduced-calorie margarine and 1 tablespoon (if desired) chopped nuts. Mix this well and sprinkle evenly over the top of your fruit pie and bake as you normally would. You can use either a purchased graham cracker piecrust or an unbaked refrigerated regular piecrust. Another almost effortless crumb topping can be made by combining 6 tablespoons Bisquick Reduced-Fat Baking Mix and 2 tablespoons Splenda or pourable Sugar Twin with 2 teaspoons of reduced-calorie margarine until the mixture becomes crumbly. Again, you can stir in 1 tablespoon of chopped nuts if you wish. Evenly sprinkle this mixture over your fruit filling and bake as usual. This works best with a purchased unbaked refrigerated piecrust.

Another trick I often use is to include tiny amounts of "real people" food, such as coconut, but **extend the flavor by using extracts**. Try it—you will be surprised by how little of the real thing you can use and still feel you are not being deprived.

If you are preparing a pie filling that has ample moisture, just line the bottom of a 9-by-9-inch cake pan with **graham crackers**. Pour the filling over the top of the crackers. Cover and refrigerate until the moisture has enough time to soften the crackers. Overnight is best. This eliminates the added **fats and sugars of a piecrust.**

One of my readers provided a smart and easy way to enjoy a **two-crust pie** without all the fat that usually comes along with those two crusts. Just use one Pillsbury refrigerated piecrust. Let it sit at room temperature for about 20 minutes. Cut the crust in half on the folded line. Gently roll each half into a ball. Wipe your counter with a wet cloth and place a sheet of wax paper on it. Put one of the balls on the wax paper, then cover with another piece of wax paper, and roll it out with your rolling pin. Carefully remove the wax paper on one side and place that side into your 8- or 9-inch pie plate. Fill with your usual pie filling, then repeat the process for the top crust. Bake as usual. Enjoy!

Here's a good tip for **avoiding a "doughy" taste when using a refrigerated piecrust**. Make sure you take the piecrust out of the refrigerator and let it sit on the counter for at least ten minutes before putting it in the pie plate and baking it. If you put the piecrust into the plate before it has a chance to "warm up," it will be stiffer than if you let it come to room temperature before using. This means that the tiny amount of flour clinging to the crust doesn't have a chance to become "one" with the crust, making the finished product "doughier."

When you are preparing a pie that uses a purchased piecrust, simply tear out the paper label on the plastic cover (but check it for a coupon good on a future purchase) and turn the cover upside down over the prepared pie. You now have a cover that protects your beautifully garnished pie from having anything fall on top of it. It makes the pie very portable when it's your turn to bring dessert to a get-together.

And for **"picture-perfect" presentation** when using a purchased piecrust, just remove the protective plastic cover, place a pizza pan over the top of the crust, invert the "tin pan" and carefully remove it so the bottom of the crust is exposed. Then, replace the "tin pan" with an attractive pottery pie plate and, with one hand holding each pan in place, flip the piecrust so that the piecrust is now sitting securely in the pottery plate. Remove the pizza pan and fill it with your favorite Healthy Exchanges pie filling. This is easier than it sounds, and it makes your dessert look extra-special!

Did you know you can make your own **fruit-flavored yogurt?** Mix 1 tablespoon of any flavor of spreadable fruit spread with ¾ cup plain yogurt. It's every bit as tasty and much cheaper. You can also make your own **lemon yogurt** by combining 3 cups plain fat-free yogurt with 1 tub Crystal Light lemonade powder. Mix well, cover, and store in the refrigerator. I think you will be pleasantly surprised by the ease, cost, and flavor of this "made from scratch" calcium-rich treat. Also, you can make any flavor you like by using any of the Crystal Light mixes—Cranberry? Iced Tea? You decide.

Other Smart Substitutions

Many people have inquired about **substituting applesauce and artificial sweetener for butter and sugar**, but what if you aren't satisfied with the result? One woman wrote to me about a recipe for her grandmother's cookies that called for 1 cup of butter and 1½ cups of sugar. Well, any recipe that depends on as much butter and sugar as this one does is generally not a good candidate for "healthy exchanges." The original recipe needed a large quantity of fat to produce a crisp cookie just like Grandma made.

Applesauce can often be used instead of vegetable oil but generally doesn't work well as a replacement for butter, margarine, or lard. If a recipe calls for ½ cup or less of vegetable oil and your recipe is for a bar cookie, quick bread, muffin, or cake mix, you can try substituting an equal amount of unsweetened applesauce. If the recipe calls for more, try using ½ cup applesauce and the rest oil. You're cutting down the fat but shouldn't end up with a taste disaster! This "applesauce shortening" works great in many recipes, but so far I haven't been able to figure out a way to deep-fat fry with it!

Another rule for healthy substitution: Up to ½ cup sugar or less can be replaced by *an artificial sweetener that can withstand the heat of baking*, like pourable Sugar Twin or Splenda. If it requires more than ½ cup sugar, cut the amount needed by 75 percent and use ½ cup sugar substitute and sugar for the rest. Other options: Reduce the butter and sugar by 25 percent and see if the finished product still satisfies you in taste and appearance. Or, make the cookies just like Grandma did, realizing they are part of your family's holiday tradition. Enjoy a *moderate* serving of a couple of cookies once or twice during the season, and just forget about them the rest of the year.

Did you know that you can replace the fat in many quick breads, muffins, and shortcakes with **fat-free mayonnaise** or **fat-free sour cream?** This can work if the original recipe doesn't call for a lot of fat *and* sugar. If the recipe is truly fat and sugar dependent, such as traditional sugar cookies, cupcakes, or pastries, it won't work. Those recipes require the large amounts of sugar and fat to make love in the dark of the oven to produce a tender finished product. But if you have a favorite quick bread that doesn't call for a lot of sugar or fat, why don't you give one of these substitutes a try?

If you enjoy beverage mixes like those from Alba, here are my Healthy Exchanges versions:

For **chocolate flavored,** use ⅓ cup nonfat dry milk powder and 2 tablespoons Nestlé Sugar-Free Chocolate Flavored Quik. Mix well and use as usual. Or, use ⅓ cup nonfat dry milk powder, 1 teaspoon unsweetened cocoa, and sugar substitute to equal 3 tablespoons sugar. Mix well and use as usual.

For **vanilla flavored,** use ⅓ cup nonfat dry milk powder, sugar substitute to equal 2 tablespoons sugar, and add 1 teaspoon vanilla extract when adding liquid.

For **strawberry flavored,** use ⅓ cup nonfat dry milk powder, sugar substitute to equal 2 tablespoons sugar, and add 1 teaspoon strawberry extract and 3-4 drops red food coloring when adding liquid.

Each of these makes one packet of drink mix. If you need to double the recipe, double everything but the extract. Use 1½ teaspoons of extract or it will be too strong. Use 1 cup cold water with one recipe mix to make a glass of flavored milk. If you want to make a shake, combine the mix, water, and 3-4 ice cubes in your blender, then process on BLEND untill smooth.

A handy tip when making **healthy punch** for a party: Prepare a few extra cups of your chosen drink, freeze it in cubes in a couple of ice trays, then keep your punch from "watering down" by cooling it with punch cubes instead of ice cubes.

What should you do if you can't find the product listed in a Healthy Exchanges recipe? You can substitute in some cases—use Lemon JELL-O if you can't find Hawaiian Pineapple, for example. But if you're determined to track down the product you need, and your own store manager hasn't been able to order it for you, why not use one of the new online grocers and order exactly what you need, no matter where you live. Try **http://www.netgrocer.com.**

Not all low-fat cooking products are interchangeable, as one of my readers recently discovered when she tried to cook pancakes on her griddle using I Can't Believe It's Not Butter! spray—and they stuck! This butter-flavored spray is wonderful for a quick squirt on air-popped popcorn or corn on the cob, and it's great for topping your pancakes once they're cooked. In fact, my tastebuds have to check twice because it tastes so much like real butter! (And this is high praise from someone who once thought butter was the most perfect food ever created.)

But I Can't Believe It's Not Butter! doesn't work well for sautéing or browning. After trying to fry an egg with it and cooking up a disaster, I knew this product had its limitations. So I decided to continue using Pam or Weight Watchers butter-flavored cooking spray whenever I'm browning anything in a skillet or on a griddle.

Many of my readers have reported difficulty finding a product I use in many recipes: JELL-O cook-and-serve puddings. I have three suggestions for those of you with this problem:

1. **Work with your grocery store manager to get this product into your store**, and then make sure you and everyone you know buys it by the bagful! Products that sell well are reordered and kept in stock, especially with today's computerized cash registers that record what's purchased. You may also want to write or call Kraft General Foods and ask for their help. They can be reached at (800) 431-1001 weekdays from 9 A.M. to 4 P.M. (EST).

2. **You can prepare a recipe that calls for cook-and-serve pudding by using instant pudding of the same flavor.** Yes, that's right, you **can** cook with the instant when making my recipes. The finished product won't be quite as wonderful, but still at least a 3 on a 4-star scale. You can never do the opposite—never use cook-and-serve in a recipe that calls for instant! One time at a cooking demonstration, I could not understand why my Blueberry Mountain Cheesecake never did set up. Then I spotted the box in the trash and noticed I'd picked the wrong type of pudding mix. Be careful—the boxes are both blue, but the instant has pudding on a silver spoon, and the cook-and-serve has a stream of milk running down the front into a bowl with a wooden spoon.

3. **You can make JO's Sugar-Free Vanilla Cook-and-Serve Pudding Mix instead of using JELL-O's.** Here's my recipe: 2 tablespoons cornstarch, ½ cup pourable Sugar Twin or Splenda, ⅔ cup Carnation Nonfat Dry Milk Powder, 1½ cups water, 2 teaspoons vanilla extract, and 4 to 5 drops yellow food coloring. Combine all this in a medium saucepan and cook over medium heat, stirring constantly, until the mixture comes to a full boil and thickens. This is for basic cooked vanilla sugar-free pudding. For a chocolate version, the recipe is 2 tablespoons cornstarch, ¼ cup pourable Sugar Twin or Splenda, 2 tablespoons sugar-free chocolate-flavored Nestle's Quik, 1½ cups water, and 1 teaspoon vanilla extract. Follow the same cooking instructions as for the vanilla.

If you're preparing this as part of a recipe that also calls for adding a package of gelatin, just stir that into the mix.

Adapting a favorite family cake recipe? Here's something to try: Replace an egg and oil in the original with ⅓ cup fat-free yogurt and ¼ cup fat-free mayonnaise. Blend these two ingredients with your liquids in a separate bowl, then add the yogurt mixture to the flour mixture and mix gently just to combine. (You don't want to overmix or you'll release the gluten in the batter and end up with a tough batter.)

Want a tasty coffee creamer without all the fat? You could use Carnation's Fat Free Coffee-mate, which is 10 calories per teaspoon, but if you drink several cups a day with several teaspoons each, that adds up quickly to nearly 100 calories a day! Why not try my version? It's not quite as creamy, but it is good. Simply combine ⅓ cup Carnation Non-fat Dry Milk Powder and ¼ cup Splenda or pourable Sugar Twin. Cover and store in your cupboard or refrigerator. At 3 calories per teaspoon, you can enjoy three teaspoons for less than the calories of one teaspoon of the purchased variety.

Some Helpful Hints

Sugar-free puddings and gelatins are important to many of my recipes, but if you prefer to avoid sugar substitutes, you could still prepare the recipes with regular puddings or gelatins. The calories would be higher, but you would still be cooking low-fat.

When a recipe calls for **chopped nuts** (and you only have whole ones), who wants to dirty the food processor just for a couple of table-spoonsfuls? You could try to chop them using your cutting board, but be prepared for bits and pieces to fly all over the kitchen. I use "Grandma's food processor." I take the biggest nuts I can find, put them in a small glass bowl, and chop them into chunks just the right size using a metal biscuit cutter.

To quickly **toast nuts** without any fuss, spread about ½ cup of nuts (any kind) in a glass pie plate and microwave on HIGH (100% power) for 6 to 7 minutes or until golden. Stir after the first three minutes, then after each minute until done. Store them in an airtight container in your refrigerator. Toasting nuts really brings out their flavor, so it seems as if you used a whole treeful instead of tiny amounts.

A quick hint about **reduced-fat peanut butter:** Don't store it in the refrigerator. Because the fat has been reduced, it won't spread as easily when it's cold. Keep it in your cupboard, and a little will spread a lot further.

Crushing **graham crackers** for topping? A self-seal sandwich bag works great!

An eleven-year-old fan e-mailed me with a great tip recently: if you can't find the **mini chocolate chips** I use in many recipes, simply purchase the regular size and put them in a nut grinder to coarsely chop them.

If you have a **leftover muffin** and are looking for something a little different for breakfast, you can make a **"breakfast sundae."** Crumble the muffin into a cereal bowl. Sprinkle a serving of fresh fruit over it and top with a couple of tablespoons of plain fat-free yogurt sweetened with sugar substitute and your choice of extract. The thought of it just might make you jump out of bed with a smile on your face. (Speaking of muffins, did you know that if you fill the unused muffin wells with water when baking muffins, you help ensure more even baking and protect the muffin pan at the same time?) Another muffin hint: Lightly spray the inside of paper baking cups with butter-flavored cooking spray before spooning the muffin batter into them. Then you won't end up with paper clinging to your fresh-baked muffins.

The secret of making **good meringues** without sugar is to use 1 tablespoon of Splenda or pourable Sugar Twin for every egg white, and a small amount of extract. Use ½ to 1 teaspoon for the batch. Almond, vanilla, and coconut are all good choices. Use the same amount of cream of tartar you usually do. Bake the meringue in the same old way. Even if you can't eat sugar, you can enjoy a healthy meringue pie when it's prepared *The Healthy Exchanges Way*. (Remember that egg whites whip up best at room temperature.)

Try **storing your Bisquick Reduced Fat Baking Mix** in the freezer. It won't freeze, and it *will* stay fresh much longer. (It works for coffee, doesn't it?)

To check if your **baking powder** is fresh, put 1 teaspoonful in a bowl and pour 2 tablespoons of very hot tap water over it. If it's fresh, it will bubble very actively. If it doesn't bubble, then it's time to replace your old can with a new one.

If you've ever wondered about **changing ingredients** in one of my recipes, the answer is that some things can be changed to suit your family's tastes, but others should not be tampered with. **Don't change** the following: the amount of flour, bread crumbs, reduced-fat baking mix, baking soda, baking powder, or liquid or dry milk powder. And if I include a small amount of salt, it's necessary for the recipe to turn out correctly. **What you can change:** an extract flavor (if you don't like coconut, choose vanilla or almond instead); a spreadable fruit flavor; the type of fruit in a pie filling (but be careful about substituting fresh for frozen and vice versa—sometimes it works, but sometimes it doesn't); the flavor of pudding or gelatin. As long as package sizes and amounts are the same, go for it. It will never hurt my feelings if you change a recipe, so please your family—don't worry about me!

Because I always say that "good enough" isn't good enough for me anymore, here's a way to make your cup of **fat-free and sugar-free hot cocoa** more special. After combining the hot chocolate mix and hot water, stir in ½ teaspoon vanilla extract and a light sprinkle of cinnamon. If you really want to feel decadent, add a tablespoon of Cool Whip Lite. Isn't life grand?

If you must limit your sugar intake, but you love the idea of sprinkling **powdered sugar** on dessert crepes or burritos, here's a pretty good substitute: Place 1 cup Splenda or pourable Sugar Twin and 1 teaspoon cornstarch in a blender container, then cover and process on HIGH until the mixture resembles powdered sugar in texture, about 45 to 60 seconds. Store in an airtight container and use whenever you want a dusting of "powdered sugar" on any dessert.

Want my "almost instant" pies to set up even more quickly? Do as one of my readers does: freeze your Keebler piecrusts. Then, when you stir up one of my pies and pour the filling into the frozen crust, it sets up within seconds.

Some of my "island-inspired" recipes call for **rum or brandy extracts** which provide the "essence" of liquor without the real thing. I'm a teetotaler by choice, so I choose not to include real liquor in any of my recipes. Extracts are cheaper than liquor, and you won't feel the need to shoo your kids away from the goodies. If you prefer not to use liquor extracts in your cooking, you can always substitute vanilla extract.

Did you know you can make your own single-serving bags of microwave popcorn? Spoon 2 tablespoons of popping kernels into a paper lunch bag, folding the top over twice to seal and placing the sealed bag in the microwave. Microwave on HIGH for 2 to 3 minutes, or until the popping stops. Then pour the popcorn into a large bowl and lightly spritz with I Can't Believe It's Not Butter! spray. You'll have 3 cups of virtually fat-free popcorn to munch on at a fraction of the price of purchased microwave popcorn.

Some Healthy Cooking Challenges and How I Solved 'Em

When you stir up one of my pie fillings, do you ever have a problem with **lumps?** Here's an easy solution for all of you "careful" cooks out there. Lumps occur when the pudding starts to set up before you can get the dry milk powder incorporated into the mixture. I always advise you to dump, pour, and stir fast with that wire whisk, letting no more than 30 seconds elapse from beginning to end.

But if you are still having problems, you can always combine the dry milk powder and the water in a separate bowl before adding the pudding mix and whisking quickly. Why don't I suggest this right from the beginning? Because that would mean an extra dish to wash every time—and you know I hate to wash dishes!

With a little practice and a light touch, you should soon get the hang of my original method. But now you've got an alternative way to lose those lumps!

I love the chemistry of foods, and so I've gotten great pleasure from analyzing what makes fat-free products tick. By dissecting these "miracle" products, I've learned how to make them work best. They require different handling than the high-fat products we're used to, but if treated properly, these slimmed-down versions can produce delicious results!

Fat-free sour cream: This product is wonderful on a hot baked potato, but have you noticed that it tends to be much gummier than regular sour cream? If you want to use it in a stroganoff dish or baked product, you must stir a tablespoon or two of skim milk into the fat-free sour cream before adding it to other ingredients.

Cool Whip Free: When the fat went out of the formula, air was stirred in to fill the void. So, if you stir it too vigorously, you release the air and *decrease* the volume. Handle it with kid gloves—gently. Since the manufacturer forgot to ask for my input, I'll share with you how to make it taste almost the same as it used to. Let the container thaw in the refrigerator, then ever so gently stir in 1 teaspoon vanilla extract. Now, put the lid back on and enjoy it a tablespoon at a time, the same way you did Cool Whip Lite.

Fat-free cream cheese: When the fat was removed from this product, water replaced it. So don't ever use an electric mixer on the fat-free version, or you risk releasing the water and having your finished product look more like dip than cheesecake! Stirring it gently with a sturdy spoon in a glass bowl with a handle will soften it just as much as it needs to be. (A glass bowl with a handle lets you see what's going on; the handle gives you control as you stir. This "user-friendly" method is good for tired cooks, young cooks, and cooks with arthritis!) And don't be alarmed if the cream cheese gets caught in your wire whisk when you start combining the pudding mix and other ingredients. Just keep knocking it back down into the bowl by hitting the whisk against the rim of the bowl, and as you continue blending, it will soften even more and drop off the whisk. When it's time to pour the filling into your crust, your whisk shouldn't have anything much clinging to it.

Reduced-fat margarine: Again, the fat was replaced by water. If you try to use the reduced-fat kind in your cookie recipe spoon for spoon, you will end up with a cakelike cookie instead of the crisp kind most of us enjoy. You have to take into consideration that some water will be released as the product bakes. Use less liquid than the recipe calls for (when re-creating family recipes *only*—I've figured that into Healthy Exchanges recipes). And never, never, never use fat-*free* margarine and expect anyone to ask for seconds!

When every minute counts, and you need 2 cups cooked noodles for a casserole, how do you **figure out how much of a box of pasta to prepare**? Here's a handy guide that should help. While your final amount might vary slightly because of how loosely or tightly you "stuff" your measuring cup, this will make life easier.

Type	Start with this amount uncooked	If you want this amount cooked
Noodles	1 cup	1 cup
(thin, medium,	1¼ cups	1½ cups
wide, and mini	1¾ cups	2 cups
lasagne)	2¼ cups	2½ cups
	2½ cups	3 cups
Macaroni	⅓ cup	½ cup
(medium shells	⅔ cup	1 cup
and elbow)	1 cup	1½ cups
	1⅓ cups	2 cups
	2 cups	3 cups
Spaghetti,	¾ cup	1 cup
fettuccine,	1 cup	1½ cups
and rotini	1½ cups	2 cups
pasta	2½ cups	3 cups

Type	Start with this amount uncooked	If you want this amount cooked
Rice (instant)	⅓ cup	½ cup
	⅔ cup	1 cup
	1 cup	1½ cups
	1⅓ cups	2 cups
	2 cups	3 cups
Rice (regular)	¼ cup	½ cup
	½ cup	1 cup
	1 cup	2 cups
	1½ cups	3 cups

Here's a handy idea for **keeping your cookbooks open** to a certain page while cooking: use two rubber bands, one wrapped vertically around the left side of the book, another on the right side. And to **keep your cookbooks clean**, try slipping the rubber-banded book into a gallon-sized Ziploc bag. (Though I'd consider it a compliment to know that the pages of my cookbooks were all splattered, because it would mean that you are really using the recipes!)

Homemade or Store-Bought?

I've been asked which is better for you: homemade from scratch, or purchased foods. My answer is *both!* Each has a place in a healthy lifestyle, and what that place is has everything to do with you.

Take **piecrusts**, for instance. If you love spending your spare time in the kitchen preparing foods, and you're using low-fat, low-sugar, and reasonably low sodium ingredients, go for it! But if, like so many people, your time is limited and you've learned to read labels, you could be better off using purchased foods.

I know that when I prepare a pie (and I experiment with a couple of pies each week, because this is Cliff's favorite dessert), I use a purchased crust. Why? Mainly because I can't make a good-tasting piecrust that is lower in fat than the brands I use. Also, purchased piecrusts fit my rule of "If it takes longer to fix than to eat, forget it!"

I've checked the nutrient information for the purchased piecrusts against recipes for traditional and "diet" piecrusts, using my computer software program. The purchased crust calculated lower in both fat and calories! I have tried some low-fat and low-sugar recipes, but they just didn't spark my tastebuds or were so complicated you needed an engineering degree just to get the crust in the pie plate.

I'm very happy with the purchased piecrusts in my recipes, because the finished product rarely, if ever, has more than 30 percent of total calories coming from fats. I also believe that we have to prepare foods our families and friends will eat with us on a regular basis and not feel deprived, or we've wasted time, energy, and money.

I could use a purchased "lite" **pie filling**, but instead I make my own. Here I can reduce both fat and sugar and still make the filling almost as fast as opening a can. The bottom line: Know what you have to spend when it comes to both time and fat/sugar calories, then make the best decision you can for you and your family. And don't go without an occasional piece of pie because you think it isn't *necessary*. A delicious pie prepared in a healthy way is one of the simple pleasures of life. It's a little thing, but it can make all the difference between just getting by with the bare minimum and living a full and healthy lifestyle.

I'm sure you'll add to this list of cooking tips as you begin preparing Healthy Exchanges recipes and discover how easy it can be to adapt your own favorite recipes using these ideas and your own common sense.

A Peek into My Pantry and My Favorite Brands

Everyone asks me what foods I keep on hand and what brands I use. There are lots of good products on the grocery shelves today—many more than we dreamed about even a year or two ago. And I can't wait to see what's out there twelve months from now. The following are my staples and, where appropriate, my favorites *at this time*. I feel that these products are healthier, tastier, easy to get—and deliver the most flavor for the least amount of fat, sugar, or calories. If you find others you like as well *or better,* please use them. This is only a guide to make your grocery shopping and cooking easier.

Plain fat-free yogurt (*Dannon—Yoplait no longer makes it*)
Nonfat dry milk powder (*Carnation*)
Evaporated skim milk (*Carnation*)
Skim milk
Fat-free cottage cheese
Fat-free cream cheese (*Philadelphia*)
Fat-free mayonnaise (*Kraft*)
Fat-free salad dressings (*Kraft*)
Fat-free sour cream (*Land O Lakes*)
Reduced-calorie margarine (*I Can't Believe It's Not Butter! Light or Promise Light*)
Cooking spray
   Olive oil–flavored and regular (*Pam*)
   Butter-flavored for sautéing (*Pam or Weight Watchers*)

Butter-flavored for spritzing *after* cooking (*I Can't Believe It's Not Butter!*)

Vegetable oil (*Puritan Canola Oil*)

Reduced-calorie whipped topping (*Cool Whip Lite or Cool Whip Free*)

Sugar substitute

if no heating is involved (*Splenda or Equal*)

if heating is required

white (*Splenda or pourable Sugar Twin*)

brown (*Brown Sugar Twin*)

Sugar-free gelatin and pudding mixes (*JELL-O*)

Baking mix (*Bisquick Reduced Fat*)

Pancake mix (*Aunt Jemima Reduced Calorie*)

Reduced-calorie pancake syrup (*Log Cabin Sugar Free and Cary's Sugar Free*)

Parmesan cheese (*Kraft fat-free*)

Reduced-fat cheese (*Kraft Reduced Fat*)

Shredded frozen potatoes (*Mr. Dell's*)

Spreadable fruit spread (*Smucker's, Welch's, or Knott's Berry Farm*)

Peanut butter (*Peter Pan reduced-fat, Jif reduced-fat, or Skippy reduced-fat*)

Chicken broth (*Healthy Request*)

Beef broth (*Swanson*)

Tomato sauce (*Hunt's—plain, Italian, or chili*)

Canned soups (*Healthy Request*)

Tomato juice (*Campbell's Reduced-Sodium*)

Ketchup (*Heinz Light Harvest or Healthy Choice*)

Purchased piecrust

unbaked (*Pillsbury—from dairy case*)

graham cracker, butter flavored, or chocolate flavored (*Keebler*)

Crescent rolls (*Pillsbury Reduced Fat*)

Pastrami and corned beef (*Carl Buddig Lean*)

Luncheon meats (*Healthy Choice or Oscar Mayer*)

Ham (*Dubuque 97% fat-free and reduced-sodium or Healthy Choice*)

Frankfurters and kielbasa sausage (*Healthy Choice*)

Canned white chicken, packed in water (*Swanson*)

Canned tuna, packed in water (*Starkist or Chicken of the Sea*)

90 to 97 percent lean ground turkey and beef

Soda crackers (*Nabisco Fat-Free*)

Reduced-calorie bread—40 calories per slice or less
Hamburger buns—80 calories each (*Less*)
Rice—instant, regular, brown, and wild
Instant potato flakes (*Betty Crocker Potato Buds*)
Noodles, spaghetti, and macaroni
Salsa (*Chi Chi's Mild Chunky*)
Pickle relish—dill, sweet, and hot dog
Mustard—Dijon, prepared, and spicy
Unsweetened apple juice
Unsweetened applesauce
Fruit—fresh, frozen (no sugar added), or canned in juice
Vegetables—fresh, frozen, or canned
Spices—JO's Spices
Lemon and lime juice (in small plastic fruit-shaped bottles found
    in the produce section)
Instant fruit beverage mixes (*Crystal Light*)
Sugar-free hot chocolate mixes (*Swiss Miss*)
Ice Cream (*Wells' Blue Bunny sugar- and fat-free*)

The items on my shopping list are everyday foods found in just about any grocery store in America. But all are as low in fat, sugar, calories, and sodium as I can find—but still taste good! I can make any recipe in my cookbooks and newsletters as long as I have my cupboards and refrigerator stocked with these items. Whenever I use the last of any one item, I just make sure I pick up another supply the next time I'm at the store.

If your grocer does not stock these items, why not ask if they can be ordered on a trial basis? If the store agrees to do so, be sure to tell your friends to stop by, so that sales are good enough to warrant restocking the new products. Competition for shelf space is fierce, so only products that sell well stay around.

Shopping "The Healthy Exchanges Way"

Sometimes, as part of a cooking demonstration, I take the group on a field trip to the nearest supermarket. There's no better place to share my discoveries about which healthy products taste best, which are best for you, and which healthy products don't deliver enough taste to include in my recipes.

While I'd certainly enjoy accompanying you to your neighborhood store, we'll have to settle for a field trip *on paper*. I've tasted and tried just about every fat- and sugar-free product on the market, but so many new ones keep coming all the time, you're going to have to learn to play detective on your own. I've turned label reading into an art, but often the label doesn't tell me everything I need to know.

Sometimes you'll find, as I have, that the product with *no* fat doesn't provide the taste satisfaction you require; other times, a no-fat or low-fat product just doesn't cook up the same way as the original product. And some foods, including even the leanest meats, can't eliminate *all* the fat. That's okay, though—a healthy diet should include anywhere from 15 to 25 percent of total calories from fat on any given day.

Take my word for it—your supermarket is filled with lots of delicious foods that can and should be part of your healthy diet for life. Come, join me as we check it out on the way to the checkout!

Before I buy anything at the store, I read the label carefully: I check the total fat plus the saturated fat; I look to see how many calories are in a realistic serving, and I say to myself, Would I eat that much—or would I eat more? I look at the sodium and I look at the total carbohydrates. I like to check those ingredients because I'm cooking for diabetics and heart patients, too. And I check the total calories from fat.

Remember that 1 fat gram equals 9 calories, while 1 protein or 1 carbohydrate gram equals 4 calories.

A wonderful new product is I Can't Believe It's Not Butter! spray, with zero calories and zero grams of fat in five squirts. It's great for your air-popped popcorn. As for **light margarine spread**, beware—most of the fat-free brands don't melt on toast, and they don't taste very good either, so I just leave them on the shelf. For the few times I do use a light margarine, I tend to buy Smart Beat Ultra, Promise Ultra, or Weight Watchers Light Ultra. The number one ingredient in them is water. I occasionally use the light margarine in cooking, but I don't really put margarine on my toast anymore. I use apple butter or make a spread with fat-free cream cheese mixed with a little spreadable fruit instead.

So far, Pillsbury hasn't released a reduced-fat **crescent roll**, so you'll only get one crescent roll per serving from me. I usually make eight of the rolls serve twelve by using them for a crust. The house brands may be lower in fat, but they're usually not as good flavorwise— and they don't quite cover the pan when you use them to make a crust. If you're going to use crescent rolls with lots of other stuff on top, then a house brand might be fine.

The Pillsbury French Loaf makes a wonderful **pizza crust** and fills a giant jelly roll pan. One fifth of this package "costs" you only 1 gram of fat (and I don't even let you have that much!). Once you use this for your pizza crust, you will never go back to anything else instead. I use it to make calzones, too.

I only use Philadelphia fat-free **cream cheese** because it has the best consistency. I've tried other brands, but I wasn't happy with them. Healthy Choice makes lots of great products, but their cream cheese just doesn't work as well with my recipes.

Let's move to the **cheese** aisle. My preferred brand is Kraft reduced-fat shredded cheeses. I will not use the fat-free versions because *they don't melt.* I would gladly give up sugar and fat, but I will not give up flavor. This is a happy compromise. I use the reduced-fat version, I use less, and I use it where your eyes "eat" it, on top of the recipe. So you walk away satisfied and with a finished product that's very low in fat. If you want to make grilled-cheese sandwiches for your kids, use the Kraft reduced-fat cheese slices, and it'll taste exactly like the ones they're used to. The fat-free will not.

Dubuque's Extra-Lean Reduced-Sodium **ham** tastes wonderful, reduces the sodium as well as the fat, and gives you a larger serving. Don't be fooled by products called turkey ham; they *may not* be lower in fat than a very lean pork product. Here's one label as an example: I checked a brand of turkey ham called Genoa. It gives you a 2-ounce serving for 70 calories and 3½ grams of fat. The Dubuque extra-lean ham, made from pork, gives you a 3-ounce serving for 90 calories, but only 2½ grams of fat. *You get more food and less fat.*

Frozen dinners can be expensive and high in sodium, but it's smart to have two or three in the freezer as a backup when your best-laid plans go awry and you need to grab something on the run. It's not a good idea to rely on them too much—what if you can't get to the store to get them, or you're short on cash? The sodium can be high in some of them because they often replace the fat with salt, so be sure to read the labels. Also ask yourself if the serving is enough to satisfy you; for many of us, it's not.

Egg substitute is expensive, and probably not necessary unless you're cooking for someone who has to worry about every bit of cholesterol in his or her diet. If you occasionally have a fried egg or an omelet, *use the real egg.* For cooking, you can usually substitute two egg whites for one whole egg. Most of the time it won't make any difference, but check your recipe carefully.

Healthy frozen desserts are hard to find except for the Weight Watchers brands. I've always felt that their portions are so small, and for their size still pretty high in fat and sugar. (This is one of the reasons I think I'll be successful marketing my frozen desserts someday. After Cliff tasted one of my earliest healthy pies—and licked the plate clean—he remarked that if I ever opened a restaurant, people would keep coming back for my desserts alone!) Keep an eye out for fat-free or very low-fat frozen yogurt or sorbet products. Even Häagen-Dazs, which makes some of the highest-fat-content ice cream, now has a fat-free fruit sorbet pop out that's pretty good. I'm sure there will be more before too long.

You have to be realistic: What are you willing to do, and what are you *not* willing to do? Let's take bread, for example. Some people just have to have the real thing—rye bread with caraway seeds or a whole-wheat version with bits of bran in it.

I prefer to use reduced-calorie **bread** because I like a *real* sandwich. This way, I can have two slices of bread and it counts as only one Bread/Starch exchange.

How I Shop for Myself

I always keep my kitchen stocked with my basic staples; that way, I can go to the cupboard and create new recipes anytime I'm inspired. I hope you will take the time (and allot the money) to stock your cupboards with items from the staples list, so you can enjoy developing your own healthy versions of family favorites without making extra trips to the market.

I'm always on the lookout for new products sitting on the grocery shelf. When I spot something I haven't seen before, I'll usually grab it, glance at the front, then turn it around and read the label carefully. I call it looking at the "promises" (the "come-on" on the front of the package) and then at the "warranty" (the ingredients list and the label on the back).

If it looks as good on the back as it does on the front, I'll say okay and either create a recipe on the spot or take it home for when I do think of something to do with it. Picking up a new product is just about the only time I buy something not on my list.

The items on my shopping list are normal, everyday foods, but as low-fat and low-sugar (*while still tasting good*) as I can find. I can make any recipe in this book as long as these staples are on my shelves. After using these products for a couple of weeks, you will find it becomes routine to have them on hand. And I promise you, I really don't spend any more at the store now than I did a few years ago when I told myself I couldn't afford some of these items. Back then, of course, plenty of unhealthy, high-priced snacks I really didn't need somehow made the magic leap from the grocery shelves into my cart. Who was I kidding?

Yes, you often have to pay a little more for fat-free or low-fat products, including meats. But since I frequently use a half pound of meat to serve four to six people, your cost per serving will be much lower.

Try adding up what you were spending before on chips and cookies, premium brand ice cream, and fatty cuts of meat, and you'll soon see that we've *streamlined* your shopping cart, and taken the weight off your pocketbook as well as your hips!

Remember, your good health is *your* business—but it's big business, too. Write to the manufacturers of products you and your family enjoy but feel are just too high in fat, sugar, or sodium to be part of your new healthy lifestyle. Companies are spending millions of dollars to respond to consumers' concerns about food products, and I bet that in the next few years, you'll discover fat-free and low-fat versions of nearly every product piled high on your supermarket shelves!

The Healthy
Exchanges
Kitchen

You might be surprised to discover that I still don't have a massive test kitchen stocked with every modern appliance and handy gadget ever made. The tiny galley kitchen where I first launched Healthy Exchanges had room for only one person at a time, but it never stopped me from feeling that the sky was the limit when it came to seeking out great healthy taste!

Now I have more room than I used to, but I still don't waste space on equipment I don't really need. Here's a list of what I consider worth having. If you notice serious gaps in your equipment, you can probably find most of what you need at a local discount store or garage sale. If your kitchen is equipped with more sophisticated appliances, don't feel guilty about using them. Enjoy every appliance you can find room for or that you can afford. Just be assured that healthy, quick, and delicious food can be prepared with the "basics."

A Healthy Exchanges Kitchen Equipment List

Good-quality nonstick skillets (medium, large)
Good-quality saucepans (small, medium, large)
Glass mixing bowls (small, medium, large)
Glass measures (1-cup, 2-cup, 4-cup, 8-cup)
Sharp knives (paring, chef, butcher)
Rubber spatulas

Wire whisks
Measuring spoons
Measuring cups
Large mixing spoons
Egg separator
Covered jar
Vegetable parer
Grater
Potato masher
Electric mixer
Electric blender
Electric skillet
Cooking timer
Slow cooker
Air popper for popcorn
Kitchen scales (unless you *always* use my recipes)
Wire racks for cooling baked goods

4-inch round custard dishes
Glass pie plates
8-by-8-inch glass baking dishes
Cake pans (9-by-9-inch, 9-by-13-inch)
10¾-by-7-by-1½-inch biscuit pan
Cookie sheets (good nonstick ones)
Jelly roll pan
Muffin tins
5-by-9-inch bread pan
Plastic colander
Cutting board
Pie wedge server
Square-shaped server
Can opener (I prefer manual)
Rolling pin

Electric toaster oven (to conserve energy for those times when only one item is being baked or for a recipe that requires a short baking time)

And of course, a slow cooker or two to prepare all the recipes in this book!

A Few Cooking Terms to Ease the Way

Everyone can learn to cook The Healthy Exchanges Way. It's simple, it's quick, and the results are delicious! If you've tended to avoid the kitchen because you find recipe instructions confusing or complicated, I hope I can help you feel more confident. I'm not offering a full cooking course here, just some terms I often use that I know you'll want to understand.

Bake: To cook food in the oven; sometimes called roasting

Beat: To mix very fast with a spoon, wire whisk, or electric mixer

Blend: To mix two or more ingredients together thoroughly so that the mixture is smooth

Boil: To cook in liquid until bubbles form

Brown: To cook at low to medium-low heat until ingredients turn brown

Chop: To cut food into small pieces with a knife, blender, or food processor

Combine: To mix ingredients together with a spoon

Cool: To let stand at room temperature until food is no longer hot to the touch

Dice: To chop into small, even-sized pieces

Drain: To pour off liquid. Sometimes you will need to reserve the liquid to use in the recipe, so please read carefully.

Drizzle: To sprinkle drops of liquid (for example, chocolate syrup) lightly over the top of food

Fold in: To combine delicate ingredients with other foods by using a gentle, circular motion. Example: adding Cool Whip Lite to an already stirred-up bowl of pudding.

Preheat: To heat your oven to the desired temperature, usually about 10 minutes before you put your food in to bake

Sauté: To cook in a skillet or frying pan until the food is soft

Simmer: To cook in a small amount of liquid over low heat; this lets the flavors blend without too much liquid evaporating.

Whisk: To beat with a wire whisk until mixture is well mixed. Don't worry about finesse here; just use some elbow grease!

How to Measure

I try to make measuring as easy as possible by providing more than one measurement for many ingredients in my recipes—both the weight in ounces and the amount measured by a measuring cup, for example. Just remember:

- You measure **solids** (flour, Cool Whip Lite, yogurt, nonfat dry milk powder) in your set of separate measuring cups ($\frac{1}{4}$, $\frac{1}{3}$, $\frac{1}{2}$, 1 cup)

- You measure **liquids** (Diet Mountain Dew, water, juice) in the clear glass or plastic measuring cups that measure ounces, cups, and pints. Set the cup on a level surface and pour the liquid into it, or you may get too much.

- You can use your measuring spoon set for liquids or solids. **Note:** Don't pour a liquid like an extract into a measuring spoon held over the bowl in case you overpour; instead, do it over the sink.

Here are a few handy equivalents:

3 teaspoons	equals	1 tablespoon
4 tablespoons	equals	$\frac{1}{4}$ cup

5⅓ tablespoons	equals	⅓ cup
8 tablespoons	equals	½ cup
10⅔ tablespoons	equals	⅔ cup
12 tablespoons	equals	¾ cup
16 tablespoons	equals	1 cup
2 cups	equals	1 pint
4 cups	equals	1 quart
8 ounces liquid	equals	1 fluid cup

That's it. Now, ready, set, cook!

How to Read
a Healthy
Exchanges Recipe

The Healthy Exchanges
Nutritional Analysis

Before using these recipes, you may wish to consult your physician or health-care provider to ensure that they are appropriate for you. The information in this book is not intended to take the place of any medical advice. It reflects my experiences, studies, research, and opinions regarding healthy eating.

Each recipe includes nutritional information calculated in three ways:

> Healthy Exchanges Weight Loss Choices™ or Exchanges
> Calories; Fat, Protein, Carbohydrates, and Fiber in grams;
>   Sodium and Calcium in milligrams
> Diabetic Exchanges

In every Healthy Exchanges recipe, the diabetic exchanges have been calculated by a registered dietitian. All the other calculations were done by computer, using the Food Processor II software. When the ingredient listing gives more than one choice, the first ingredient listed is the one used in the recipe analysis. Due to inevitable variations in the ingredients you choose to use, the nutritional values should be considered approximate.

The annotation "(limited)" following Protein counts in some recipes indicates that consumption of whole eggs should be limited to four per week.

Please note the following symbols:

☆ This star means that you should read the recipe's directions carefully for special instructions about **division** of ingredients.

❋ This symbol indicates **FREEZES WELL.**

The Recipes

Sensational

Soups

If ever there was an appliance perfectly suited to making soups, soups, and more soups, it would be the slow cooker. The very best soups are made better simply by spending time bubbling away so that all their flavors can weave together a spectacular tapestry of taste. No matter which ingredients you choose to include in your potful of pleasure, they become more than they are to begin with once they cook slowly and surely into a memorable dish.

The section also features some wonderful hearty stews and chowders that are sure to be warmly welcomed by your family whenever they appear on the menu. At our house, soup was never viewed as simply an appetizer or quick lunch from a can. As far back as I can remember, soup was a cozy-warm, terrifically thrifty, and supremely satisfying occasion for my sisters and I to gather round the table with my parents and feast on whatever combination of ingredients had inspired my mother!

You'll find an abundance of choices here, from the creamiest, cheesiest soups of any low-fat cookbook (Cheesy Crock Soup is a favorite) to the thickest, richest down-home stews that ever graced a Midwestern kitchen table (Pepper Steak Stew and Barleyburger Stew come to mind). If you're looking to use up leftovers, Hobo Stew will serve you well; and if you're hungry for the kind of soup your grandma used to make, you'll be pleased to savor Pioneer Vegetable Soup and Grandma's Cabbage Soup. Whatever you choose, you'll be warmed inside and out before you know it!

Sensational

Soups

Simply Good Vegetable Soup

The name says it all—a great-tasting but easy recipe that provides a delicious way to get the veggies you need for good health every day! Make a pot and enjoy it for days.　　◑　Serves 6 (1⅓ cups)

2½ cups reduced-sodium tomato juice

1½ cups hot water

1 cup chopped onion

2 cups diced carrots

1½ cups diced unpeeled zucchini

3 cups shredded cabbage

2 cups (one 16-ounce can) tomatoes, chopped and undrained

1 tablespoon pourable Splenda or Sugar Twin

2 teaspoons dried parsley flakes

⅛ teaspoon black pepper

Spray a slow cooker container with butter-flavored cooking spray. In prepared container, combine tomato juice and water. Stir in onion, carrots, zucchini, and cabbage. Add undrained tomatoes, Splenda, parsley flakes, and black pepper. Mix well to combine. Cover and cook on LOW for 6 to 8 hours. Mix well before serving.

Each serving equals:

HE: 3½ Vegetable • 1 Optional Calorie

76 Calories • 0 gm Fat • 3 gm Protein •
16 gm Carbohydrate • 228 mg Sodium • 62 mg Calcium •
4 gm Fiber

DIABETIC: 3 Vegetable

Grandma's Cabbage Soup

There's no need to deprive yourself by going on a diet that allows *only* cabbage soup, as one popular fad diet suggests. But as part of a healthy lifestyle, this soothing version is just about perfect.

☻ Serves 6 (1½ cups)

> 2 cups shredded cabbage
> ⅔ cup uncooked instant rice
> 2 cups (one 16-ounce can) Healthy Request Chicken Broth
> 2½ cups hot water
> 1 cup (one 8-ounce can) Hunt's Tomato Sauce
> ½ cup shredded carrots
> ½ cup finely chopped onion
> 2 cups (one 16-ounce can) tomatoes, chopped and undrained
> 1 tablespoon pourable Splenda or Sugar Twin
> 1 teaspoon dried dill weed
> ⅛ teaspoon black pepper

Spray a slow cooker container with butter-flavored cooking spray. In prepared container, combine cabbage, uncooked rice, chicken broth, water, and tomato sauce. Stir in carrots and onion. Add undrained tomatoes, Splenda, dill weed, and black pepper. Mix well to combine. Cover and cook on LOW for 8 hours. Mix well before serving.

Each serving equals:

HE: 2 Vegetable • ⅓ Bread • 6 Optional Calories

84 Calories • 0 gm Fat • 3 gm Protein •
18 gm Carbohydrate • 543 mg Sodium • 44 mg Calcium •
3 gm Fiber

DIABETIC: 2 Vegetable • ½ Starch

Cheesy Cheese Soup

Instead of a no-no (as many cheese-based soups would be if you're watching your cholesterol), this cheesiest of cheese soups is an unqualified YES! It tastes so luscious it ought to be sinful, but if you're looking for culinary "trouble," you'll need to look elsewhere.

○ Serves 6 (1 cup)

> 1 (10¾-ounce) can Healthy Request Cream of Celery Soup
> 1½ cups (one 12-fluid-ounce can) Carnation Evaporated Skim Milk
> 1½ cups hot water
> 2 teaspoons dried onion flakes
> 1 teaspoon Worcestershire sauce
> ¼ teaspoon paprika
> 1 full cup Cheez Whiz Light
> 1½ cups frozen mixed vegetables, thawed

Spray a slow cooker container with butter-flavored cooking spray. In prepared container, combine celery soup, evaporated skim milk, water, onion flakes, Worcestershire sauce, and paprika. Add Cheez Whiz Light. Mix well to combine. Stir in vegetables. Cover and cook on LOW for 3 to 4 hours. Mix well before serving.

HINT: Thaw vegetables by placing them in a colander and rinsing them under hot water for one minute.

Each serving equals:

HE: 1½ Protein • ½ Skim Milk • ½ Vegetable • ¼ Slider •
8 Optional Calories

---

168 Calories • 4 gm Fat • 13 gm Protein •
20 gm Carbohydrate • 941 mg Sodium • 405 mg Calcium •
1 gm Fiber

DIABETIC: 1½ Meat • ½ Skim Milk • ½ Vegetable

Cheesy Crock Soup

So creamy good, this vegetable cheese soup is ideal for those wintry days when you think you'll never be warm again! A cupful of this will convince you that spring is just around the corner.

● Serves 6 (1 full cup)

> 1 (10¾-ounce) can Healthy Request Cream of Mushroom Soup
> 1 cup Carnation Nonfat Dry Milk Powder
> 3 cups hot water
> ½ cup finely diced onion
> 2 cups finely chopped celery
> ½ cup (one 2.5-ounce can) sliced mushrooms, drained
> 1 teaspoon Worcestershire sauce
> 1 teaspoon dried parsley flakes
> 1½ cups shredded Kraft reduced-fat Cheddar cheese

Spray a slow cooker container with butter-flavored cooking spray. In prepared container, combine mushroom soup, dry milk powder, and water. Add onion, celery, and mushrooms. Mix well to combine. Stir in Worcestershire sauce, parsley flakes, and Cheddar cheese. Cover and cook on LOW for 4 to 6 hours or until vegetables are tender. Mix well before serving.

Each serving equals:

HE: 1⅓ Protein • 1 Vegetable • ½ Skim Milk • ¼ Slider • 8 Optional Calories

149 Calories • 5 gm Fat • 12 gm Protein • 14 gm Carbohydrate • 580 mg Sodium • 393 mg Calcium • 1 gm Fiber

DIABETIC: 1 Meat • ½ Vegetable • ½ Skim Milk

Tomato-Potato Soup

Here's a pantry-friendly recipe that makes a terrific soup—without any special ingredients, just what most of us always have on hand. It takes only minutes to get this one under way, but I think you'll find that the result is truly special. ❂ Serves 4 (1½ cups)

1 (10¾-ounce) can Healthy Request Tomato Soup
2½ cups reduced-sodium tomato juice
1 cup finely diced onion
3 cups finely diced raw potatoes
1 teaspoon dried parsley flakes

Spray a slow cooker container with butter-flavored cooking spray. In prepared container, combine tomato soup and tomato juice. Stir in onion, potatoes, and parsley flakes. Cover and cook on LOW for 8 hours. Mix well before serving.

Each serving equals:

HE: 1¾ Vegetable • ¾ Bread • ½ Slider •
5 Optional Calories

165 Calories • 1 gm Fat • 4 gm Protein •
35 gm Carbohydrate • 307 mg Sodium • 32 mg Calcium •
3 gm Fiber

DIABETIC: 2 Vegetable • 1½ Starch

French Onion Soup Pot

True French onion soup is based on soup stock that takes hours of effort to prepare, and which one of us has that kind of time? I'm happy to say that this recipe delivers the hearty flavors of the "real thing" with much less work!　　　◐　　　Serves 4

> $1^3/4$ cups (one 15-ounce can) Swanson Beef Broth
> $1^1/4$ cups hot water
> 2 teaspoons dried parsley flakes
> $1/8$ teaspoon black pepper
> 2 teaspoons Worcestershire sauce
> $1/4$ cup grated Kraft fat-free Parmesan cheese
> 3 cups thinly sliced onion
> 4 slices reduced-calorie white bread, toasted and cubed

Spray a slow cooker container with butter-flavored cooking spray. In prepared container, combine beef broth, water, parsley flakes, black pepper, and Worcestershire sauce. Stir in Parmesan cheese. Add onion. Mix well to combine. Cover and cook on LOW for 8 hours. For each serving, spoon 1 cup soup mixture into a bowl and sprinkle $1/4$ of bread cubes over the top.

Each serving equals:

HE: $1^1/2$ Vegetable • $1/2$ Bread • $1/4$ Protein •
8 Optional Calories

---

121 Calories • 1 gm Fat • 5 gm Protein •
23 gm Carbohydrate • 575 mg Sodium • 44 mg Calcium •
5 gm Fiber

DIABETIC: $1^1/2$ Vegetable • $1/2$ Meat

French Broccoli-Rice Soup

Oh-so-luscious and creamy, this soup delivers plenty of nourishment in one tasty bowl! It's quicker than many of the soups in this book, so try it some day when time is definitely at a premium.

♥ Serves 4 (1½ cups)

> 1 (10¾-ounce) can Healthy Request Cream of Mushroom Soup
> 1½ cups (one 12-fluid-ounce can) Carnation Evaporated Skim Milk
> 1½ cups hot water
> ¾ cup shredded Kraft reduced-fat Cheddar cheese
> ⅓ cup uncooked instant rice
> ½ cup shredded carrots
> ½ cup diced onion
> 2 cups frozen cut broccoli, thawed
> 1 teaspoon dried parsley flakes

Spray a slow cooker container with butter-flavored cooking spray. In prepared container, combine mushroom soup, evaporated skim milk, water, and Cheddar cheese. Stir in uncooked rice, carrots, onion, broccoli, and parsley flakes. Cover and cook on LOW for 3 to 4 hours. Mix well before serving.

HINT: Thaw broccoli by placing it in a colander and rinsing it under hot water for one minute.

Each serving equals:

HE: 1½ Vegetable • 1 Protein • ¾ Skim Milk •
¼ Bread • ½ Slider • 1 Optional Calorie

229 Calories • 5 gm Fat • 15 gm Protein •
31 gm Carbohydrate • 618 mg Sodium •
496 mg Calcium • 3 gm Fiber

DIABETIC: 1½ Vegetable • 1 Meat • 1 Skim Milk •
1 Starch/Carbohydrate

Tomato Bean Pot

Beans are a great soup starter—high in fiber and sturdy as they come. Hours of cooking make them even more delicious, and this tomato-based dish is fantastically filling as well.

⏺ Serves 6 (1 full cup)

20 ounces (two 16-ounce cans) navy beans, rinsed and drained

1 cup finely chopped onion

1 cup finely chopped celery

2 cups (one 16-ounce can) tomatoes, chopped and undrained

1 cup hot water

1 tablespoon sweet pickle relish

¼ cup pourable Splenda or Sugar Twin

2 tablespoons Brown Sugar Twin

2 teaspoons prepared yellow mustard

⅛ teaspoon black pepper

Spray a slow cooker container with butter-flavored cooking spray. In prepared container, combine navy beans, onion, celery, and undrained tomatoes. Stir in water, pickle relish, Splenda, Brown Sugar Twin, mustard, and black pepper. Cover and cook on LOW for 6 to 8 hours. Mix well before serving.

Each serving equals:

HE: 1⅔ Protein • 1⅓ Vegetable • 8 Optional Calories

140 Calories • 0 gm Fat • 8 gm Protein • 27 gm Carbohydrate • 530 mg Sodium • 73 mg Calcium • 6 gm Fiber

DIABETIC: 1 Meat • 1 Vegetable • 1 Starch

Creamy Baked Potato Soup

The restaurant version of this pub favorite is way too high in fat and calories for most of us to enjoy very often, but I've worked some healthy magic on its basic ingredients, and now it's yours to relish anytime at all!

♥ Serves 6 (1 full cup)

1 (10¾-ounce) can Healthy Request Cream of Mushroom Soup

1½ cups (one 12-fluid-ounce can) Carnation Evaporated Skim Milk

¼ cup (one 2-ounce jar) chopped pimiento, undrained

3 cups diced cooked unpeeled potatoes

6 tablespoons Hormel Bacon Bits

¾ cup finely chopped green onion

1 teaspoon dried parsley flakes

⅛ teaspoon black pepper

6 tablespoons shredded Kraft reduced-fat Cheddar cheese

Spray a slow cooker container with butter-flavored cooking spray. In prepared container, combine mushroom soup, evaporated skim milk, and undrained pimiento. Add potatoes, bacon bits, and green onion. Mix well to combine. Stir in parsley flakes and black pepper. Cover and cook on LOW for 2 to 3 hours. Mix well before serving. When serving, top each bowl with 1 tablespoon Cheddar cheese.

Each serving equals:

HE: ⅔ Bread • ½ Skim Milk • ⅓ Protein • ¼ Vegetable • ½ Slider • 13 Optional Calories

228 Calories • 4 gm Fat • 11 gm Protein • 37 gm Carbohydrate • 595 mg Sodium • 258 mg Calcium • 3 gm Fiber

DIABETIC: 1½ Starch • 1 Meat • ½ Skim Milk

Tuna, Potato and Corn Chowder

It's hard to think of a dish that's heartier than corn chowder—and this version adds lots of healthy protein to the mix, along with potatoes to make it extra thick and yummy. It's another pantry pleasure, made from healthy and convenient packaged foods that are easy to keep on hand.

○ Serves 6 (1½ cups)

> *2 cups (one 16-ounce can) Healthy Request Chicken Broth*
> *1 (10¾-ounce) can Healthy Request Cream of Mushroom Soup*
> *1 cup hot water*
> *1½ teaspoons dried dill weed*
> *⅛ teaspoon black pepper*
> *1½ cups frozen whole-kernel corn, thawed*
> *¾ cup diced cooked potatoes*
> *2 (6-ounce) cans white tuna, packed in water, drained and flaked*
> *1½ cups (one 12-fluid-ounce can) Carnation Evaporated Skim Milk*
> *⅔ cup instant potato flakes*

Spray a slow cooker container with butter-flavored cooking spray. In prepared container, combine chicken broth, mushroom soup, and water. Stir in dill weed and black pepper. Add corn, potatoes, and tuna. Mix well to combine. Cover and cook on HIGH for 2 hours. Stir in evaporated skim milk and potato flakes. Re-cover and continue cooking on HIGH for 30 minutes. Mix well before serving.

HINT: Thaw corn by placing it in a colander and rinsing it under hot water for one minute.

Each serving equals:

> HE: 1 Bread • 1 Protein • ½ Skim Milk •
> ¼ Slider • 13 Optional Calories
>
> ---
>
> 223 Calories • 3 gm Fat • 21 gm Protein •
> 28 gm Carbohydrate • 635 mg Sodium •
> 217 mg Calcium • 1 gm Fiber
>
> ---
>
> DIABETIC: 2 Meat • 1½ Starch • ½ Skim Milk

Calico Chicken Chowder

Part of the fun of this recipe is finding all the tasty ingredients in each and every spoonful! Just like the delightful multicolored fabric that inspired its title, this dish is a tapestry of festive flavors!

◑ Serves 6 (1⅓ cups)

1 (10¾-ounce) can Healthy Request Cream of Chicken Soup
1½ cups (one 12-fluid-ounce can) Carnation Evaporated Skim Milk
1 cup hot water
1 teaspoon dried parsley flakes
⅛ teaspoon black pepper
¾ cup finely chopped onion
1 cup frozen whole-kernel corn, thawed
2 cups finely chopped raw potatoes
2 full cups diced cooked chicken breast
1 cup frozen peas, thawed

Spray a slow cooker container with butter-flavored cooking spray. In prepared container, combine chicken soup, evaporated skim milk, water, parsley flakes, and black pepper. Stir in onion, corn, and potatoes. Add chicken. Mix well to combine. Cover and cook on LOW for 6 to 8 hours. Mix well before serving. Just before serving, stir in peas.

HINTS: 1. Thaw corn and peas by placing them in a colander and rinsing them under hot water for one minute.
2. If you don't have leftovers, purchase a chunk of cooked chicken breast from your local deli.

Each serving equals:

HE: 2 Protein • 1 Bread • ½ Skim Milk •
¼ Vegetable • ¼ Slider • 10 Optional Calories

251 Calories • 3 gm Fat • 25 gm Protein •
31 gm Carbohydrate • 349 mg Sodium •
183 mg Calcium • 3 gm Fiber

DIABETIC: 2 Meat • 1½ Starch • ½ Skim Milk

Mexican Chicken Stew

This simple blend of vegetables and poultry couldn't be easier to prepare for the pot, but long, slow cooking transforms these sturdy basics into something wonderful. Olé!   ☻   Serves 4 (1½ cups)

> 3 cups coarsely chopped cabbage
>
> 2 cups thinly sliced carrots
>
> ¼ cup chopped onion
>
> 1¾ cups (one 14½-ounce can) stewed tomatoes, coarsely chopped and
>   drained
>
> 1 tablespoon pourable Splenda or Sugar Twin
>
> 1 teaspoon chili seasoning
>
> 16 ounces skinned and boned uncooked chicken breast, cut into 24
>   pieces

Spray a slow cooker container with olive oil–flavored cooking spray. In prepared container, combine cabbage, carrots, onion, stewed tomatoes, Splenda, and chili seasoning. Stir in chicken pieces. Cover and cook on LOW for 6 to 8 hours. Mix well before serving.

Each serving equals:

HE: 3 Protein • 2¾ Vegetable • 2 Optional Calories

199 Calories • 3 gm Fat • 25 gm Protein •
18 gm Carbohydrate • 307 mg Sodium • 95 mg Calcium •
5 gm Fiber

DIABETIC: 3 Meat • 2½ Vegetable

Chicken Pot Stew

Speedy and substantial, this quick-fix chicken stew is a great idea on those days when you really need a break—not the fast-food kind, but the fast and homemade-in-a-slow-cooker kind!

○ Serves 4 (1 cup)

1 (10¾-ounce) can Healthy Request Cream of Chicken Soup
1 teaspoon dried parsley flakes
1 teaspoon dried onion flakes
1 (16-ounce) package frozen cauliflower, broccoli, and carrot blend
16 ounces skinned and boned uncooked chicken breast, cut into 16
    pieces

Spray a slow cooker container with butter-flavored cooking spray. In prepared container, combine chicken soup, parsley flakes, and onion flakes. Stir in frozen vegetables and chicken pieces. Cover and cook on LOW for 8 hours. Mix well before serving.

Each serving equals:

HE: 3 Protein • 1½ Vegetable • ½ Slider •
5 Optional Calories

196 Calories • 4 gm Fat • 26 gm Protein •
14 gm Carbohydrate • 386 mg Sodium • 52 mg Calcium •
3 gm Fiber

DIABETIC: 3 Meat • 1½ Vegetable • ½ Starch/Carbohydrate

Southwestern Chicken Stew

The great thing about canned beans is that they don't need soaking, so you can use them right away in a favorite recipe. Stock your pantry with a few cans of beans, and you'll always have the fixings for a high-fiber soup!   ❍   Serves 6 (1 full cup)

> 10 ounces (one 16-ounce can) pinto beans, rinsed and drained
> 2 cups diced cooked chicken breast
> 1½ cups frozen whole-kernel corn, thawed
> 2 cups (one 16-ounce can) Healthy Request Chicken Broth
> 1½ cups chunky salsa (mild, medium, or hot)
> 1½ teaspoons chili seasoning
> 1 teaspoon dried parsley flakes

Spray a slow cooker container with butter-flavored cooking spray. In prepared container, combine pinto beans, chicken, and corn. Add chicken broth and salsa. Mix well to combine. Stir in chili seasoning and parsley flakes. Cover and cook on LOW for 6 to 8 hours. Mix well before serving.

HINTS: 1. If you don't have leftovers, purchase a chunk of cooked chicken breast from your local deli.
2. Thaw corn by placing it in a colander and rinsing it under hot water for one minute.

Each serving equals:

HE: 2½ Protein • ½ Bread • ½ Vegetable • 6 Optional Calories

182 Calories • 2 gm Fat • 19 gm Protein • 22 gm Carbohydrate • 642 mg Sodium • 31 mg Calcium • 4 gm Fiber

DIABETIC: 2 Meat • 1 Starch • ½ Vegetable

Creamy Chicken Stew

You might not want to stand over a hot stove for hours on end to produce a stew this scrumptious—no one has that much time these days! But with your handy kitchen helper, a dish that takes hours to reach perfection needs no supervision.   ☻   Serves 4 (1¼ cups)

16 ounces skinned and boned uncooked chicken breast, cut into 32
    pieces
1½ cups chopped carrots
1 cup chopped onion
1½ cups chopped celery
1 (10¾-ounce) can Healthy Request Cream of Chicken Soup
1 teaspoon dried basil leaves
⅛ teaspoon black pepper

Spray a slow cooker container with butter-flavored cooking spray. Place chicken pieces in prepared container. Layer carrots, onion, and celery over chicken. In a small bowl, combine chicken soup, basil, and black pepper. Spoon soup mixture evenly over top. Cover and cook on LOW for 6 to 8 hours. Mix well before serving.

Each serving equals:

HE: 3 Protein • 2 Vegetable • ½ Slider •
5 Optional Calories

204 Calories • 4 gm Fat • 25 gm Protein •
17 gm Carbohydrate • 404 mg Sodium • 56 mg Calcium •
3 gm Fiber

DIABETIC: 3 Meat • 1½ Vegetable • ½ Starch

Country Italian Chicken Stew

I love using chicken breasts in the slow cooker because hours in the pot only make this healthy cut more tender. You'll be astonished how the rich flavors in a modest amount of healthy salad dressing transform some basic veggies and chicken into a bit of heaven.

○ Serves 4 (1¼ cups)

> 2 cups diced raw potatoes
>
> 1 cup sliced carrots
>
> 1 cup chopped celery
>
> ½ cup chopped onion
>
> 16 ounces skinned and boned uncooked chicken breast, cut into 16 pieces
>
> 1 (10¾-ounce) can Healthy Request Tomato Soup
>
> ¼ cup Kraft Fat Free Italian Dressing

Spray a slow cooker container with olive oil–flavored cooking spray. Evenly arrange potatoes, carrots, and celery in prepared container. Sprinkle onion over top. Place chicken pieces evenly over vegetables. In a small bowl, combine tomato soup and Italian dressing. Spoon mixture evenly over top. Cover and cook on LOW for 6 to 8 hours. Gently stir just before serving.

Each serving equals:

> HE: 3 Protein • 1¼ Vegetable • ½ Bread • ½ Slider • 14 Optional Calories
>
> ---
>
> 260 Calories • 4 gm Fat • 29 gm Protein • 27 gm Carbohydrate • 530 mg Sodium • 41 mg Calcium • 3 gm Fiber
>
> ---
>
> DIABETIC: 3 Meat • 1 Vegetable • 1 Starch

Dilled Turkey Chowder

Here's a great solution when you've got big-bird leftovers! Slow cooking with this fragrant herb produces astonishingly tasty results—and happy families! ☻ Serves 6 (1½ cups)

2 cups (one 16-ounce can) Healthy Request Chicken Broth

1 (10¾-ounce) can Healthy Request Cream of Mushroom Soup

1 teaspoon dried dill weed

1½ cups frozen whole-kernel corn, thawed

3 cups finely diced raw potatoes

1 cup sliced carrots

½ cup chopped onion

2 full cups diced cooked turkey breast

Spray a slow cooker container with butter-flavored cooking spray. In prepared container, combine chicken broth, mushroom soup, and dill weed. Add corn, potatoes, carrots, and onion. Mix well to combine. Stir in turkey. Cover and cook on LOW for 8 hours. Mix well before serving.

HINTS: 1. Thaw corn by placing it in a colander and rinsing it under hot water for one minute.

2. If you don't have leftovers, purchase a chunk of cooked turkey breast from your local deli.

Each serving equals:

HE: 2 Protein • 1 Bread • ½ Vegetable • ¼ Slider • 13 Optional Calories

218 Calories • 2 gm Fat • 21 gm Protein • 29 gm Carbohydrate • 398 mg Sodium • 65 mg Calcium • 3 gm Fiber

DIABETIC: 2 Meat • 1½ Starch • ½ Vegetable

Terrific Turkey Soup

What a great soup to take to school or work for a healthy, energy-producing lunch. Everyone will want a taste—and then the recipe, too!

● Serves 6 (1½ cups)

4 cups (two 16-ounce cans) Healthy Request Chicken Broth
1 cup hot water
2 cups frozen whole-kernel corn, thawed
⅔ cup uncooked instant rice
1 cup finely chopped celery
½ cup finely chopped onion
¼ cup (one 2-ounce jar) chopped pimiento, undrained
2 full cups diced cooked turkey breast
2 teaspoons dried parsley flakes
⅛ teaspoon black pepper

Spray a slow cooker container with butter-flavored cooking spray. In prepared container, combine chicken broth and water. Stir in corn, uncooked rice, celery, onion, and undrained pimiento. Add turkey, parsley flakes, and black pepper. Mix well to combine. Cover and cook on LOW for 6 to 8 hours. Mix well before serving.

HINTS: 1. Thaw corn by placing it in a colander and rinsing it under hot water for one minute.
       2. If you don't have leftovers, purchase a chunk of cooked turkey breast from your local deli.

Each serving equals:

HE: 2 Protein • 1 Bread • ½ Vegetable •
8 Optional Calories

181 Calories • 1 gm Fat • 22 gm Protein •
21 gm Carbohydrate • 371 mg Sodium • 24 mg Calcium •
2 gm Fiber

DIABETIC: 2 Meat • 1 Starch • ½ Vegetable

German Meatball Stew

Men will love this imaginative way to serve meatballs with some old-world flair! You'll be pleased to find that long, slow cooking without interruption doesn't lead to "mushy" meat. ♥ Serves 6

3½ cups (two 15-ounce cans) stewed tomatoes, undrained
1¾ cups (one 14½-ounce can) Frank's Bavarian-style sauerkraut, drained
¾ cup finely chopped onion ☆
4 cups diced raw potatoes
16 ounces extra lean ground turkey or beef
6 tablespoons dried fine bread crumbs
¼ cup skim milk
1 teaspoon dried parsley flakes

Spray a slow cooker container with butter-flavored cooking spray. In prepared container, combine undrained stewed tomatoes, sauerkraut, ½ cup onion, and potatoes. In a large bowl, combine meat, remaining ¼ cup onion, bread crumbs, skim milk, and parsley flakes. Mix well. Form into 12 (2-inch) meatballs. Arrange meatballs on top of vegetables. Cover and cook on LOW for 8 hours. For each serving, place 2 meatballs and 1 cup vegetable mixture on a plate.

HINT: If you can't find Bavarian sauerkraut, use regular sauerkraut, ½ teaspoon caraway seeds, and 1 teaspoon Brown Sugar Twin.

Each serving equals:

HE: 2 Protein • 2 Vegetable • 1 Bread •
4 Optional Calories

275 Calories • 7 gm Fat • 19 gm Protein •
34 gm Carbohydrate • 808 mg Sodium • 88 mg Calcium •
4 gm Fiber

DIABETIC: 2 Meat • 2 Vegetable • 1 Starch

Cabbage Taco Soup

My husband, Cliff, goes for Southwestern flavors wherever he finds them, and believe me, he found his way into the kitchen when we were testing this recipe! The beans deliver healthy protein and fiber, but this dish is so low in calories and fat, you've got plenty of room left for dessert. ☻ Serves 6 (1 cup)

> 8 ounces extra lean ground turkey or beef
> 1³⁄₄ cups (one 15-ounce can) Hunt's Tomato Sauce
> 1¹⁄₂ cups hot water
> 1 tablespoon taco seasoning
> 2 teaspoons pourable Splenda or Sugar Twin
> 1 teaspoon dried parsley flakes
> 6 ounces (one 8-ounce can) red kidney beans, rinsed and drained
> 4 cups shredded cabbage
> ¹⁄₂ cup chopped onion

In a large skillet sprayed with olive oil–flavored cooking spray, brown meat. Spray a slow cooker container with olive oil–flavored cooking spray. In prepared container, combine tomato sauce, water, taco seasoning, Splenda, and parsley flakes. Add kidney beans, cabbage, and onion. Mix well to combine. Stir in browned meat. Cover and cook on LOW for 6 to 8 hours. Mix well before serving.

Each serving equals:

HE: 2 Vegetable • 1¹⁄₂ Protein

---

127 Calories • 3 gm Fat • 11 gm Protein •
14 gm Carbohydrate • 580 mg Sodium • 50 mg Calcium •
5 gm Fiber

DIABETIC: 2 Vegetable • 1¹⁄₂ Meat

Hobo Stew

The tradition of this recipe, named after the men who rode the rails and traveled from town to town, is that you "dump" in whatever you've got to make a meal. When you can make a pound of meat serve six hungry people this well, you've got a budget meal that doesn't taste like you scrimped!   ❤   Serves 6 (1⅓ cups)

> *16 ounces extra lean ground turkey or beef*
> *1 cup diced onion*
> *2 cups diced celery*
> *2 cups diced carrots*
> *3 cups diced raw potatoes*
> *1 (10¾-ounce) can Healthy Request Cream of Mushroom Soup*
> *1 (10¾-ounce) can Healthy Request Tomato Soup*
> *⅓ cup hot water*
> *2 teaspoons dried parsley flakes*
> *⅛ teaspoon black pepper*

In a large skillet sprayed with butter-flavored cooking spray, brown meat. Spray a slow cooker container with butter-flavored cooking spray. Place browned meat in prepared container. Add onion, celery, carrots, and potatoes. Mix well to combine. In a medium bowl, combine mushroom soup, tomato soup, water, parsley flakes, and black pepper. Spoon mixture evenly over top. Mix well to combine. Cover and cook on LOW for 6 to 8 hours. Mix well before serving.

Each serving equals:

> HE: 2 Protein • 1⅔ Vegetable • ½ Bread • ½ Slider • 18 Optional Calories
>
> ---
>
> 239 Calories • 7 gm Fat • 16 gm Protein • 28 gm Carbohydrate • 508 mg Sodium • 78 mg Calcium • 3 gm Fiber
>
> ---
>
> DIABETIC: 2 Meat • 1½ Starch/Carbohydrate • 1 Vegetable

Barleyburger Stew

There's something to remember about cooking with barley—it's very absorbent, so be sure to measure it carefully. My friend Barb once poured a cup of this grain into a soup she was making, and suddenly there was no more liquid in the pot. ☻ Serves 6 (1½ cups)

8 ounces extra lean ground turkey or beef
1 cup chopped onion
1 cup chopped carrots
1 cup chopped celery
4½ cups reduced-sodium tomato juice
1½ cups hot water
1½ teaspoons chili seasoning
⅛ teaspoon black pepper
½ cup uncooked barley

In a large skillet sprayed with butter-flavored cooking spray, brown meat and onion. Spray a slow cooker container with butter-flavored cooking spray. Place meat mixture in prepared container. Stir in carrots, celery, tomato juice, water, chili seasoning, and black pepper. Add uncooked barley. Mix well to combine. Cover and cook on MEDIUM for 6 to 8 hours. Mix well before serving.

Each serving equals:

HE: 2½ Vegetable • 1 Protein • ⅔ Bread

172 Calories • 4 gm Fat • 10 gm Protein •
24 gm Carbohydrate • 161 mg Sodium • 33 mg Calcium •
5 gm Fiber

DIABETIC: 1½ Vegetable • 1 Meat • 1 Starch

Savory Vegetable Soup

If you're looking for a vegetable soup that's so chockful of goodies it's a meal worth writing home about, this is the one! Make sure you slice your veggies the same thickness so they'll all cook in the same time.

● Serves 6 (1½ cups)

16 ounces extra lean ground turkey or beef	Swanson Beef Broth
1 cup chopped onion	2 cups hot water
1 cup sliced carrots	2 cups (one 16-ounce can) tomatoes, coarsely chopped and undrained
1 cup sliced celery	
1 cup frozen cut green beans, thawed	
⅔ cup uncooked instant rice	1 teaspoon dried parsley flakes
1¾ cups (one 15-ounce can)	½ teaspoon dried basil leaves
	⅛ teaspoon black pepper

In a large skillet sprayed with butter-flavored cooking spray, brown meat. Spray a slow cooker container with butter-flavored cooking spray. In prepared container, combine browned meat, onion, carrots, celery, green beans, and uncooked rice. Add beef broth, water, and undrained tomatoes. Mix well to combine. Stir in parsley flakes, basil leaves, and black pepper. Cover and cook on LOW for 8 hours. Mix well before serving.

HINT: Thaw green beans by placing them in a colander and rinsing them under hot water for one minute.

Each serving equals:

HE: 2 Protein • 2 Vegetable • ⅓ Bread • 6 Optional Calories

187 Calories • 7 gm Fat • 16 gm Protein • 15 gm Carbohydrate • 483 mg Sodium • 45 mg Calcium • 3 gm Fiber

DIABETIC: 2 Meat • 2 Vegetable • ½ Starch

Cookstove Vegetable Soup

One of my most favorite spices is lemon pepper, which makes vegetables truly sparkle! When used in a long-cooking recipe like this one, it enriches and deepens their natural flavors.

☻ Serves 4 (1½ cups)

> 8 ounces extra lean ground turkey or beef
> 2 cups reduced-sodium tomato juice
> 1½ cups hot water
> 1 cup diced raw potatoes
> 1 cup diced celery
> ½ cup chopped onion
> 1 cup diced carrots
> ⅓ cup uncooked instant rice
> ⅛ teaspoon black pepper
> 1 teaspoon lemon pepper

In a large skillet sprayed with butter-flavored cooking spray, brown meat. Spray a slow cooker container with butter-flavored cooking spray. In prepared container, combine browned meat, tomato juice, and water. Add potatoes, celery, onion, carrots, uncooked rice, black pepper, and lemon pepper. Mix well to combine. Cover and cook on LOW for 6 to 8 hours. Mix well before serving.

Each serving equals:

HE: 2¼ Vegetable • 1½ Protein • ½ Bread

165 Calories • 5 gm Fat • 12 gm Protein •
18 gm Carbohydrate • 267 mg Sodium • 29 mg Calcium •
2 gm Fiber

DIABETIC: 2 Vegetable • 1½ Meat • ½ Starch

Swedish Cabbage Stew

If you're hunting for a tasty, nutritious, and thrifty meal, this savory stew is an excellent option. The nutmeg gives it a unique flavor I think you'll like a lot. ☑ Serves 6 (1 full cup)

16 ounces extra lean ground turkey or beef
1 cup chopped onion
3 cups shredded cabbage
1½ cups cooked instant rice
1 (10¾-ounce) can Healthy Request Cream of Mushroom Soup
½ cup (one 2.5-ounce jar) sliced mushrooms, undrained
¼ cup skim milk
1 tablespoon dried parsley flakes
⅛ teaspoon black pepper
¼ teaspoon ground nutmeg

In a large skillet sprayed with butter-flavored cooking spray, brown meat. Spray a slow cooker container with butter-flavored cooking spray. In prepared container, combine browned meat, onion, cabbage, and rice. Stir in mushroom soup, undrained mushrooms, skim milk, parsley flakes, black pepper, and nutmeg. Cover and cook on LOW for 6 to 8 hours. Mix well before serving.

HINT: 1 cup uncooked instant rice usually cooks to about 1½ cups.

Each serving equals:

HE: 2 Protein • 1½ Vegetable • ½ Bread • ¼ Slider • 11 Optional Calories

203 Calories • 7 gm Fat • 16 gm Protein • 19 gm Carbohydrate • 338 mg Sodium • 86 mg Calcium • 2 gm Fiber

DIABETIC: 2 Meat • 1 Vegetable • 1 Starch

Brunswick Soup

Here's a perfect way to use up some "bits and pieces" in a delectable recipe that doesn't taste like leftover stew! This soup is as rich as it is nourishing—perfect for a crisp fall evening.

● Serves 4 (1½ cups)

> 8 ounces extra lean ground turkey or beef
> ½ cup chopped onion
> 1 cup diced cooked chicken breast
> 1¾ cups (one 15-ounce can) Hunt's Tomato Sauce
> 1 cup hot water
> 2 cups (one 16-ounce can) cream-style corn
> 1 tablespoon Worcestershire sauce
> ⅛ teaspoon black pepper
> 1 teaspoon dried parsley flakes

In a large skillet sprayed with butter-flavored cooking spray, brown meat. Spray a slow cooker container with butter-flavored cooking spray. In prepared container, combine browned meat, onion, and chicken. Add tomato sauce and water. Mix well to combine. Stir in corn, Worcestershire sauce, black pepper, and parsley flakes. Cover and cook on LOW for 6 to 8 hours. Mix well before serving.

HINT: If you don't have leftovers, purchase a chunk of cooked chicken breast from your local deli.

Each serving equals:

HE: 2¾ Protein • 2 Vegetable • 1 Bread

288 Calories • 8 gm Fat • 24 gm Protein •
30 gm Carbohydrate • 871 mg Sodium • 18 mg Calcium •
4 gm Fiber

DIABETIC: 3 Meat • 2 Vegetable • 1 Starch

Chili Mac Pot

This is another of those handy recipes I consider my "pantry prides." All you need to do is defrost a pound of meat, then find the rest of the ingredients on your cabinet shelves, and you've got a family-pleasing meal with very little fuss.　❂　Serves 6 (1 full cup)

> 16 ounces extra lean ground turkey or beef
> 1 cup chopped onion
> 2 cups (one 16-ounce can) tomatoes, coarsely chopped and undrained
> 1 (10¾-ounce) can Healthy Request Tomato Soup
> 1 cup reduced-sodium tomato juice
> 2 teaspoons chili seasoning
> 6 ounces (one 8-ounce can) red kidney beans, rinsed and drained
> 1 cup uncooked elbow macaroni

In a large skillet sprayed with olive oil–flavored cooking spray, brown meat. Meanwhile, in a slow cooker container sprayed with olive oil–flavored cooking spray, combine onion, undrained tomatoes, tomato soup, tomato juice, and chili seasoning. Stir in kidney beans and uncooked macaroni. Add browned meat. Mix well to combine. Cover and cook on LOW for 6 to 8 hours. Mix well before serving.

Each serving equals:

HE: 2½ Protein • 1⅓ Vegetable • ½ Bread •
¼ Slider • 10 Optional Calories

---

218 Calories • 6 gm Fat • 15 gm Protein •
26 gm Carbohydrate • 519 mg Sodium • 33 mg Calcium •
3 gm Fiber

DIABETIC: 2½ Meat • 1 Vegetable • 1 Starch

Comfort Pot Soup

From the time we're children, soup is a comfort food we rely on and trust to make us feel warm inside. This veggie-beef melange provides enough cozy comfort to soothe kids of all ages!

◐ Serves 6 (1½ cups)

> 8 ounces extra lean ground turkey or beef
> 3 cups reduced-sodium tomato juice
> 1¾ cups (one 15-ounce can) Swanson Beef Broth
> 1½ cups frozen cut green beans
> 1 cup frozen sliced carrots
> 1 cup frozen peas
> 1 cup frozen whole-kernel corn
> 2 cups diced raw potatoes
> ½ cup (one 2.5-ounce jar) sliced mushrooms, drained
> 1 teaspoon Italian seasoning

In a large skillet sprayed with olive oil–flavored cooking spray, brown meat. Spray a slow cooker container with olive oil–flavored cooking spray. In prepared container, place browned meat. Add tomato juice, beef broth, green beans, carrots, peas, corn, potatoes, mushrooms, and Italian seasoning. Mix well to combine. Cover and cook on MEDIUM for 8 hours. Mix well before serving.

Each serving equals:

HE: 2⅓ Vegetable • 1 Bread • 1 Protein •
6 Optional Calories

---

192 Calories • 4 gm Fat • 12 gm Protein •
27 gm Carbohydrate • 447 mg Sodium • 39 mg Calcium •
5 gm Fiber

DIABETIC: 2 Vegetable • 1 Starch • 1 Meat

Slow Cooker Stew

The trick to a truly satisfying stew is a happy mix of tender ingredients—and slow cooking is ideal for this culinary mainstay. Are you surprised to find tapioca in the ingredients list? Just enjoy how it makes the gravy wonderfully thick and rich.   ☾   Serves 6 (1½ cups)

16 ounces lean beef stew meat, cubed
½ cup chopped onion
2 cups chopped carrots
1½ cups chopped celery
4 cups diced raw potatoes
1¾ cups (one 15-ounce can) Swanson Beef Broth
1 tablespoon parsley flakes
½ teaspoon Italian seasoning
⅛ teaspoon black pepper
2 tablespoons Quick Cooking Minute Tapioca

In a large skillet sprayed with butter-flavored cooking spray, brown stew meat. Spray a slow cooker container with butter-flavored cooking spray. Place browned meat in prepared container. Add onion, carrots, celery, and potatoes. Mix well to combine. In a small bowl, combine beef broth, parsley flakes, Italian seasoning, black pepper, and uncooked tapioca. Pour mixture over vegetables. Cover and cook on LOW for 8 hours. Mix well before serving.

Each serving equals:

HE: 2 Protein • 1⅓ Vegetable • ⅔ Bread •
16 Optional Calories
***
243 Calories • 7 gm Fat • 20 gm Protein •
25 gm Carbohydrate • 451 mg Sodium • 37 mg Calcium •
3 gm Fiber
***
DIABETIC: 2 Meat • 1 Vegetable • 1 Starch

Mushroom Stew

Layering flavors is a smart cook's secret, and here I'm using both soup and veggies to give this dish that luscious mushroom sizzle. You could make this with fresh mushrooms if you prefer, though the canned ones are likely to be sturdier through the long cooking time.

○ Serves 6 (1 cup)

2 tablespoons all-purpose flour
1 teaspoon dried parsley flakes
16 ounces lean beef stew meat, cut into small pieces
½ cup sliced onion
1 cup sliced celery
1 cup (one 4-ounce can) sliced mushrooms, undrained
1 (10¾-ounce) can Healthy Request Cream of Mushroom Soup
2 teaspoons Worcestershire sauce
1¾ cups (one 15-ounce can) Hunt's Tomato Sauce
½ cup hot water

Spray a slow cooker container with butter-flavored cooking spray. In a large bowl, combine flour and parsley flakes. Add stew meat. Mix well to coat meat with flour mixture. Place meat in prepared slow cooker container. Evenly sprinkle onion, celery, and undrained mushrooms over meat. In a small bowl, combine mushroom soup, Worcestershire sauce, tomato sauce, and water. Pour mixture over top. Cover and cook on LOW for 6 to 8 hours. Mix well before serving.

Each serving equals:

HE: 2 Protein • 2 Vegetable • ¼ Slider •
18 Optional Calories

---

182 Calories • 6 gm Fat • 17 gm Protein •
15 gm Carbohydrate • 809 mg Sodium • 72 mg Calcium •
2 gm Fiber

DIABETIC: 2 Meat • 2 Vegetable

Cowboy Stew

No one is more ravenous or ready to eat hearty than cowboys on a cattle drive! Here's a stew to satisfy that never-ending hunger—even if your "campfire crowd" did nothing tougher than play golf or mow the lawn!

● Serves 6 (1½ cups)

2 cups (one 16-ounce can) tomatoes, coarsely chopped and undrained
1 tablespoon chili seasoning
1½ cups frozen whole-kernel corn, thawed
3 cups chopped raw potatoes
6 ounces (one 8-ounce can) red kidney beans, rinsed and drained
½ cup chopped onion
1 cup chopped carrots
1 cup chopped celery
16 ounces lean round steak, cut into 24 pieces

Spray a slow cooker container with butter-flavored cooking spray. In prepared container, combine undrained tomatoes and chili seasoning. Add corn, potatoes, kidney beans, onion, carrots, and celery. Mix well to combine. Stir in steak pieces. Cover and cook on LOW for 6 to 8 hours. Mix well before serving.

HINT: Thaw corn by placing it in a colander and rinsing it under hot water for one minute.

Each serving equals:

HE: 2½ Protein • 1½ Vegetable • 1 Bread

252 Calories • 4 gm Fat • 25 gm Protein •
29 gm Carbohydrate • 307 mg Sodium • 47 mg Calcium •
5 gm Fiber

DIABETIC: 2½ Meat • 1½ Vegetable • 1 Starch

New World Borscht

This rosy soup presents the glorious beet in all its culinary charm! Not all borschts are prepared with meat, but I think this recipe will please the appetites of men who might otherwise have mixed opinions about a soup that's a shade of pink.   ☻   Serves 6 (1½ cups)

16 ounces lean round steak, cut into 36 pieces
1¾ cups (one 15-ounce can) Swanson Beef Broth
1¼ cups hot water
¼ teaspoon dried dill weed
3½ cups finely shredded cabbage
1 cup chopped onion
1 cup thinly sliced carrots
1 cup finely chopped celery
¾ cup reduced-sodium tomato juice
1 tablespoon lemon juice
2 cups (one 16-ounce can) julienne beets, drained
6 tablespoons Land O Lakes no-fat sour cream

Spray a slow cooker container with butter-flavored cooking spray. In prepared container, combine steak pieces, beef broth, and water. Stir in dill weed, cabbage, onion, carrots, celery, and tomato juice. Cover and cook on LOW for 8 hours. Add lemon juice and beets. Mix well to combine. Re-cover and cook on HIGH for 15 minutes. Mix well before serving. When serving, top each bowl with 1 tablespoon sour cream.

Each serving equals:

HE: 2½ Vegetable • 2 Protein • ¼ Slider • 1 Optional Calorie

187 Calories • 3 gm Fat • 24 gm Protein • 16 gm Carbohydrate • 480 mg Sodium • 67 mg Calcium • 3 gm Fiber

DIABETIC: 2 Vegetable • 2 Meat

Beefy Minestrone

The famed Italian "kitchen sink" soup is high in fiber and just jammed with delicious ingredients. For a soup that "eats like a meal," I'd choose this one. (So would my meat-lover son, James.)

⚫ Serves 6 (1½ cups)

1¾ cups (one 15-ounce can) Swanson Beef Broth
2¾ cups hot water
2 cups (one 16-ounce can) tomatoes, coarsely chopped and undrained
8 ounces lean round steak, cut into 36 pieces
½ cup chopped onion
½ cup chopped celery
2 cups shredded cabbage
1 cup thinly sliced unpeeled zucchini
1 cup sliced carrots
6 ounces (one 8-ounce can) red kidney beans, rinsed and drained
⅔ cup uncooked small elbow macaroni

Spray a slow cooker container with butter-flavored cooking spray. In prepared container, combine beef broth, water, and undrained tomatoes. Stir in steak pieces, onion, celery, cabbage, zucchini, and carrots. Add kidney beans and uncooked macaroni. Mix well to combine. Cover and cook on LOW for 6 to 8 hours. Stir well before serving.

Each serving equals:

HE: 2 Vegetable • 1½ Protein • ⅓ Bread •
6 Optional Calories

---

150 Calories • 2 gm Fat • 15 gm Protein •
18 gm Carbohydrate • 520 mg Sodium • 51 mg Calcium •
4 gm Fiber

DIABETIC: 2 Vegetable • 1½ Meat • ½ Starch

Creamy Pot Stew

With this collection of recipes and a family that loves meat and potatoes, you can prepare a different "beefy" stew as often as you like! Use a sturdy potato for best results—Yukon Gold are great if you can get 'em.

◐ Serves 6 (1¼ cups)

> 1¾ cups (one 15-ounce can) Swanson Beef Broth
> 1 (10¾-ounce) can Healthy Request Cream of Mushroom Soup
> 2 teaspoons dried parsley flakes
> ¼ teaspoon black pepper
> 1½ cups sliced carrots
> 1 cup chopped celery
> ½ cup chopped onion
> 2 cups diced raw potatoes
> 16 ounces lean round steak, cut into 36 pieces

Spray a slow cooker container with butter-flavored cooking spray. In prepared container, combine beef broth, mushroom soup, parsley flakes, and black pepper. Stir in carrots, celery, onion, and potatoes. Add steak pieces. Mix well to combine. Cover and cook on LOW for 8 hours. Mix well before serving.

Each serving equals:

> HE: 2 Protein • 1 Vegetable • ⅓ Bread • ¼ Slider • 13 Optional Calories
>
> ---
>
> 205 Calories • 5 gm Fat • 23 gm Protein • 17 gm Carbohydrate • 495 mg Sodium • 66 mg Calcium • 2 gm Fiber
>
> ---
>
> DIABETIC: 2 Meat • 1 Vegetable • 1 Starch

Easy Beef Stew

If you and yours enjoy chunks of potatoes and carrots as well as tasty bites of beef, this simple but satisfying stew is bound to please both taste buds and tummies around the table!

O Serves 6 (1½ cups)

1 (10¾-ounce) can Healthy Request Tomato Soup
1 cup hot water
1 teaspoon dried parsley flakes
16 ounces lean round steak, cut into 36 pieces
3 cups diced raw potatoes
2 cups sliced carrots
1½ cups sliced celery
1 cup chopped onion

Spray a slow cooker container with butter-flavored cooking spray. In prepared container, combine tomato soup, water, and parsley flakes. Stir in meat. Add potatoes, carrots, celery, and onion. Mix well to combine. Cover and cook on LOW for 8 hours. Mix well before serving.

Each serving equals:

HE: 2 Protein • 1½ Vegetable • ½ Bread • ¼ Slider • 10 Optional Calories

224 Calories • 4 gm Fat • 23 gm Protein • 24 gm Carbohydrate • 257 mg Sodium • 35 mg Calcium • 3 gm Fiber

DIABETIC: 2 Meat • 1 Vegetable • 1 Starch

Pepper Steak Stew

Something wonderful happens to peppers when they're cooked long and slow in beef gravy. They take on so much hearty flavor, you'll wonder why you didn't always serve them like this. If you've got red or yellow peppers, you can mix those in, too, for a bit more color.

● Serves 6 (1 full cup)

16 ounces lean round steak, cut into 24 pieces
2½ cups coarsely chopped green bell pepper
½ cup chopped onion
3 cups diced raw potatoes
1 (12-ounce) jar Heinz Fat Free Beef Gravy
¼ teaspoon dried minced garlic

Spray a slow cooker container with butter-flavored cooking spray. In prepared container, combine steak pieces, green pepper, onion, and potatoes. Stir in gravy and garlic. Cover and cook on LOW for 6 to 8 hours. Mix well before serving.

Each serving equals:

HE: 2 Protein • 1 Vegetable • ½ Bread • ¼ Slider • 5 Optional Calories

196 Calories • 4 gm Fat • 23 gm Protein • 17 gm Carbohydrate • 361 mg Sodium • 15 mg Calcium • 2 gm Fiber

DIABETIC: 2 Meat • 1 Starch • ½ Vegetable

Pioneer Vegetable Soup

One of the first tasks of the brave settlers who staked their claims in the harsh new land of the plains and prairies was planting a vegetable garden. A good harvest of root vegetables meant food (like this soup) to sustain them and their families through a long winter.

Serves 6 (1½ cups)

1¾ cups (one 15-ounce can) Swanson Beef Broth
1¼ cups water
1 cup chopped onion
1 cup sliced carrots
2 cups diced raw potatoes
1 cup diced turnips
1 cup diced celery
2 cups (one 16-ounce can) tomatoes, coarsely chopped and undrained
⅛ teaspoon black pepper
16 ounces lean round steak, cut into 36 pieces

Spray a slow cooker container with butter-flavored cooking spray. In prepared container, combine beef broth and water. Stir in onion, carrots, potatoes, turnips, celery, undrained tomatoes, and black pepper. Add steak pieces. Mix well to combine. Cover and cook on LOW for 8 hours. Mix well before serving.

Each serving equals:

HE: 2 Protein • 2 Vegetable • ⅓ Bread •
6 Optional Calories

188 Calories • 4 gm Fat • 23 gm Protein •
15 gm Carbohydrate • 451 mg Sodium • 42 mg Calcium •
3 gm Fiber

DIABETIC: 2 Meat • 2 Vegetable • ½ Starch

Trail's End Stew

While it's not always good to think of food as a reward (especially junky, fat-laden treats), here's a perfect and well-earned dish to serve in celebration of some challenge or journey. Though the journey can be as important as the destination, finding this waiting for you at the end of a stressful day will be a true reward.   ☾   Serves 6 (1 cup)

> 1 cup (one 8-ounce can) Hunt's Tomato Sauce
> 1 teaspoon prepared yellow mustard
> 1 tablespoon Brown Sugar Twin
> ⅛ teaspoon black pepper
> 20 ounces (two 16-ounce cans) red kidney beans, rinsed and drained
> 12 ounces lean round steak, cut into 36 pieces
> 1½ cups chopped onion
> 1 cup finely chopped celery

Spray a slow cooker container with butter-flavored cooking spray. In prepared container, combine tomato sauce, mustard, Brown Sugar Twin, and black pepper. Add kidney beans, steak pieces, onion, and celery. Mix well to combine. Cover and cook on LOW for 8 hours. Mix well before serving.

Each serving equals:

HE: 3 Protein • 1½ Vegetable • 11 Optional Calories

227 Calories • 3 gm Fat • 23 gm Protein •
27 gm Carbohydrate • 297 mg Sodium • 26 mg Calcium •
9 gm Fiber

DIABETIC: 2½ Meat • 1½ Starch • 1 Vegetable

Pot Roast Soup

It's one of America's favorite home-cooked entrees, and now it's also a spectacular soup! Meaty and filling, it's a terrific way to use up leftovers in a dish that is definitely not "second-best."

● Serves 6 (1 cup)

1½ cups diced cooked lean roast beef
1½ cups sliced carrots
1 cup chopped celery
½ cup chopped onion
2 cups diced raw potatoes
1 (10¾-ounce) can Healthy Request Tomato Soup
1 teaspoon dried parsley flakes
¾ cup hot water
⅛ teaspoon black pepper
1 (12-ounce) jar Heinz Fat Free Beef Gravy

Spray a slow cooker container with butter-flavored cooking spray. In prepared container, combine roast beef, carrots, celery, onion, and potatoes. Stir in tomato soup, parsley flakes, water, and black pepper. Add gravy. Mix well to combine. Cover and cook on LOW for 6 to 8 hours. Mix well before serving.

HINT: If you don't have leftovers, purchase a chunk of cooked lean roast beef from your local deli.

Each serving equals:

HE: 1⅓ Protein • 1 Vegetable • ⅓ Bread • ½ Slider • 15 Optional Calories

172 Calories • 4 gm Fat • 13 gm Protein •
21 gm Carbohydrate • 595 mg Sodium • 25 mg Calcium •
2 gm Fiber

DIABETIC: 1 Meat • 1 Vegetable • 1 Starch/Carbohydrate

Sauerkraut Tomato Soup

This soup recalls my family's Bohemian roots in Old-World Europe. I made this with regular sauerkraut, but it would also be tasty prepared with the Bavarian-style sauerkraut, too!

○ Serves 6 (1¼ cups)

> 2 cups (one 16-ounce can) sauerkraut, rinsed and drained
> 2 cups (one 16-ounce can) tomatoes, chopped and undrained
> ½ cup finely chopped onion
> 2 cups hot water
> 1 tablespoon pourable Splenda or Sugar Twin
> 2 full cups diced cooked lean roast beef
> 2 teaspoons dried parsley flakes
> ⅛ teaspoon black pepper

Spray a slow cooker container with butter-flavored cooking spray. In prepared container, combine sauerkraut, undrained tomatoes, onion, and water. Stir in Splenda. Add roast beef, parsley flakes, and black pepper. Mix well to combine. Cover and cook on LOW for 6 to 8 hours. Mix well before serving.

HINT: If you don't have leftovers, purchase a chunk of lean cooked roast beef from your local deli.

Each serving equals:

HE: 2 Protein • 1½ Vegetable • 1 Optional Calorie

149 Calories • 5 gm Fat • 17 gm Protein •
9 gm Carbohydrate • 689 mg Sodium • 23 mg Calcium •
1 gm Fiber

DIABETIC: 2 Meat • 1½ Vegetable

Mexicali Pork Soup Pot

You don't often think of pork as a Mexican favorite, even though it's a regular on South-of-the-Border menus. Cliff liked this dish's tangy flavors—of course, he also added some hot-hot-hot salsa to his serving!

◐ Serves 6 (1⅓ cups)

16 ounces lean pork tenderloin, cut into 36 pieces
1½ cups reduced-sodium tomato juice
1 (10¾-ounce) can Healthy Request Tomato Soup
½ cup chopped onion
1 cup sliced carrots
10 ounces (one 16-ounce can) red kidney beans, rinsed and drained

1½ cups frozen whole-kernel corn, thawed
½ teaspoon dried minced garlic
2 teaspoons chili seasoning
2 teaspoons dried parsley flakes
⅛ teaspoon black pepper

Spray a slow cooker container with olive oil–flavored cooking spray. In prepared container, combine meat, tomato juice, and tomato soup. Stir in onion, carrots, kidney beans, and corn. Add garlic, chili seasoning, parsley flakes, and black pepper. Mix well to combine. Cover and cook on LOW for 6 to 8 hours. Mix well before serving.

HINT: Thaw corn by placing it in a colander and rinsing it under hot water for one minute.

Each serving equals:

HE: 2¾ Protein • 1 Vegetable • ½ Bread • ¼ Slider • 15 Optional Calories

236 Calories • 4 gm Fat • 21 gm Protein • 29 gm Carbohydrate • 509 mg Sodium • 35 mg Calcium • 4 gm Fiber

DIABETIC: 2½ Meat • 1½ Starch • 1 Vegetable

Bean Pot Soup

One of my friends, who is always on the lookout for high-fiber soups, gave this one a thumbs-up! It's low in fat but full of flavor, so you'll feel delightfully satisfied by its sturdy goodness.

● Serves 6 (1 full cup)

> 1½ cups diced Dubuque 97% fat-free ham or any extra-lean ham
> 1 cup diced onion
> 1 cup chopped celery
> 1 cup shredded carrots
> 1 cup (one 8-ounce can) Hunt's Tomato Sauce
> 2 cups hot water
> 20 ounces (two 16-ounce cans) great northern beans, rinsed and
>   drained
> 1 tablespoon pourable Splenda or Sugar Twin
> 1 teaspoon dried parsley flakes

Spray a slow cooker container with butter-flavored cooking spray. In prepared container, combine ham, onion, celery, carrots, tomato sauce, and water. Add great northern beans, Splenda, and parsley flakes. Mix well to combine. Cover and cook on LOW for 6 to 8 hours. Mix well before serving.

Each serving equals:

HE: 2⅔ Protein • 1⅔ Vegetable • 1 Optional Calorie

154 Calories • 2 gm Fat • 13 gm Protein •
21 gm Carbohydrate • 704 mg Sodium • 25 mg Calcium •
7 gm Fiber

DIABETIC: 2 Meat • 1 Vegetable • 1 Starch

Bean and Cabbage Soup

Do you ever find yourself standing in front of a display of canned beans at the store, wondering what kind to use in which recipe? This book will give you lots of options, including this one, which shines a spotlight on the special pleasures of the splendid navy bean!

○ Serves 4 (1½ cups)

2 cups coarsely chopped cabbage

1 cup chopped onion

1 cup sliced carrots

1 cup chopped celery

2 cups hot water

10 ounces (one 16-ounce can) navy beans, rinsed and drained

1½ cups diced Dubuque 97% fat-free ham or any extra-lean ham

1 teaspoon dried parsley flakes

⅛ teaspoon black pepper

Spray a slow cooker container with butter-flavored cooking spray. In prepared container, combine cabbage, onion, carrots, celery, and water. Add navy beans, ham, parsley flakes, and black pepper. Mix well to combine. Cover and cook on LOW for 8 hours. Mix well before serving.

Each serving equals:

HE: 2¾ Protein • 2 Vegetable

---

191 Calories • 3 gm Fat • 17 gm Protein •
24 gm Carbohydrate • 877 mg Sodium • 71 mg Calcium •
6 gm Fiber

DIABETIC: 2 Meat • 2 Vegetable • 1 Starch

Cream of Potato and Ham Soup

My daughter-in-law Pam loves creamy dishes like Fettuccine Alfredo, so I was sure she'd enjoy this luscious combination! It packs an amazing amount of good taste into just a single serving, so try it on the "creamy" dish lovers at your house soon. ☻ Serves 6 (1½ cups)

> 6 cups shredded loose-packed frozen potatoes,
>   thawed
> 1 cup chopped celery
> ½ cup chopped onion
> ½ cup shredded carrots
> 2 full cups Dubuque 97% fat-free ham or any
>   extra-lean ham
> 1 cup + 2 tablespoons shredded Kraft reduced-fat
>   Cheddar cheese
> 2 cups hot water
> 1 cup Carnation Nonfat Dry Milk Powder
> 1 (10¾-ounce) can Healthy Request Cream of
>   Mushroom Soup
> 1 teaspoon dried parsley flakes
> ⅛ teaspoon black pepper

Spray a slow cooker container with butter-flavored cooking spray. In prepared container, combine potatoes, celery, onion, carrots, ham, and Cheddar cheese. In a large bowl, combine water and dry milk powder. Add mushroom soup, parsley flakes, and black pepper. Mix well to combine. Stir milk mixture into potato mixture. Cover and cook on LOW for 8 hours. Mix well before serving.

HINT: Mr. Dell's frozen shredded potatoes are a good choice, or raw shredded potatoes may be used in place of frozen potatoes.

Each serving equals:

HE: 2⅓ Protein • ⅔ Bread • ⅔ Vegetable • ½ Skim Milk • ¼ Slider • 8 Optional Calories

258 Calories • 6 gm Fat • 21 gm Protein • 30 gm Carbohydrate • 902 mg Sodium • 355 mg Calcium • 3 gm Fiber

DIABETIC: 2 Meat • 1 Starch • ½ Vegetable • ½ Skim Milk

Chunky Ham and Corn Chowder

What a "super" dish to serve at a Super Bowl buffet—it's as man-pleasing (and fan-pleasing) as they come! If you can't find cream of celery soup, mushroom will do just fine.   ☻   Serves 6 (1 full cup)

2 full cups diced Dubuque 97% fat-free ham or any extra-lean ham
½ cup diced onion
1½ cups chopped celery
1½ cups frozen whole-kernel corn, thawed
1 cup (one 8-ounce can) cream-style corn
1½ cups (one 12-fluid-ounce can) Carnation Evaporated Skim Milk
1 (10¾-ounce) can Healthy Request Cream of Celery Soup
1 cup diced raw potatoes
1 teaspoon dried parsley flakes
⅛ teaspoon black pepper

Spray a slow cooker container with butter-flavored cooking spray. In prepared container, combine ham, onion, celery, and corn. Stir in evaporated skim milk, celery soup, potatoes, parsley flakes, and black pepper. Cover and cook on LOW for 6 to 8 hours. Mix well before serving.

HINT: Thaw corn by placing it in a colander and rinsing it under hot water for one minute.

Each serving equals:

HE: 1⅓ Protein • 1 Bread • ⅔ Vegetable • ½ Skim Milk

235 Calories • 3 gm Fat • 17 gm Protein •
35 gm Carbohydrate • 907 mg Sodium •
241 mg Calcium • 3 gm Fiber

DIABETIC: 1½ Meat • 1 Starch • ½ Vegetable •
½ Skim Milk

Ham-Vegetable Soup

When you give a vegetable soup hours to mingle with delectable chunks of ham, you deepen the flavor satisfaction beyond all expectations. A great time-saver—buy your cabbage already shredded at the market if you can. ● Serves 6 (1 full cup)

1 (10¾-ounce) can Healthy Request Tomato Soup

1 cup reduced-sodium tomato juice

1½ cups hot water

1½ cups diced Dubuque 97% fat-free ham or any extra-lean ham

2 cups diced raw potatoes

2 cups finely shredded cabbage

1½ cups thinly sliced carrots

½ cup chopped onion

1 teaspoon dried parsley flakes

Spray a slow cooker container with butter-flavored cooking spray. In prepared container, combine tomato soup, tomato juice, and water. Stir in ham and potatoes. Add cabbage, carrots, onion, and parsley flakes. Mix well to combine. Cover and cook on LOW for 6 to 8 hours or until vegetables are tender. Mix well before serving.

Each serving equals:

HE: 1⅓ Vegetable • 1 Protein • ⅓ Bread

154 Calories • 2 gm Fat • 9 gm Protein •
25 gm Carbohydrate • 678 mg Sodium • 33 mg Calcium •
3 gm Fiber

DIABETIC: 1 Vegetable • 1 Meat • 1 Starch

Cottage Pea Soup

Frozen peas provide a terrifically intense taste in a slow-cooked soup—and it's because those peas are flash frozen moments after they're picked. Whether you live in an old farmhouse or in a big-city studio apartment, this soup will convince you that you're ensconced in a lovely cottage by a lake. ☻ Serves 6 (1 full cup)

> 2 cups (one 16-ounce can) Healthy Request Chicken Broth
> 3 cups frozen peas, thawed ☆
> 1 (10¾-ounce) can Healthy Request Cream of Mushroom Soup
> 1 cup chopped onion
> 1 cup finely chopped celery
> 1 cup shredded carrots
> 1½ cups diced Dubuque 97% fat-free ham or any extra-lean ham
> ⅛ teaspoon black pepper

In a blender container, combine broth and 2½ cups peas. Cover and process on PUREE for 15 seconds. In a slow cooker container sprayed with butter-flavored cooking spray, combine pureed pea mixture and mushroom soup. Stir in remaining ½ cup peas, onion, celery, and carrots. Add ham and black pepper. Mix well to combine. Cover and cook on LOW for 6 to 8 hours. Mix well before serving.

HINT: Thaw peas by placing them in a colander and rinsing them under hot water for one minute.

Each serving equals:

HE: 1 Bread • 1 Protein • 1 Vegetable • ¼ Slider •
13 Optional Calories

---

147 Calories • 3 gm Fat • 12 gm Protein •
18 gm Carbohydrate • 794 mg Sodium • 70 mg Calcium •
4 gm Fiber

DIABETIC: 1 Starch • 1 Meat • 1 Vegetable

Chunky Pepperoni Pizza Soup

If your kids would rather eat pizza than any other food in the world, here's the perfect soup to please them! And if you're feeling like a kid today, dig in! ☻ Serves 6 (1 full cup)

1 (10¾-ounce) can Healthy Request Tomato Soup

2 cups (one 16-ounce can) tomatoes, finely chopped and undrained

2 cups water

1½ teaspoons Italian seasoning

1 cup uncooked rotini pasta

1 cup chopped onion

2 (3.5-ounce) packages Hormel reduced-fat pepperoni slices, chopped

6 tablespoons grated Kraft fat-free Parmesan cheese

Spray a slow cooker container with olive oil–flavored cooking spray. In prepared container, combine tomato soup, undrained tomatoes, water, and Italian seasoning. Stir in uncooked pasta, onion, and chopped pepperoni. Cover and cook on LOW for 6 to 8 hours. Mix well before serving. When serving, top each bowl with 1 tablespoon Parmesan cheese.

Each serving equals:

HE: 1 Protein • 1 Vegetable • ½ Bread • ¼ Slider • 10 Optional Calories

159 Calories • 3 gm Fat • 9 gm Protein • 24 gm Carbohydrate • 769 mg Sodium • 79 mg Calcium • 2 gm Fiber

DIABETIC: 1 Meat • 1 Vegetable • 1 Starch

Everything-But-the-Kitchen-Sink Soup

Okay, time to clean out the refrigerator and cabinet to feed a hungry crowd! If you're one of those people who enjoys lots of surprise ingredients in every spoonful, this soup should have your name on it!

○ Serves 8 (1¼ cups)

> 2 cups (one 16-ounce can) Healthy Request Chicken Broth
> 2 cups water
> 1 (10¾-ounce) can Healthy Request Cream of Mushroom
>   Soup
> 2 tablespoons white vinegar
> 2 teaspoons dried dill weed
> 2 cups (one 16-ounce can) sauerkraut, drained
> 1 cup (one 4-ounce can) sliced mushrooms, drained
> 3 cups diced raw potatoes
> 1½ cups chopped carrots
> 1 cup chopped onion
> ½ cup frozen whole-kernel corn, thawed
> 1½ cups chopped celery
> 8 ounces Healthy Choice 97% lean Polish Kielbasa, cut into
>   ½-inch pieces
> 1 full cup diced cooked chicken breast
> 2 tablespoons Hormel Bacon Bits
> 2 hard-boiled eggs, chopped

Spray a slow cooker container with butter-flavored cooking spray. In prepared container, combine chicken broth, water, mushroom soup, vinegar, and dill weed. Stir in sauerkraut and mushrooms. Add potatoes, carrots, onion, corn, celery, Polish Kielbasa, and chicken. Mix well to combine. Cover and cook on LOW for 8 hours. Mix well before serving. When serving, top each bowl with ¾ teaspoon bacon bits and ¼ of a chopped egg.

HINTS: 1. Thaw corn by placing it in a colander and rinsing it under hot water for one minute.

2. If you don't have leftovers, purchase a chunk of cooked chicken breast from your local deli.

3. If you want the look and feel of egg without the cholesterol, toss out the yolk and dice the whites.

Each serving equals:

HE: 1¾ Vegetable • 1⅔ Protein • ½ Bread • ¼ Slider • 11 Optional Calories

205 Calories • 5 gm Fat • 16 gm Protein • 24 gm Carbohydrate • 810 mg Sodium • 86 mg Calcium • 3 gm Fiber

DIABETIC: 2 Meat • 1½ Vegetable • 1 Starch

Beans and Frankfurter Stew

Everybody loves franks and beans, so I thought I'd see how those tra-ditional summer favorites worked together in a savory stew. The enthu-siastic cheers and quickly emptied bowls of my tasters told me I was on the right track.   ○   Serves 6 (1 full cup)

1 (10¾-ounce) can Healthy Request Tomato Soup

1 cup hot water

1 teaspoon Worcestershire sauce

1 teaspoon dried parsley flakes

20 ounces (two 16-ounce cans) great northern beans, rinsed and drained

1½ cups chopped carrots

1 cup diced celery

½ cup chopped onion

8 ounces Healthy Choice 97% Fat Free Frankfurters, diced

Spray a slow cooker container with butter-flavored cooking spray. In prepared container, combine tomato soup, water, Worcestershire sauce, and parsley flakes. Stir in great northern beans, carrots, celery, and onion. Add diced frankfurters. Mix well to combine. Cover and cook on LOW for 8 hours. Mix well before serving.

Each serving equals:

HE: 2½ Protein • 1 Vegetable • ¼ Slider •
13 Optional Calories

174 Calories • 2 gm Fat • 11 gm Protein •
28 gm Carbohydrate • 681 mg Sodium • 20 mg Calcium •
7 gm Fiber

DIABETIC: 2 Meat • 1½ Starch/Carbohydrate • ½ Vegetable

Savory
Side Dishes

Do you often feel that mealtime is a juggling act and you're about to be booed by the audience when you drop all those precariously balanced plates on the floor? I've always marveled at cooks who manage to get everything on the table at the same time, still steaming hot and looking as delicious as it tastes. Well, using your slow cooker to prepare a savory side dish is a solution to this hectic problem. The pot can also work as a serving dish, so you don't have to go searching for one!

Cliff, as some of my readers already know, is America's number one fan of canned green beans. He's always liked them best, as many husbands seem to, especially when they're bathed in a rich, creamy sauce. Whenever we go food shopping, he's happy to let me do the picking while he does the pushing of the cart, but when we approach the canned vegetable aisle, he usually asks me if we've got enough green beans on hand. "Oh, yes," I always say, because it's true. We should buy them by the case, as we used to when we ran JO's Cafe!

I sometimes feel as if I could make a meal of delectable side dishes offered on a restaurant menu, especially if there's a great selection of regional vegetable recipes that are full of flavor but still low in calories and fat. If you've always struggled with a weight-loss program because you find the entree portions a little small, here's your solution: never plan a dinner menu that doesn't include at least a couple of scrumptious side dishes. I mean, who would worry about a moderate portion of meat when you've also got Celery Scalloped Potatoes and Bavarian Red Cabbage! You can go a more elegant route with Beans and Mushrooms Almondine, or revel in old-fashioned flavor with Grandma's Custard Corn Pudding. Whatever you choose, you'll never feel deprived again!

Savory
Side Dishes

Savory Harvard Beets

I love the vivid color of beets on the plate, so I've tried a variety of preparations to bring out their best qualities. This has a kind of sweet-and-sour flavor to it that is easy to love! (And rah-rah for the good old Crimson!) ☻ Serves 6 (½ cup)

½ cup pourable Splenda or Sugar Twin
2 tablespoons all-purpose flour
¼ cup hot water
¼ cup white vinegar
1 teaspoon dried parsley flakes
½ cup finely chopped onion
4 cups (two 16-ounce cans) whole beets, rinsed and drained

Spray a slow cooker container with butter-flavored cooking spray. In prepared container, combine Splenda, flour, water, vinegar, and parsley flakes. Add onion and beets. Mix well to combine. Cover and cook on LOW for 6 to 8 hours. Mix well before serving.

Each serving equals:

HE: 1½ Vegetable • 18 Optional Calories

64 Calories • 0 gm Fat • 2 gm Protein •
14 gm Carbohydrate • 384 mg Sodium • 25 mg Calcium •
2 gm Fiber

DIABETIC: 1½ Vegetable

Beans and Mushrooms Almondine

If there was ever a perfect nut to partner with green beans, it's got to be the almond—crisp, crunchy, and a wonderful color contrast! This is a very pretty dish to offer your guests, but it's also just right for treating yourself like company.   ◗   Serves 6 (1 cup)

> 6 cups frozen cut green beans, thawed
> ½ cup finely chopped onion
> 1 cup (one 4-ounce can) sliced mushrooms, drained
> ¼ cup slivered almonds
> 2 teaspoons reduced-calorie margarine

Spray a slow cooker container with butter-flavored cooking spray. In prepared container, combine green beans, onion, and mushrooms. Stir in almonds and margarine. Cover and cook on LOW for 4 hours. Mix well before serving.

HINT: Thaw green beans by placing them in a colander and rinsing them under hot water for one minute.

Each serving equals:

HE: 2½ Vegetable • ½ Fat • 10 Optional Calories

95 Calories • 3 gm Fat • 4 gm Protein •
13 gm Carbohydrate • 130 mg Sodium • 70 mg Calcium •
5 gm Fiber

DIABETIC: 2½ Vegetable • ½ Fat

Garlic French Green Bean Bake

Remember the old Rolling Stones song about having "time on your side"? This recipe demonstrates the power of time coupled with a very short list of ingredients. The result: magic in your mouth!

❍ Serves 6 (1 cup)

> ²⁄₃ *cup Kraft Fat Free French Dressing*
> ¼ *cup Hormel Bacon Bits*
> ½ *teaspoon dried minced garlic*
> 1 *teaspoon dried onion flakes*
> 6 *cups frozen cut green beans, thawed*

Spray a slow cooker container with butter-flavored cooking spray. In prepared container, combine French dressing, bacon bits, garlic, and onion flakes. Stir in green beans. Cover and cook on LOW for 6 hours. Mix well before serving.

HINT: Thaw green beans by placing them in a colander and rinsing them under hot water for one minute.

Each serving equals:

HE: 2 Vegetable • ¾ Slider • 1 Optional Calorie

---

109 Calories • 1 gm Fat • 4 gm Protein •
21 gm Carbohydrate • 434 mg Sodium • 53 mg Calcium •
4 gm Fiber

DIABETIC: 2 Vegetable • ½ Starch/Carbohydrate

Green Beans in Bacon-Cheese Sauce

When Cliff poked his head into the kitchen while we were preparing this recipe, he knew from the aroma that he was going to be in "green bean lover's heaven" for dinner that night! When he heard the dish's name, he gave me a big smile. There's nothing like a little cheese and bacon to win a husband's heart.   ☺   Serves 6 (1 cup)

1 (10¾-ounce) can Healthy Request Cream of Mushroom Soup
¼ cup (one 2-ounce can) chopped pimiento, undrained
1 cup + 2 tablespoons shredded Kraft reduced-fat Cheddar cheese
⅛ teaspoon black pepper
1 cup (one 4-ounce can) sliced mushrooms, undrained
½ cup finely chopped onion
6 tablespoons Hormel Bacon Bits
6 cups frozen cut green beans, thawed

Spray a slow cooker container with butter-flavored cooking spray. In prepared container, combine mushroom soup, undrained pimiento, Cheddar cheese, and black pepper. Stir in undrained mushrooms, onion, and bacon bits. Add green beans. Mix well to combine. Cover and cook on LOW for 4 to 6 hours. Mix well before serving.

HINT: Thaw green beans by placing them in a colander and rinsing them under hot water for one minute.

Each serving equals:

HE: 2½ Vegetable • 1 Protein • ½ Slider • 13 Optional Calories

174 Calories • 6 gm Fat • 12 gm Protein • 18 gm Carbohydrate • 740 mg Sodium • 239 mg Calcium • 4 gm Fiber

DIABETIC: 2½ Vegetable • 1 Meat • ½ Starch/Carbohydrate

Savory Green Beans

If the men and kids in your house could eat green beans every single night, you need a repertoire of recipes to keep life just a little interesting. When you pour some tomato sauce into the pot, you get a surprising amount of fresh and exciting flavor. ☻ Serves 6 (1 cup)

> 1 (10¾-ounce) can Healthy Request Tomato Soup
> ¼ cup (one 2-ounce jar) chopped pimiento, undrained
> 1 teaspoon dried basil leaves
> ⅛ teaspoon black pepper
> 6 cups frozen cut green beans, thawed
> 1½ cups finely chopped onion

Spray a slow cooker container with butter-flavored cooking spray. In prepared container, combine tomato soup, undrained pimiento, basil, and black pepper. Add green beans and onion. Mix well to combine. Cover and cook on LOW for 8 hours. Mix well before serving.

HINT: Thaw green beans by placing them in a colander and rinsing them under hot water for one minute.

Each serving equals:

HE: 2½ Vegetable • ¼ Slider • 10 Optional Calories

101 Calories • 1 gm Fat • 3 gm Protein •
20 gm Carbohydrate • 195 mg Sodium • 66 mg Calcium •
5 gm Fiber

DIABETIC: 2½ Vegetable • ½ Starch/Carbohydrate

Green Beans in Cheesy Mustard Sauce

I bet you'll love the extra zing a dollop of mustard gives this creamy cheese sauce—and how that sauce transforms some basic beans! It takes so little to make the ordinary extraordinary—and you deserve it!

♥ Serves 6 (1 cup)

> 1 (10¾-ounce) can Healthy Request Cream of Mushroom Soup
> 1 cup + 2 tablespoons shredded Kraft reduced-fat Cheddar cheese
> ¼ cup (one 2-ounce jar) chopped pimiento, undrained
> 1½ teaspoons prepared yellow mustard
> 1 teaspoon dried onion flakes
> 1 teaspoon dried parsley flakes
> ⅛ teaspoon black pepper
> 6 cups frozen cut green beans, thawed

Spray a slow cooker container with butter-flavored cooking spray. In prepared container, combine mushroom soup, Cheddar cheese, and undrained pimiento. Stir in mustard, onion flakes, parsley flakes, and black pepper. Add green beans. Mix well to combine. Cover and cook on LOW for 6 hours. Mix well before serving.

HINT: Thaw green beans by placing them in a colander and rinsing them under hot water for one minute.

Each serving equals:

HE: 2 Vegetable • 1 Protein • ¼ Slider •
8 Optional Calories

137 Calories • 5 gm Fat • 8 gm Protein •
15 gm Carbohydrate • 396 mg Sodium •
236 mg Calcium • 4 gm Fiber

DIABETIC: 2 Vegetable • 1 Meat

Green Beans and Ham

Sometimes children who turn up their noses at eating their veggies can be successfully "seduced" with a few additions to the pot, like the ham and lemon pepper that give this dish real pizzazz! Try it and see.

● Serves 4 (1½ cups)

> 3 cups frozen cut green beans, thawed
> ½ cup diced onion
> 1 full cup diced Dubuque 97% fat-free ham or any extra-lean ham
> 2 cups diced raw potatoes
> ¾ cup hot water
> 1 tablespoon dried parsley flakes
> ½ teaspoon lemon pepper

Spray a slow cooker container with butter-flavored cooking spray. In prepared container, combine green beans, onion, ham, and potatoes. Stir in water, parsley flakes, and lemon pepper. Cover and cook on LOW for 8 hours. Mix well before serving.

HINT: Thaw green beans by placing them in a colander and rinsing them under hot water for one minute.

Each serving equals:

HE: 1¾ Vegetable • 1 Protein • ½ Bread

134 Calories • 2 gm Fat • 10 gm Protein •
19 gm Carbohydrate • 366 mg Sodium • 48 mg Calcium •
4 gm Fiber

DIABETIC: 2 Vegetable • 1 Meat • ½ Starch

Green Bean Side Pot

This dish has a wonderfully smoky, barbecue-type flavor, making it a delightful accompaniment for pork tenderloins or lean roast beef.

● Serves 6 (¾ cup)

2 cups (one 16-ounce can) tomatoes, chopped and undrained
½ cup hot water
1 teaspoon Worcestershire sauce
1 tablespoon Brown Sugar Twin
1 teaspoon dried parsley flakes
⅛ teaspoon black pepper
2 cups frozen cut green beans, thawed
½ cup chopped onion
⅔ cup uncooked instant rice

Spray a slow cooker container with butter-flavored cooking spray. In prepared container, combine undrained tomatoes, water, Worcestershire sauce, Brown Sugar Twin, parsley flakes, and black pepper. Add green beans and onion. Mix well to combine. Stir in uncooked rice. Cover and cook on LOW for 6 to 8 hours. Mix well before serving.

HINT: Thaw green beans by placing them in a colander and rinsing them under hot water for one minute.

Each serving equals:

HE: 1½ Vegetable • ⅓ Bread • 1 Optional Calorie

64 Calories • 0 gm Fat • 2 gm Protein •
14 gm Carbohydrate • 159 mg Sodium • 38 mg Calcium •
2 gm Fiber

DIABETIC: 1½ Vegetable • ½ Starch

South Seas Green Beans

It's not just your tummy that gets tired of eating the same old thing—it's also your soul! Climb out of your vegetable rut today with this aromatic way to be sure to "get your greens."

○ Serves 6 (1 cup)

> *4 cups frozen cut green beans, thawed*
> *½ cup chopped onion*
> *¼ cup Hormel Bacon Bits*
> *¼ cup hot water*
> *¼ cup cider vinegar*
> *¼ cup (one 2-ounce jar) chopped pimiento, undrained*
> *2 tablespoons pourable Splenda or Sugar Twin*
> *⅛ teaspoon black pepper*

Spray a slow cooker container with butter-flavored cooking spray. In prepared container, combine green beans, onion, and bacon bits. Stir in water, vinegar, and undrained pimiento. Add Splenda and black pepper. Mix well to combine. Cover and cook on LOW for 6 to 8 hours. Mix well before serving.

HINT: Thaw green beans by placing them in a colander and rinsing them under hot water for one minute.

Each serving equals:

HE: 1½ Vegetable • 19 Optional Calories

65 Calories • 1 gm Fat • 4 gm Protein •
10 gm Carbohydrate • 171 mg Sodium • 41 mg Calcium •
3 gm Fiber

DIABETIC: 2 Vegetable

Scalloped Carrots

Here's something a little different to do with those old standbys, frozen carrots. The creamy-cheesy sauce that surrounds those orange circles will make your family sit up and take notice.

○ Serves 6 (full ¾ cup)

> 1 (10¾-ounce) can Healthy Request Cream of Celery Soup
>
> ¼ cup water
>
> ½ cup + 1 tablespoon shredded Kraft reduced-fat Cheddar cheese
>
> ⅛ teaspoon black pepper
>
> 5 cups frozen cut carrots, thawed
>
> 1 cup chopped onion
>
> 15 Ritz Reduced Fat Crackers, made into crumbs

Spray a slow cooker container with butter-flavored cooking spray. In prepared container, combine celery soup, water, Cheddar cheese, and black pepper. Stir in carrots and onion. Add cracker crumbs. Mix well to combine. Cover and cook on LOW for 4 hours. Mix well before serving.

HINTS: 1. Thaw carrots by placing them in a colander and rinsing them under hot water for one minute.
2. A self-seal sandwich bag works great for crushing crackers.

Each serving equals:

HE: 2 Vegetable • ½ Bread • ½ Protein • ¼ Slider • 8 Optional Calories

144 Calories • 4 gm Fat • 5 gm Protein • 22 gm Carbohydrate • 417 mg Sodium • 179 mg Calcium • 4 gm Fiber

DIABETIC: 2 Vegetable • ½ Starch/Carbohydrate • ½ Meat

Carrots Lyonnaise

Prepared in the style of the French town of Lyon, these carrots just shimmer with scrumptious goodness! This is a terrific time to use that bag or two of shredded carrots you picked up at the store.

○ Serves 6 (²/₃ cup)

> 6 cups shredded carrots
> 1½ cups chopped onion
> 1 (10¾-ounce) can Healthy Request Cream of Chicken Soup
> 2 teaspoons dried parsley flakes
> ⅛ teaspoon black pepper

Spray a slow cooker container with butter-flavored cooking spray. In prepared container, combine carrots and onion. Add chicken soup, parsley flakes, and black pepper. Mix well to combine. Cover and cook on LOW for 6 to 8 hours. Mix well before serving.

Each serving equals:

HE: 2½ Vegetable • ¼ Slider • 10 Optional Calories

93 Calories • 1 gm Fat • 2 gm Protein • 19 gm Carbohydrate • 237 mg Sodium • 40 mg Calcium • 4 gm Fiber

DIABETIC: 2½ Vegetable • ½ Starch/Carbohydrate

Southern Sunshine Glazed Carrots

There's a different quality to the sunlight down South, especially in that state of intoxicating orange flavor, Florida! Even on a rainy day, you've got all the sunny sweetness anyone could ever want when you put these on the menu.   ☻   Serves 6 (full ½ cup)

3 cups frozen sliced carrots, thawed

3 tablespoons chopped pecans

¼ cup orange marmalade spreadable fruit

2 tablespoons reduced-calorie margarine

1 teaspoon dried onion flakes

1 teaspoon dried parsley flakes

Spray a slow cooker container with butter-flavored cooking spray. In prepared container, combine carrots and pecans. In a small bowl, combine spreadable fruit, margarine, onion flakes, and parsley flakes. Stir fruit mixture into carrot mixture. Cover and cook on LOW for 6 to 8 hours. Mix gently before serving.

HINT: Thaw carrots by placing them in a colander and rinsing them under hot water for one minute.

Each serving equals:

HE: 1 Fat • 1 Vegetable • ⅔ Fruit

96 Calories • 4 gm Fat • 1 gm Protein •
14 gm Carbohydrate • 89 mg Sodium • 27 mg Calcium •
3 gm Fiber

DIABETIC: 1 Fat • 1 Vegetable • ½ Fruit

Celery Stuffing Side Dish

Whether or not you're having turkey for dinner, you can serve this savory stuffing recipe anytime you wish! Why did I use cream of chicken soup instead of cream of celery? Taste it and see.

❍ Serves 8 (¾ cup)

> 1 (10¾-ounce) can Healthy Request Cream of Chicken Soup
> 1½ cups (one 12-fluid-ounce can) Carnation Evaporated Skim Milk
> 1½ teaspoons ground sage
> ½ teaspoon poultry seasoning
> 2 cups finely chopped celery
> 1 cup chopped onion
> 16 slices reduced-calorie dry white bread, cut into 1-inch cubes

Spray a slow cooker container with butter-flavored cooking spray. In prepared container, combine chicken soup, evaporated skim milk, sage, and poultry seasoning. Stir in celery and onion. Add bread cubes. Mix well to combine. Cover and cook on LOW for 6 to 8 hours. Mix well before serving.

Each serving equals:

HE: 1 Bread • ¾ Vegetable • ⅓ Skim Milk •
¼ Slider • 7 Optional Calories

165 Calories • 1 gm Fat • 9 gm Protein •
30 gm Carbohydrate • 464 mg Sodium •
174 mg Calcium • 2 gm Fiber

DIABETIC: 1½ Starch • ½ Vegetable

California Vegetable Cheese Bake

What a wonderful way to get your veggies today! If you haven't tried it yet, let me tantalize you: Velveeta Light is a cheese lover's dream come true.　　❍　Serves 6 (²/₃ cup)

4 cups frozen carrot, broccoli, and cauliflower blend, thawed
½ cup finely chopped onion
1 (10¾-ounce) can Healthy Request Cream of Mushroom Soup
¼ cup (one 2-ounce jar) chopped pimiento, drained
1½ cups cubed Velveeta Light processed cheese

Spray a slow cooker container with butter-flavored cooking spray. In prepared container, combine thawed vegetables and onion. Add mushroom soup, pimiento, and cheese. Mix well to combine. Cover and cook on LOW for 4 to 6 hours. Mix well before serving.

HINT:　　Thaw vegetables by placing them in a colander and rinsing them under hot water for one minute.

Each serving equals:

HE: 2 Protein • 1½ Vegetable • ¼ Slider •
8 Optional Calories

140 Calories • 4 gm Fat • 13 gm Protein •
13 gm Carbohydrate • 236 mg Sodium •
373 mg Calcium • 3 gm Fiber

DIABETIC: 1½ Meat • 1½ Vegetable

Broccoli Rice Melange

We keep reading that broccoli is one of the healthiest vegetables around, so I've created lots of tasty ways to serve that great green. Cliff was almost tempted (I said *almost*) to sample a bite, this dish looked and smelled so irresistible. But he just couldn't break his no-broccoli rule. (P.S. The rest of us loved it!) ☻ Serves 6 (1 cup)

1 cup uncooked instant rice
4 cups frozen chopped broccoli, thawed
½ cup chopped onion
1½ cups (one 12-fluid-ounce can) Carnation Evaporated Skim Milk
1 (10¾-ounce) can Healthy Request Cream of Mushroom Soup
1 cup + 2 tablespoons shredded Kraft reduced-fat Cheddar cheese

Spray a slow cooker container with butter-flavored cooking spray. In prepared container, combine uncooked rice, broccoli, and onion. Add evaporated skim milk and mushroom soup. Mix well to combine. Stir in Cheddar cheese. Cover and cook on LOW for 5 to 6 hours. Mix well before serving.

HINT: Thaw broccoli by placing it in a colander and rinsing it under hot water for one minute.

Each serving equals:

HE: 1½ Vegetable • 1 Protein • ½ Skim Milk •
½ Bread • ¼ Slider • 8 Optional Calories

217 Calories • 5 gm Fat • 14 gm Protein •
29 gm Carbohydrate • 481 mg Sodium •
405 mg Calcium • 3 gm Fiber

DIABETIC: 1½ Vegetable • 1 Starch • 1 Meat •
½ Skim Milk

Veggie Rice Pot

I have always preferred my rice sprinkled with lots of lovely, healthy colors. Here, the bright bits of green and orange vegetables remind me just how good this dish is for me, instead of just good.

⚫ Serves 4 (1 cup)

1 (10¾-ounce) can Healthy Request Tomato Soup

1¼ cups hot water

1 teaspoon chili seasoning

1 teaspoon dried parsley flakes

⅛ teaspoon black pepper

1⅓ cups uncooked instant rice

1½ cups frozen cut carrots, thawed

1 cup frozen cut green beans, thawed

½ cup chopped onion

Spray a slow cooker container with butter-flavored cooking spray. In prepared container, combine tomato soup, water, chili seasoning, parsley flakes, and black pepper. Stir in uncooked rice. Add carrots, green beans, and onion. Mix well to combine. Cover and cook on LOW for 4 hours. Mix well before serving.

HINT: Thaw carrots and green beans by placing them in a colander and rinsing them under hot water for 30 seconds.

Each serving equals:

HE: 1½ Vegetable • 1 Bread • ½ Slider •
5 Optional Calories

---

173 Calories • 1 gm Fat • 4 gm Protein •
37 gm Carbohydrate • 315 mg Sodium • 41 mg Calcium •
4 gm Fiber

DIABETIC: 1½ Vegetable • 1½ Starch

Cauliflower in Cheesy Tomato Sauce

Here's a recipe that gets better and better as it bubbles away. Are you surprised to discover you can relish a zippy cheese sauce with your cauliflower and not feel guilty for a second? You CAN!

● Serves 6 (⅔ cup)

> 4 cups frozen chopped cauliflower, thawed
>
> ½ cup chopped onion
>
> 1 (10¾-ounce) can Healthy Request Tomato Soup
>
> 1 cup + 2 tablespoons shredded Kraft reduced-fat Cheddar cheese
>
> ¼ cup Hormel Bacon Bits
>
> 2 teaspoons dried parsley flakes
>
> ⅛ teaspoon black pepper

Spray a slow cooker container with butter-flavored cooking spray. In prepared container, combine cauliflower and onion. Stir in tomato soup. Add Cheddar cheese, bacon bits, parsley flakes, and black pepper. Mix well to combine. Cover and cook on LOW for 4 to 6 hours. Mix well before serving.

HINT: Thaw cauliflower by placing it in a colander and rinsing it under hot water for one minute.

Each serving equals:

HE: 1½ Vegetable • 1 Protein • ½ Slider •
7 Optional Calories

141 Calories • 5 gm Fat • 10 gm Protein •
14 gm Carbohydrate • 555 mg Sodium •
164 mg Calcium • 3 gm Fiber

DIABETIC: 1½ Vegetable • 1 Meat • ½ Starch

Bavarian Red Cabbage

This splendidly colorful side dish makes a festive meal even more beautiful with its rosy hue and tangy crunch. I'd serve it with something like grilled chicken for extra sparkle and fun.

Serves 6 (1 full cup)

8 cups coarsely sliced red cabbage

1 cup chopped onion

1½ cups cored, peeled, and chopped Granny Smith apples

½ cup cider vinegar

2 tablespoons pourable Splenda or Sugar Twin

3 tablespoons Hormel Bacon Bits

Spray a slow cooker container with butter-flavored cooking spray. In prepared container, combine red cabbage, onion, and apples. In a small bowl, combine vinegar, Splenda, and bacon bits. Drizzle mixture evenly over top. Cover and cook on LOW for 6 to 8 hours. Mix well before serving.

Each serving equals:

HE: 1½ Vegetable • ½ Fruit • 15 Optional Calories

81 Calories • 1 gm Fat • 3 gm Protein •
15 gm Carbohydrate • 139 mg Sodium • 69 mg Calcium •
3 gm Fiber

DIABETIC: 1½ Vegetable • ½ Fruit

Savory Scalloped Cabbage

You can make this dish even easier by using pre-shredded vegetables, though I usually use a grater or food processor for all my chopping. Never had baked cabbage before? This will be a delectable new experience you won't soon forget.　❂　Serves 6 (1 cup)

> 1 (10¾-ounce) can Healthy Request Cream of Mushroom Soup
> ¼ cup (one 2-ounce jar) chopped pimiento, drained
> ¾ cup shredded Kraft reduced-fat Cheddar cheese
> 8 cups shredded cabbage
> 1½ cups shredded carrots
> ½ cup chopped onion

Spray a slow cooker container with butter-flavored cooking spray. In prepared container, combine mushroom soup, pimiento, and Cheddar cheese. Add cabbage, carrots, and onion. Mix well to combine. Cover and cook on LOW for 3 to 4 hours. Mix well before serving.

Each serving equals:

HE: 2 Vegetable • ⅔ Protein • ¼ Slider •
8 Optional Calories

120 Calories • 4 gm Fat • 6 gm Protein •
15 gm Carbohydrate • 348 mg Sodium •
200 mg Calcium • 4 gm Fiber

DIABETIC: 2 Vegetable • 1 Meat

Country Sweet-Sour Cabbage

I've been growing cabbage in my garden for as long as I can remember. This is a delicious way to experience the memorable marriage of fruits and vegetables in one fragrant, good-for-you dish.

● Serves 6 (1 cup)

> 8 cups shredded cabbage
> 1½ cups cored, peeled, and diced cooking apples
> ½ cup chopped onion
> ½ cup hot water
> ½ cup cider vinegar
> ½ cup pourable Splenda or Sugar Twin
> 2 tablespoons reduced-calorie margarine

Spray a slow cooker container with butter-flavored cooking spray. In prepared container, combine cabbage, apples, and onion. In a small bowl, combine water, vinegar, and Splenda. Add water mixture to cabbage mixture. Mix well to combine. Drop margarine by teaspoon over top. Cover and cook on LOW for 3 to 4 hours. Mix well before serving.

Each serving equals:

HE: 1½ Vegetable • ½ Fruit • ½ Fat • 8 Optional Calories

78 Calories • 2 gm Fat • 2 gm Protein •
13 gm Carbohydrate • 67 mg Sodium • 62 mg Calcium •
4 gm Fiber

DIABETIC: 1½ Vegetable • ½ Fruit • ½ Fat

Dutch Corn and Cabbage

Here's a combination that goes together as perfectly as tulips and windmills! The vivid yellow and green colors complement each other just beautifully. ☕ Serves 6 (1 full cup)

> 4½ cups shredded cabbage
>
> 3 cups frozen whole-kernel corn, thawed
>
> ¼ cup hot water
>
> 6 tablespoons Hormel Bacon Bits
>
> 1 tablespoon pourable Splenda or Sugar Twin
>
> 1 teaspoon dried parsley flakes
>
> ⅛ teaspoon black pepper

Spray a slow cooker container with butter-flavored cooking spray. In prepared container, combine cabbage, corn, and water. Add bacon bits, Splenda, parsley flakes, and black pepper. Mix well to combine. Cover and cook on LOW for 4 hours. Mix well before serving.

HINT: Thaw corn by placing it in a colander and rinsing it under hot water for one minute.

Each serving equals:

HE: 1 Bread • ¾ Vegetable • ¼ Slider • 6 Optional Calories

130 Calories • 2 gm Fat • 6 gm Protein •
22 gm Carbohydrate • 265 mg Sodium • 36 mg Calcium •
3 gm Fiber

DIABETIC: 1 Starch • 1 Vegetable • ½ Meat

Mushroom Pasta Bake

Oh-so-creamy and outrageously good, this recipe is especially tasty served with lean sliced meats. Instead of potatoes or rice as a side dish, try this tonight!   ♥   Serves 4 (1 cup)

1 (10¾-ounce) can Healthy Request Cream of Mushroom Soup

½ cup water

¼ cup Land O Lakes no-fat sour cream

1 cup (one 4-ounce can) sliced mushrooms, undrained

1 teaspoon dried parsley flakes

¼ teaspoon dried minced garlic

½ cup finely chopped onion

1⅓ cups uncooked rotini pasta

Spray a slow cooker container with butter-flavored cooking spray. In prepared container, combine mushroom soup, water, and sour cream. Stir in undrained mushrooms, parsley flakes, and garlic. Add onion and uncooked rotini pasta. Mix well to combine. Cover and cook on LOW for 6 to 8 hours. Mix well before serving.

Each serving equals:

HE: 1 Bread • ¾ Vegetable • ½ Slider •
16 Optional Calories

166 Calories • 2 gm Fat • 5 gm Protein •
32 gm Carbohydrate • 482 mg Sodium • 96 mg Calcium •
2 gm Fiber

DIABETIC: 1½ Starch • 1 Vegetable

Farmhouse Escalloped Tomatoes

Whenever I see a bowl of red, ripe tomatoes, my creative mind starts whirring away with imaginative new ways to serve them! So much flavor, so few calories—and zero fat! ☻ Serves 6 (1 cup)

5 cups peeled and chopped fresh tomatoes
½ cup finely chopped onion
½ cup finely chopped green bell pepper
2 tablespoons pourable Splenda or Sugar Twin
1 teaspoon dried basil leaves
⅛ teaspoon black pepper
4 slices reduced-calorie bread, toasted and cut into cubes

Spray a slow cooker container with butter-flavored cooking spray. In prepared container, combine tomatoes, onion, and green pepper. Stir in Splenda, basil, and black pepper. Add bread cubes. Mix well to combine. Cover and cook on LOW for 6 hours. Mix well before serving.

Each serving equals:

HE: 2 Vegetable • ⅓ Bread • 2 Optional Calories

72 Calories • 0 gm Fat • 3 gm Protein •
15 gm Carbohydrate • 91 mg Sodium • 28 mg Calcium •
2 gm Fiber

DIABETIC: 2 Vegetable • ½ Starch

Texas Tomatoes with Rice

If you ask a Texan (and believe me, I have), everything needs to be big on taste down there. When you want a smoky, spicy, hot-off-the-grill flavor, sample this veggie-rice combo, especially when it's too chilly to cook outside. ❍ Serves 6 (1 full cup)

3 cups (one 28-ounce can) tomatoes, chopped and undrained
2 cups hot water
2 cups uncooked instant rice
¾ cup finely chopped onion
1½ teaspoons chili seasoning
2 teaspoons dried parsley flakes
1 tablespoon Brown Sugar Twin
⅛ teaspoon black pepper

Spray a slow cooker container with butter-flavored cooking spray. In prepared container, combine undrained tomatoes and water. Stir in uncooked rice and onion. Add chili seasoning, parsley flakes, Brown Sugar Twin, and black pepper. Mix well to combine. Cover and cook on LOW for 4 to 6 hours. Mix well before serving.

Each serving equals:

HE: 1¼ Vegetable • 1 Bread • 1 Optional Calorie

120 Calories • 0 gm Fat • 3 gm Protein •
27 gm Carbohydrate • 230 mg Sodium • 36 mg Calcium •
2 gm Fiber

DIABETIC: 1 Vegetable • 1 Starch

Corn-Tomato Pot

This melange of colors and flavors is comfort food at its most appealing! It adds interest to the plate and can be served any time of the year, so it's an ideal recipe for busy cooks everywhere.

● Serves 6 (1 cup)

3 cups (one 28-ounce can) tomatoes, chopped and undrained
½ cup chopped green bell pepper
1 cup chopped onion
3 cups frozen whole-kernel corn, thawed
1 tablespoon Brown Sugar Twin
1 teaspoon dried parsley flakes
⅛ teaspoon black pepper

Spray a slow cooker container with butter-flavored cooking spray. In prepared container, combine undrained tomatoes, green pepper, and onion. Stir in corn. Add Brown Sugar Twin, parsley flakes, and black pepper. Mix well to combine. Cover and cook on LOW for 3 to 4 hours. Mix well before serving.

HINT: Thaw corn by placing it in a colander and rinsing it under hot water for one minute.

Each serving equals:

HE: 1½ Vegetable • 1 Bread • 1 Optional Calorie

120 Calories • 0 gm Fat • 4 gm Protein •
24 gm Carbohydrate • 223 mg Sodium • 31 mg Calcium •
3 gm Fiber

DIABETIC: 1½ Vegetable • 1 Starch

Creamed Corn

Dazzle your favorite creamed-corn lover with this spectacularly good "homemade" version that tastes way too good to be so healthy! No one will believe this dish is fat-free, so you have my permission to pass along the recipe. (Not that you need it, of course . . .)

○ Serves 8 (scant ½ cup)

4 cups frozen whole-kernel corn, thawed

1 cup chopped onion

1 (8-ounce) package Philadelphia fat-free cream cheese

2 teaspoons dried parsley flakes

⅛ teaspoon black pepper

Spray a slow cooker container with butter-flavored cooking spray. In prepared container, combine corn and onion. Add cream cheese, parsley flakes, and black pepper. Mix well to combine. Cover and cook on HIGH for 2 hours. Mix well before serving.

HINT: Thaw corn by placing it in a colander and rinsing it under hot water for one minute.

Each serving equals:

HE: 1 Bread • ½ Protein • ¼ Vegetable

108 Calories • 0 gm Fat • 6 gm Protein •
21 gm Carbohydrate • 140 mg Sodium • 90 mg Calcium •
2 gm Fiber

DIABETIC: 1 Starch • ½ Meat

Grandma's Custard Corn Pudding

When you come home from a busy day at the office and lift the lid on this old-fashioned wonder, you'll be convinced that a grandmotherly elf slipped into your kitchen while you were out—and made supper while you were gone! ☻ Serves 8 (½ cup)

⅔ cup Carnation Nonfat Dry Milk Powder

½ cup water

2 eggs or equivalent in egg substitute

1 tablespoon pourable Splenda or Sugar Twin

1 teaspoon dried onion flakes

1 teaspoon dried parsley flakes

⅛ teaspoon black pepper

1 cup (one 8-ounce can) cream-style corn

3 cups frozen whole-kernel corn, thawed

Spray a slow cooker container with butter-flavored cooking spray. In prepared container, combine dry milk powder and water. Add eggs, Splenda, onion flakes, parsley flakes, and black pepper. Mix well to combine. Stir in cream-style corn and whole-kernel corn. Cover and cook on LOW for 2 to 3 hours. Mix well before serving.

HINT: Thaw corn by placing it in a colander and rinsing it under hot water for one minute.

Each serving equals:

HE: 1 Bread • ¼ Skim Milk • ¼ Protein •
1 Optional Calorie

---

130 Calories • 2 gm Fat • 6 gm Protein •
22 gm Carbohydrate • 140 mg Sodium • 85 mg Calcium •
2 gm Fiber

DIABETIC: 1½ Starch/Carbohydrate

Olé Scalloped Corn

My scalloped corn recipes have always been popular with my husband, but when I gave this old standby some added sizzle, Cliff applauded my efforts with "a kiss for the cook"!   ♥   Serves 6 (½ cup)

1 cup (one 8-ounce can) cream-style corn
½ cup frozen whole-kernel corn, thawed
¼ cup Land O Lakes no-fat sour cream
1 egg, slightly beaten, or equivalent in egg substitute
1 cup chopped onion
½ cup chopped green bell pepper
¼ cup (one 2-ounce jar) chopped pimiento, undrained
21 small fat-free saltine crackers, made into crumbs
1 teaspoon dried parsley flakes
⅛ teaspoon black pepper

Spray a slow cooker container with olive oil–flavored cooking spray. In prepared container, combine corn, sour cream, and egg. Stir in onion, green pepper, undrained pimiento, and cracker crumbs. Add parsley flakes, and black pepper. Mix well to combine. Cover and cook on LOW for 3 to 4 hours. Mix well before serving.

HINTS: 1. Thaw corn by placing it in a colander and rinsing it under hot water for one minute.
2. A self-seal sandwich bag works great for crushing crackers.

Each serving equals:

HE: 1 Bread • ½ Vegetable • ¼ Slider

121 Calories • 1 gm Fat • 4 gm Protein •
24 gm Carbohydrate • 274 mg Sodium • 27 mg Calcium •
2 gm Fiber

DIABETIC: 1½ Starch/Carbohydrate

Herbed Corn Bake

When my son Tommy tasted this dish on a visit to my kitchen, he voted it "most likely to succeed!" He and Angie have passed their love of corn (every Iowan's pride) on to their daughter Cheyanne.

● Serves 6 (²⁄₃ cup)

> ²⁄₃ cup Carnation Nonfat Dry Milk Powder
>
> 1 cup hot water
>
> ½ cup Kraft fat-free mayonnaise
>
> 1 egg, slightly beaten, or equivalent in egg substitute
>
> 1 teaspoon dried parsley flakes
>
> 2½ cups frozen whole-kernel corn, thawed
>
> 1 cup herb-seasoned dry bread cubes
>
> ¾ cup finely chopped onion

Spray a slow cooker container with butter-flavored cooking spray. In prepared container, combine dry milk powder, water, and mayonnaise. Stir in egg and parsley flakes. Add corn, bread cubes, and onion. Mix well to combine. Cover and cook on LOW for 2 to 3 hours. Mix well before serving.

HINTS: 1. Thaw corn by placing it in a colander and rinsing it under hot water for one minute.
2. Pepperidge Farm bread cubes work great.

Each serving equals:

HE: 1 Bread • ⅓ Skim Milk • ¼ Vegetable • ¼ Slider • 3 Optional Calories

149 Calories • 1 gm Fat • 7 gm Protein • 28 gm Carbohydrate • 301 mg Sodium • 111 mg Calcium • 2 gm Fiber

DIABETIC: 1½ Starch/Carbohydrate • ½ Skim Milk

Kidney Bean Bake

If you're one of those people who could happily eat chili every other evening, why not vary your menu with this hearty baked-bean dish that's as tangy as it is terrific! Because it's high in fiber, your body will thank you—and even your taste buds will raise a cheer.

● Serves 6 (1 cup)

1 cup (one 8-ounce can) Hunt's Tomato Sauce
¼ cup sweet pickle relish
⅛ teaspoon black pepper
30 ounces (three 16-ounce cans) red kidney beans, rinsed and drained
1 cup finely chopped celery
1 cup finely chopped onion

Spray a slow cooker container with butter-flavored cooking spray. In prepared container, combine tomato sauce, pickle relish, and black pepper. Add kidney beans, celery, and onion. Mix well to combine. Cover and cook on LOW for 6 to 8 hours. Mix well before serving.

Each serving equals:

HE: 2½ Protein • 1⅓ Vegetable • 10 Optional Calories

205 Calories • 1 gm Fat • 11 gm Protein •
38 gm Carbohydrate • 348 mg Sodium • 19 mg Calcium •
14 gm Fiber

DIABETIC: 1½ Meat • 1½ Starch • 1 Vegetable

Yummy Kidney Beans

What a wonderful "cookout" twang this savory bean dish delivers! This saucy combo is healthy, sure, but it'll also satisfy you heart and soul.

❍ Serves 6 (1 cup)

> 30 ounces (three 16-ounce cans) red kidney beans, rinsed and drained
> 1/4 cup Hormel Bacon Bits
> 1 cup chopped onion
> 1 cup (one 8-ounce can) Hunt's Tomato Sauce
> 1 teaspoon chili seasoning
> 1/4 cup pourable Splenda or Sugar Twin
> 2 tablespoons Brown Sugar Twin
> 1 teaspoon dried parsley flakes

Spray a slow cooker container with butter-flavored cooking spray. In prepared container, combine kidney beans, bacon bits, and onion. Stir in tomato sauce, chili seasoning, Splenda, Brown Sugar Twin, and parsley flakes. Cover and cook on LOW for 4 to 6 hours. Mix well before serving.

Each serving equals:

HE: 2½ Protein • 1 Vegetable • ¼ Slider •
2 Optional Calories

---

210 Calories • 2 gm Fat • 13 gm Protein •
35 gm Carbohydrate • 418 mg Sodium • 13 mg Calcium •
14 gm Fiber

DIABETIC: 2 Meat • 1½ Starch • 1 Vegetable

Three Bean Pot

If you're a fan of three-bean salad, here's a cold-weather way to get that summer-salad fix! If you've got a vegetarian in the family, you can leave the bacon bits out and just sprinkle them on top of everyone else's finished dish. The flavor won't be quite as blended, but it'll still be very, very good.   ☻   Serves 6 (1 full cup)

> 10 ounces (one 16-ounce can) great northern beans, rinsed and drained
> 10 ounces (one 16-ounce can) pinto beans, rinsed and drained
> 10 ounces (one 16-ounce can) red kidney beans, rinsed and drained
> 1¾ cups (one 14½-ounce can) stewed tomatoes, coarsely chopped and undrained
> ½ cup (one 2.5-ounce jar) sliced mushrooms, drained
> ¾ cup chopped onion
> 1 cup chopped celery
> 1 cup sliced carrots
> ¼ cup Hormel Bacon Bits
> ⅛ teaspoon black pepper
> ¼ teaspoon dried minced garlic

Spray a slow cooker container with butter-flavored cooking spray. In prepared container, combine great northern beans, pinto beans, and kidney beans. Stir in undrained tomatoes, mushrooms, and onion. Add celery, carrots, bacon bits, black pepper, and garlic. Mix well to combine. Cover and cook on LOW for 6 to 8 hours. Mix gently before serving.

Each serving equals:

HE: 2½ Protein • 1⅔ Vegetable • 17 Optional Calories

---

214 Calories • 2 gm Fat • 12 gm Protein •
37 gm Carbohydrate • 504 mg Sodium • 80 mg Calcium •
10 gm Fiber

DIABETIC: 1½ Meat • 1½ Vegetable • 1½ Starch

Sensational Baked Beans

I especially love the slow cooker for making baked beans, and this recipe serves up some of the best you'll ever taste! Isn't it great to be able to stir up a pot of these for a summer cookout without turning on the oven and heating up the house?   ☻   Serves 6 (¾ cup)

> 1 cup (one 8-ounce can) Hunt's Tomato Sauce
>
> 1 teaspoon prepared yellow mustard
>
> 2 tablespoons pourable Splenda or Sugar Twin
>
> 1 teaspoon Worcestershire sauce
>
> 30 ounces (three 16-ounce cans) great northern beans, rinsed and drained
>
> 1 cup finely chopped onion
>
> 6 tablespoons Hormel Bacon Bits

Spray a slow cooker container with butter-flavored cooking spray. In prepared container, combine tomato sauce, mustard, Splenda, and Worcestershire sauce. Stir in great northern beans. Add onion and bacon bits. Mix well to combine. Cover and cook on LOW for 6 to 8 hours. Mix well before serving.

Each serving equals:

HE: 2½ Protein • 1 Vegetable • ¼ Slider •
5 Optional Calories

---

166 Calories • 2 gm Fat • 11 gm Protein •
26 gm Carbohydrate • 527 mg Sodium • 13 mg Calcium •
8 gm Fiber

DIABETIC: 2 Meat • 1 Vegetable • 1 Starch

Hawaiian Baked Beans

Trust me on this one—the flavor combo sounds odd but tastes astonishingly good! Your family will be willing to hula for their supper once they taste this tropical treat.   ❍   Serves 6 (1 cup)

> 30 ounces (three 16-ounce cans) great northern beans, rinsed and
>   drained
> 1½ cups finely chopped onion
> 1 tablespoon prepared yellow mustard
> ¼ cup chili sauce
> 1 cup (one 8-ounce can) crushed pineapple, packed in fruit juice,
>   undrained
> ¾ cup Hormel Bacon Bits

Spray a slow cooker container with butter-flavored cooking spray. In prepared container, combine great northern beans, onion, mustard, and chili sauce. Stir in undrained pineapple and bacon bits. Cover and cook on LOW for 6 to 8 hours. Mix well before serving.

Each serving equals:

HE: 2½ Protein • ½ Vegetable • ⅓ Fruit • ¾ Slider

228 Calories • 4 gm Fat • 14 gm Protein •
34 gm Carbohydrate • 695 mg Sodium • 18 mg Calcium •
9 gm Fiber

DIABETIC: 2½ Meat • 1½ Starch • ½ Vegetable

Celery Scalloped Potatoes

Here's another recipe you can vary if you wish—served as written, of course, but also stirred up with another flavor of healthy cream soup. Choose mushroom if you like, or even broccoli (but only if Cliff isn't coming over for supper).   ☻   Serves 6 (1 cup)

9 cups shredded loose-packed frozen potatoes
2 cups finely chopped celery
1 cup finely chopped onion
1 (10¾-ounce) can Healthy Request Cream of Celery Soup
⅛ teaspoon black pepper

Spray a slow cooker container with butter-flavored cooking spray. In prepared container, combine potatoes, celery, and onion. Add celery soup and black pepper. Mix well to combine. Cover and cook on LOW for 4 to 6 hours. Mix well before serving.

HINTS: 1. Mr. Dell's frozen shredded potatoes are a good choice, or raw shredded potatoes may be used in place of frozen potatoes.
2. Also good with 1 cup + 2 tablespoons shredded Kraft reduced-fat Cheddar cheese stirred in with soup. If using, add 1 Protein to each serving.

Each serving equals:

HE: 1 Bread • 1 Vegetable • ¼ Slider • 8 Optional Calories

149 Calories • 1 gm Fat • 4 gm Protein •
31 gm Carbohydrate • 232 mg Sodium • 96 mg Calcium •
5 gm Fiber

DIABETIC: 1½ Starch • 1 Vegetable

Scalloped Potatoes

You have to love a recipe that simply asks you to combine the ingredients in a pot, then tells you to go live your busy life for a few hours and return hours later to a splendid meal. Here's a classic dish that will free you from the kitchen for more important (or more fun) activities.

⬤ Serves 6 (1 full cup)

> 9 cups shredded loose-packed frozen potatoes
> 1½ cups finely chopped onion
> 1 (10¾-ounce) can Healthy Request Cream of Mushroom Soup
> 1½ cups (one 12-fluid-ounce can) Carnation Evaporated Skim Milk
> 1 cup + 2 tablespoons shredded Kraft reduced-fat Cheddar cheese
> ¼ cup (one 2-ounce jar) chopped pimiento, drained
> ⅛ teaspoon black pepper

Spray a slow cooker container with butter-flavored cooking spray. In prepared container, combine potatoes, onion, mushroom soup, and evaporated skim milk. Stir in Cheddar cheese, pimiento, and black pepper. Cover and cook on LOW for 6 to 8 hours. Mix gently before serving.

HINT: Mr. Dell's frozen shredded potatoes are a good choice, or raw shredded potatoes may be used in place of frozen potatoes.

Each serving equals:

HE: 1 Bread • 1 Protein • ½ Skim Milk • ½ Vegetable • ¼ Slider • 6 Optional Calories

---

244 Calories • 4 gm Fat • 14 gm Protein • 38 gm Carbohydrate • 457 mg Sodium • 362 mg Calcium • 4 gm Fiber

---

DIABETIC: 1½ Starch • 1 Meat • ½ Skim Milk • ½ Vegetable

Peas and Carrots au Gratin

This family pleaser just gets better and better with the addition of cheese, doesn't it? Drain the veggies well so there's little danger of the sauce being watery. ☻ Serves 6 (¾ cup)

> 1 (10¾-ounce) can Healthy Request Cream of Mushroom Soup
> 1 cup + 2 tablespoons shredded Kraft reduced-fat Cheddar cheese
> 1 teaspoon dried onion flakes
> 1 teaspoon dried parsley flakes
> 3 cups frozen peas, thawed
> 3 cups frozen sliced carrots, thawed

Spray a slow cooker container with butter-flavored cooking spray. In prepared container, combine mushroom soup, Cheddar cheese, onion flakes, and parsley flakes. Stir in peas and carrots. Cover and cook on LOW for 6 hours. Mix well before serving.

HINT: Thaw peas and carrots by placing them in a colander and rinsing them under hot water for one minute.

Each serving equals:

> HE: 1 Bread • 1 Protein • 1 Vegetable • ¼ Slider •
> 8 Optional Calories
> _____
> 165 Calories • 5 gm Fat • 10 gm Protein •
> 20 gm Carbohydrate • 493 mg Sodium •
> 218 mg Calcium • 5 gm Fiber
> _____
> DIABETIC: 1½ Starch • 1 Meat • 1 Vegetable

Three Cheese Macaroni

Not one, not two, but three tasty and terrific cheeses transform a delicious standard into a dish worthy of special attention! Any mac and cheese lovers at your house? Serve this and revel in the applause you're sure to receive. ☯ Serves 6 (⅔ cup)

1 (10¾-ounce) can Healthy Request Cream of Mushroom Soup
1 cup hot water
¼ cup (one 2-ounce jar) chopped pimiento, undrained
¼ cup (¾ ounce) grated Kraft fat-free Parmesan cheese
⅛ teaspoon black pepper
¾ cup shredded Kraft reduced-fat Cheddar cheese
¾ cup shredded Kraft reduced-fat mozzarella cheese
2 cups uncooked elbow macaroni

Spray a slow cooker container with butter-flavored cooking spray. In prepared container, combine mushroom soup, water, undrained pimiento, Parmesan cheese, and black pepper. Stir in Cheddar cheese and mozzarella cheese. Add uncooked macaroni. Mix well to combine. Cover and cook on LOW for 4 hours. Mix well before serving.

Each serving equals:

HE: 1½ Protein • 1 Bread • ¼ Slider • 8 Optional Calories

190 Calories • 6 gm Fat • 11 gm Protein •
23 gm Carbohydrate • 464 mg Sodium •
231 mg Calcium • 1 gm Fiber

DIABETIC: 1½ Starch • 1 Meat

Italian Zucchini

This is an August standby, a super solution to the abundant zucchini in gardens all across America! This can be served hot or cold—it's definitely delectable both ways.   ☻   Serves 6 (1 full cup)

3 cups sliced unpeeled zucchini
1½ cups chopped onion
3 cups (one 28-ounce can) tomatoes, chopped and undrained
¼ cup Kraft Fat Free Italian Dressing
2 tablespoons pourable Splenda or Sugar Twin

Spray a slow cooker container with olive oil–flavored cooking spray. In prepared container, combine zucchini and onion. Add undrained tomatoes, Italian dressing, and Splenda. Mix well to combine. Cover and cook on LOW for 4 to 6 hours. Mix well before serving.

Each serving equals:

HE: 2½ Vegetable • 7 Optional Calories

48 Calories • 0 gm Fat • 2 gm Protein •
10 gm Carbohydrate • 319 mg Sodium • 38 mg Calcium •
3 gm Fiber

DIABETIC: 2 Vegetable

Zucchini Souffle Pot

Are you shocked by the idea of making a souffle in your slow cooker? This took a few tries to get a result to be proud of, but I think you'll be thrilled by the uniqueness of this dish.　❂　Serves 6

1 cup + 2 tablespoons Bisquick Reduced Fat Baking Mix

3 eggs, beaten, or equivalent in egg substitute

1/4 cup Kraft Fat Free Italian Dressing

1/4 cup grated Kraft fat-free Parmesan cheese

3/4 cup shredded Kraft reduced-fat Cheddar cheese

3 1/2 cups finely chopped unpeeled zucchini

1 cup diced onion

Spray a slow cooker container with butter-flavored cooking spray. In a large bowl, combine baking mix, eggs, and Italian dressing. Add Parmesan cheese and Cheddar cheese. Mix well to combine. Stir in zucchini and onion. Pour mixture into prepared container. Cover and cook on LOW for 6 to 8 hours. Cut into 6 wedges.

Each serving equals:

HE: 1 1/2 Vegetable • 1 1/3 Protein • 1 Bread •
4 Optional Calories

190 Calories • 6 gm Fat • 10 gm Protein •
24 gm Carbohydrate • 564 mg Sodium •
145 mg Calcium • 2 gm Fiber

DIABETIC: 1 Vegetable • 1 Meat • 1 Starch

Must-Have Main Dishes

When I was raising my children, working full-time at Iowa Mutual Insurance Company, and also going to college at night, my slow cooker was a real lifesaver. Knowing that supper would be ready whenever we all got home, and also knowing that it would stay warm in the pot if one of us arrived late was a real comfort. It also made it possible for us to eat well on a modest budget, because I could purchase less expensive cuts of meat and turn them into tender and terrific entrees tasty enough to please my growing boys (and my daughter Becky, too)!

I think I must have prepared chicken just about every way anyone ever has, back in those days, but I particularly remember stirring up lots of different versions of hamburger casserole (doesn't every Mom? I think so!). Tommy could eat hamburger milk gravy seven nights a week, and while James preferred my pot roasts, he would happily tuck into anything Italian with ground meat and tomato sauce. Testing the recipes for this section brought back a lot of memories—of the struggle and the satisfaction of nourishing my family when I was more than a little short on time (and sometimes money, too).

For every working mom (and dad), slow cooker entrees are more than timesavers; they're stress-reducers, problem-solvers, and the handy-dandy answer to the often-asked question, "What's for dinner?" (And the follow-up—"When do we eat?") If the store's got a special on chicken breasts, you're ready to roll with Hot Chicken Salad or my Spicy Apricot-Glazed Chicken; if the only meat left in the freezer is some pork tenderloins, you've got the makings for Pork and Sweet Potato Casserole or Green Beans and Pork; and instead of rushing home to make Sloppy Joes from an envelope mix, wouldn't it be wonderful to come home to find a potful of hearty beef already made—and much tastier than the "easy" kind? Whatever your pleasure, a delicious dinner is only hours away!

Must-Have
Main Dishes

Fisherman's Wharf Tuna Noodle Dish

Even if you never get to San Francisco's famous Fisherman's Wharf, you can imagine the spray of the Pacific Ocean on your cheeks as you feast on this classic tuna casserole. 🖤 Serves 6 (²/₃ cup)

2 (6-ounce) cans white tuna, packed in water, drained and flaked
1³/₄ cups uncooked noodles
1 cup (one 4-ounce can) sliced mushrooms, drained
½ cup finely chopped onion
1 (10³/₄-ounce) can Healthy Request Cream of Mushroom Soup
¼ cup hot water
¼ cup (one 2-ounce jar) chopped pimiento, undrained
1 cup (one 8-ounce can) peas, rinsed and drained
1 teaspoon dried parsley flakes

Spray a slow cooker container with butter-flavored cooking spray. In prepared container, combine tuna, uncooked noodles, mushrooms, and onion. Stir in mushroom soup, water, undrained pimiento, peas, and parsley flakes. Cover and cook on LOW for 4 hours. Mix well before serving.

Each serving equals:

HE: 1 Bread • 1 Protein • ½ Vegetable • ¼ Slider •
8 Optional Calories

171 Calories • 3 gm Fat • 17 gm Protein •
19 gm Carbohydrate • 596 mg Sodium • 65 mg Calcium •
2 gm Fiber

DIABETIC: 2 Meat • 1 Starch • ½ Vegetable

Savory Salmon Scallop

If you're in a tuna-eating rut (and I know it happens, I've been there!), here's just the recipe to reawaken your tired taste buds! This rosy-pink fish just pleaded to be bathed in a creamy sauce, so it is!

● Serves 6 (1 cup)

> 1 (10¾-ounce) can Healthy Request Cream of Celery Soup
> ¼ cup Land O Lakes no-fat sour cream
> ¼ cup (one 2-ounce jar) chopped pimiento, undrained
> 1 teaspoon dried dill weed
> 1½ cups frozen peas, thawed
> 1 cup finely chopped celery
> ½ cup finely chopped onion
> 6 slices reduced-calorie white bread, torn into small pieces
> 1 (14¾-ounce) can pink salmon, drained, boned, and flaked

Spray a slow cooker container with butter-flavored cooking spray. In prepared container, combine celery soup, sour cream, undrained pimiento, and dill weed. Stir in peas, celery, onion, and bread pieces. Add salmon. Mix well to combine. Cover and cook on LOW for 6 to 8 hours. Mix well before serving.

HINT: Thaw peas by placing them in a colander and rinsing them under hot water for one minute.

Each serving equals:

HE: 2¼ Protein • 1 Bread • ½ Vegetable

218 Calories • 6 gm Fat • 19 gm Protein •
22 gm Carbohydrate • 683 mg Sodium •
225 mg Calcium • 4 gm Fiber

DIABETIC: 2½ Meat • 1 Starch • ½ Vegetable

Salmon Cheese Casserole

A little cheese can go a very long way when you give it a chance to "shake hands and mingle" with the other flavors in this luscious supper dish. ☕ Serves 6 (¾ cup)

> 1 (14¾-ounce) can pink salmon, drained, boned, and flaked
> 1 (10¾-ounce) can Healthy Request Cream of Celery Soup
> 1 cup (one 4-ounce can) sliced mushrooms, drained
> 1 cup finely chopped onion
> 1 cup finely chopped celery
> ¾ cup shredded Kraft reduced-fat Cheddar cheese
> 6 slices reduced-calorie white bread, torn into small pieces
> 1 teaspoon dried parsley flakes

Spray a slow cooker container with butter-flavored cooking spray. In prepared container, combine salmon, celery soup, mushrooms, onion, and celery. Add Cheddar cheese, bread pieces, and parsley flakes. Mix well to combine. Cover and cook on LOW for 6 to 8 hours. Mix well before serving.

Each serving equals:

HE: 2⅔ Protein • 1 Vegetable • ½ Bread • ¼ Slider •
8 Optional Calories

189 Calories • 5 gm Fat • 18 gm Protein •
18 gm Carbohydrate • 493 mg Sodium •
244 mg Calcium • 2 gm Fiber

DIABETIC: 3 Meat • 1 Vegetable •
1 Starch/Carbohydrate

Cheesy Shrimp and Rice Dish

Many people view shrimp as a treat for special occasions, but the truth is that this sumptuous shellfish is more reasonably priced than ever before. I think you'll be pleasantly surprised what a rich sauce this recipe creates. ☻ Serves 6 (1 cup)

½ cup chopped celery

½ cup chopped onion

½ cup (one 2.5-ounce jar) sliced mushrooms, drained

1½ cups (one 12-fluid-ounce can) Carnation Evaporated Skim Milk

2 tablespoons reduced-sodium ketchup

1 cup + 2 tablespoons shredded Kraft reduced-fat Cheddar cheese

2 (6-ounce) packages frozen shrimp, thawed

1⅓ cups uncooked instant rice

1 tablespoon dried parsley flakes

⅛ teaspoon black pepper

Spray a slow cooker container with butter-flavored cooking spray. In prepared container, combine celery, onion, and mushrooms. Stir in evaporated skim milk and ketchup. Add Cheddar cheese, shrimp, uncooked rice, parsley flakes, and black pepper. Mix well to combine. Cover and cook on LOW for 4 hours. Mix well before serving.

HINTS: 1. Thaw shrimp by placing them in a colander and rinsing them under hot water for one minute.

2. Canned shrimp, rinsed and drained, may be substituted for frozen.

Each serving equals:

HE: 3 Protein • ⅔ Bread • ½ Skim Milk • ½ Vegetable • 5 Optional Calories

240 Calories • 4 gm Fat • 24 gm Protein • 27 gm Carbohydrate • 491 mg Sodium • 327 mg Calcium • 1 gm Fiber

DIABETIC: 2½ Meat • 1 Starch • ½ Skim Milk • ½ Vegetable

Fish in Cheesy Cream Sauce

Sometimes simple and easy equals elegant—just as it does in this recipe! Flounder, sole, haddock or halibut would all be wonderful when served this way. ☻ Serves 4

16 ounces white fish, cut into 4 pieces
1 (10¾-ounce) can Healthy Request Cream of Mushroom Soup
¾ cup shredded Kraft reduced-fat Cheddar cheese
1 teaspoon dried dill weed

Spray a slow cooker container with butter-flavored cooking spray. Evenly arrange fish pieces in prepared container. In a small bowl, combine mushroom soup, Cheddar cheese, and dill weed. Evenly spoon sauce mixture over fish pieces. Cover and cook on LOW for 3 to 4 hours. When serving, evenly spoon sauce over fish pieces.

Each serving equals:

HE: 2½ Protein • ½ Slider • 1 Optional Calorie

170 Calories • 6 gm Fat • 22 gm Protein •
7 gm Carbohydrate • 542 mg Sodium •
238 mg Calcium • 0 gm Fiber

DIABETIC: 4 Meat • ½ Starch/Carbohydrate

Hot Chicken Salad

No, I didn't make a mistake in the title of this recipe, although I wouldn't suggest this for your next picnic, either. But as something fresh and new to do with chicken, it's fantastically appetizing and flavorful.

● Serves 6 (²/₃ cup)

1 (10³/₄-ounce) can Healthy Request Cream of Chicken Soup
³/₄ cup Kraft fat-free mayonnaise
2 teaspoons dried parsley flakes
2 full cups diced cooked chicken breast
³/₄ cup diced celery
¹/₄ cup finely chopped onion
¹/₄ cup (one 2-ounce jar) diced pimiento, drained
¹/₄ cup slivered almonds
1 cup crushed Lay's "WOW" potato chips
2 hard-boiled eggs, chopped

In a slow cooker container, combine chicken soup, mayonnaise, and parsley flakes. Stir in chicken, celery, onion, pimiento, and almonds. Add crushed potato chips and eggs. Mix gently to combine. Cover and cook on LOW for 3 to 4 hours. Mix well before serving.

HINTS: 1. If you don't have leftovers, purchase a chunk of cooked chicken breast from your local deli.
2. If you want the look and feel of egg without the cholesterol, toss out the yolk and dice the whites.

Each serving equals:

HE: 2¹/₂ Protein • ¹/₂ Bread • ¹/₃ Fat • ¹/₃ Vegetable •
¹/₂ Slider • 10 Optional Calories

---

231 Calories • 7 gm Fat • 23 gm Protein •
19 gm Carbohydrate • 561 mg Sodium • 38 mg Calcium •
1 gm Fiber

DIABETIC: 2¹/₂ Meat • 1 Starch/Carbohydrate • ¹/₂ Fat

Chicken Pot Macaroni

What a cozy and comforting family meal this simple combination makes! It also freezes beautifully, so you can cook up a batch and have it ready for those "too-tired-to-cook" nights.

● Serves 6 (1 cup)

1 (10¾-ounce) can Healthy Request Cream of Chicken Soup

¼ cup (one 2-ounce jar) chopped pimiento, undrained

1½ cups hot water

1 teaspoon dried parsley flakes

⅛ teaspoon black pepper

2 full cups diced cooked chicken breast

1 cup finely chopped celery

½ cup diced onion

1½ cups frozen sliced carrots, thawed

2 cups uncooked elbow macaroni

Spray a slow cooker container with butter-flavored cooking spray. In prepared container, combine chicken soup, undrained pimiento, and water. Stir in parsley flakes and black pepper. Add chicken, celery, onion, carrots, and uncooked macaroni. Mix well to combine. Cover and cook on LOW for 6 to 8 hours. Mix well before serving.

HINTS: 1. If you don't have leftovers, purchase a chunk of cooked chicken breast from your local deli.

2. Thaw carrots by placing them in a colander and rinsing them under hot water for one minute.

Each serving equals:

HE: 2 Protein • 1 Bread • 1 Vegetable • ¼ Slider • 10 Optional Calories

---

219 Calories • 3 gm Fat • 22 gm Protein • 26 gm Carbohydrate • 278 mg Sodium • 35 mg Calcium • 2 gm Fiber

---

DIABETIC: 2 Meat • 1½ Starch • 1 Vegetable

Broccoli Chicken Pot

I like to keep plenty of cans of chicken broth on hand. It's a low-fat staple at the heart of many of my easy and delicious recipes. When your shelves are well-stocked, you're truly prepared to live a healthy lifestyle, so the next time there's a sale, stack 'em up!

● Serves 6 (scant 1 cup)

> 2 cups (one 16-ounce can) Healthy Request Chicken Broth
> 1 teaspoon dried onion flakes
> 1 teaspoon dried parsley flakes
> ⅛ teaspoon black pepper
> 3 cups frozen chopped broccoli, partially thawed
> 3 cups unseasoned dry bread cubes
> 2 full cups diced cooked chicken breast

Spray a slow cooker container with butter-flavored cooking spray. In prepared container, combine chicken broth, onion flakes, parsley flakes, and black pepper. Stir in broccoli. Add bread cubes and chicken. Mix well to combine. Cover and cook on LOW for 6 to 8 hours. Mix well before serving.

HINTS: 1. Place broccoli in a colander and rinse under hot water for 30 seconds.
2. Pepperidge Farm bread cubes work great.
3. If you don't have leftovers, purchase a chunk of cooked chicken breast from your local deli.

Each serving equals:

HE: 2 Protein • 1 Vegetable • ½ Bread •
5 Optional Calories

208 Calories • 4 gm Fat • 23 gm Protein •
20 gm Carbohydrate • 369 mg Sodium • 69 mg Calcium •
3 gm Fiber

DIABETIC: 2 Meat • 1 Vegetable • 1 Starch

Spicy Apricot Glazed Chicken

This sweet-and-tangy chicken dish provides a fresh and fruity way to enjoy those good old reliable chicken breasts. This recipe can be doubled as long as the cooking time is adjusted. ◐ Serves 4

> 16 ounces skinned and boned uncooked chicken breast, cut into 4
>   pieces
> ¼ cup apricot spreadable fruit
> ¼ cup Kraft Fat Free Catalina or Russian Dressing
> 1 tablespoon dried onion flakes
> 2 teaspoons dried parsley flakes

Spray a slow cooker container with butter-flavored cooking spray. Evenly arrange chicken pieces in prepared container. In a small bowl, combine spreadable fruit, Catalina dressing, onion flakes, and parsley flakes. Evenly spread fruit mixture over chicken pieces. Cover and cook on LOW for 6 to 8 hours. When serving, evenly spoon sauce over chicken pieces.

Each serving equals:

HE: 3 Protein • 1 Fruit • ¼ Slider • 5 Optional Calories

187 Calories • 3 gm Fat • 23 gm Protein •
17 gm Carbohydrate • 235 mg Sodium • 15 mg Calcium •
0 gm Fiber

DIABETIC: 3 Meat • 1 Fruit

Chicken and Stuffing Bake

I think this cookbook has more stuffing recipes than any of my others—and there's a good reason why. Slow cooking at a low temperature is great for a bread-based recipe. The flavors deepen without the dish drying out.   ❤   Serves 6 (1 cup)

2 full cups diced cooked chicken breast
1 (10¾-ounce) can Healthy Request Cream of Chicken Soup
1½ cups (one 12-fluid-ounce can) Carnation Evaporated Skim Milk
1 cup finely chopped celery
½ cup finely chopped onion
2 teaspoons dried parsley flakes
⅛ teaspoon black pepper
3 cups unseasoned dry bread cubes

Spray a slow cooker container with butter-flavored cooking spray. In prepared container, combine chicken, chicken soup, and evaporated skim milk. Stir in celery, onion, parsley flakes, and black pepper. Add bread cubes. Mix well to combine. Cover and cook on LOW for 6 hours. Mix well before serving.

HINTS: 1. If you don't have leftovers, purchase a chunk of cooked chicken breast from your local deli.
2. Pepperidge Farm bread cubes work great.

Each serving equals:

HE: 2 Protein • ½ Skim Milk • ½ Bread •
½ Vegetable • ¼ Slider • 10 Optional Calories

256 Calories • 4 gm Fat • 25 gm Protein •
30 gm Carbohydrate • 485 mg Sodium •
197 mg Calcium • 2 gm Fiber

DIABETIC: 2 Meat • 1 Starch • ½ Skim Milk •
½ Vegetable

Chicken and Corn Hash

What a pleasing pair the corn and potatoes make—and when you stir in all that chicken, you've got a real recipe for success! My grandkids voted this one of my best. ☻ Serves 6 (1 cup)

4½ cups shredded loose-packed frozen potatoes

1½ cups frozen whole-kernel corn, thawed

1 cup chopped onion

¼ cup (one 2-ounce jar) chopped pimiento, undrained

½ cup (one 2.5-ounce jar) sliced mushrooms, drained

1 (10¾-ounce) can Healthy Request Cream of Chicken Soup

1 teaspoon dried parsley flakes

⅛ teaspoon black pepper

2 full cups diced cooked chicken breast

Spray a slow cooker container with butter-flavored cooking spray. In prepared container, combine potatoes, corn, onion, undrained pimiento, and mushrooms. Stir in chicken soup, parsley flakes, and black pepper. Add chicken. Mix well to combine. Cover and cook on LOW for 6 to 8 hours. Mix well before serving.

HINTS: 1. Mr. Dell's frozen shredded potatoes are a good choice, or raw shredded potatoes may be used in place of frozen potatoes.

2. Thaw corn by placing it in a colander and rinsing it under hot water for one minute.

3. If you don't have leftovers, purchase a chunk of cooked chicken breast from your local deli.

Each serving equals:

HE: 2 Protein • 1 Bread • ½ Vegetable • ¼ Slider • 10 Optional Calories

---

231 Calories • 3 gm Fat • 22 gm Protein • 29 gm Carbohydrate • 298 mg Sodium • 25 mg Calcium • 4 gm Fiber

---

DIABETIC: 2 Meat • 1½ Starch • ½ Vegetable

Baked Chicken Breasts with Mushroom Sauce

You'll run out of adjectives (and your family, out of compliments) when you offer this luscious, creamy, downright dreamy dish for dinner sometime soon. ☺ Serves 4

16 ounces skinned and boned uncooked chicken breast,
    cut into 4 pieces
1 (10¾-ounce) can Healthy Request Cream of Chicken Soup
2 tablespoons Land O Lakes no-fat sour cream
1 cup (one 4-ounce can) sliced mushrooms, drained
1 teaspoon dried parsley flakes

Spray a slow cooker container with butter-flavored cooking spray. Evenly arrange chicken pieces in prepared container. In a medium bowl, combine chicken soup, sour cream, mushrooms, and parsley flakes. Spoon sauce mixture evenly over chicken pieces. Cover and cook on LOW for 6 to 8 hours. When serving, evenly spoon sauce over chicken.

Each serving equals:

HE: 3 Protein • ½ Vegetable • ½ Slider •
12 Optional Calories

180 Calories • 4 gm Fat • 25 gm Protein •
11 gm Carbohydrate • 525 mg Sodium • 26 mg Calcium •
1 gm Fiber

DIABETIC: 3 Meat • ½ Vegetable • ½ Starch/Carbohydrate

Almond Chicken

This delightful "chicken-in-every-pot" recipe has an Asian magic all its own. (Not to mention lots of crunch, crunch, crunch . . .) It's a winner that will please both young and old.   ☻   Serves 6 (¾ cup)

1 (10¾-ounce) can Healthy Request Cream of Chicken Soup

2 tablespoons reduced-sodium soy sauce

16 ounces skinned and boned uncooked chicken breast, cut into 36
    pieces

1½ cups chopped celery

½ cup chopped onion

1 cup (one 4-ounce can) sliced mushrooms, drained

½ cup slivered almonds

Spray a slow cooker container with butter-flavored cooking spray. In prepared container, combine chicken soup and soy sauce. Stir in chicken, celery, onion, and mushrooms. Add almonds. Mix well to combine. Cover and cook on LOW for 6 to 8 hours. Mix well before serving.

HINT: Good served with hot rice.

Each serving equals:

HE: 2⅓ Protein • 1 Vegetable • ⅔ Fat • ¼ Slider •
10 Optional Calories

183 Calories • 7 gm Fat • 19 gm Protein •
11 gm Carbohydrate • 549 mg Sodium • 49 mg Calcium •
2 gm Fiber

DIABETIC: 2 Meat • 1 Vegetable • 1 Fat •
½ Starch/Carbohydrate

Special Chicken Cacciatore

You see it on most Italian restaurant menus, but maybe you don't often try to fix it at home. Well, there's no better time than right now to experience this most *bellissima classico*—this beautiful classic.

○ Serves 4

> 1 cup (one 8-ounce can) tomatoes, finely chopped and undrained
> 1 (10³/4-ounce) can Healthy Request Tomato Soup
> 1½ teaspoons Italian seasoning
> ½ teaspoon dried minced garlic
> ½ cup (one 2.5-ounce jar) sliced mushrooms, drained
> ½ cup chopped green bell pepper
> ½ cup chopped onion
> 16 ounces skinned and boned uncooked chicken breast,
>   cut into 4 pieces

In a slow cooker container sprayed with olive oil–flavored cooking spray, combine undrained tomatoes, tomato soup, Italian seasoning, and garlic. Stir in mushrooms, green pepper, and onion. Add chicken pieces. Mix well to combine. Cover and cook on LOW for 6 to 8 hours. When serving, evenly spoon sauce over chicken.

Each serving equals:

HE: 3 Protein • 1¼ Vegetable • ½ Slider •
5 Optional Calories

---

204 Calories • 4 gm Fat • 25 gm Protein •
17 gm Carbohydrate • 531 mg Sodium • 29 mg Calcium •
2 gm Fiber

DIABETIC: 3 Meat • 1 Vegetable • ½ Starch/Carbohydrate

French Chicken Pot

Cooking with a tasty, fat-free dressing is as smart as it is easy. Someone has already devoted time and effort to perfecting a delectable blend of flavors—and you get the benefit of that wisdom (plus the *merci mille fois*—a thousand thanks!)   ☻   Serves 6

> 6 (4-ounce) skinned and boned uncooked chicken breast pieces
> ¼ cup Kraft Fat Free French Dressing
> 6 tablespoons apricot spreadable fruit
> 2 teaspoons dried onion flakes
> 2 teaspoons dried parsley flakes

Spray a slow cooker container with butter-flavored cooking spray. Evenly arrange chicken pieces in prepared container. In a medium bowl, combine French dressing and spreadable fruit. Stir in onion flakes and parsley flakes. Drizzle dressing mixture evenly over chicken pieces. Cover and cook on LOW for 6 to 8 hours. When serving, evenly spoon sauce over chicken.

Each serving equals:

HE: 3 Protein • 1 Fruit • 17 Optional Calories

175 Calories • 3 gm Fat • 23 gm Protein •
14 gm Carbohydrate • 155 mg Sodium • 13 mg Calcium •
0 gm Fiber

DIABETIC: 3 Meat • 1 Fruit

Chicken Zucchini Pot Supper

Did you know that "Parmesan" means "in the style of Parma," a lovely town in Italy? If it's only half as wonderful as the cheese that bears its name, I'm tempted to put it on my itinerary very soon.

○ Serves 4 (1 cup)

> *3 tablespoons all-purpose flour*
> *¼ cup grated Kraft fat-free Parmesan cheese*
> *¼ teaspoon lemon pepper*
> *½ teaspoon paprika*
> *16 ounces skinned and boned uncooked chicken breast, cut into 24*
>   *pieces*
> *2 cups thinly sliced unpeeled zucchini*
> *½ cup (one 2.5-ounce can) sliced mushrooms, drained*

Spray a slow cooker container with butter-flavored cooking spray. In a brown paper bag, combine flour, Parmesan cheese, lemon pepper, and paprika. Place chicken pieces in bag. Shake well to coat chicken. Place chicken pieces in prepared container. Add zucchini and mushrooms. Mix gently to combine. Cover and cook on LOW for 6 to 8 hours. Mix well before serving.

Each serving equals:

HE: 3 Protein • 1¼ Vegetable • ¼ Bread

---

171 Calories • 3 gm Fat • 25 gm Protein • 11 gm Carbohydrate • 248 mg Sodium • 25 mg Calcium • 2 gm Fiber

---

DIABETIC: 3 Meat • 1 Vegetable • ½ Starch

Chicken Divan Pot

Can a sauce for chicken be *too* creamy? Can a dish that contains broccoli ever win my husband's heart? A happy "no" to question number one, and a regretful "no" to question number two!

⚫ Serves 6 (1 cup)

> 1 (10¾-ounce) can Healthy Request Cream of Chicken Soup
> ½ cup Kraft fat-free mayonnaise
> 3 full cups diced cooked chicken breast
> 1 cup finely chopped onion
> 3½ cups frozen chopped broccoli, thawed

Spray a slow cooker container with butter-flavored cooking spray. In prepared container, combine chicken soup and mayonnaise. Stir in chicken and onion. Add broccoli. Mix well to combine. Cover and cook on LOW for 6 to 8 hours. Mix well before serving.

HINTS: 1. If you don't have leftovers, purchase a chunk of cooked chicken breast from your local deli.
2. Thaw broccoli by placing it in a colander and rinsing it under hot water for one minute.
3. Good served over pasta or potatoes.

Each serving equals:

HE: 3 Protein • 1½ Vegetable • ½ Slider •
3 Optional Calories

---

212 Calories • 4 gm Fat • 30 gm Protein •
14 gm Carbohydrate • 422 mg Sodium • 69 mg Calcium •
3 gm Fiber

DIABETIC: 3 Meat • 1½ Vegetable • ½ Starch/Carbohydrate

Chicken and Rice Casserole

This dish made me want to sing, "Chicken and rice, chicken and rice, it's just so nice, I'll say it twice." Once your kids get a taste of this dish, they're likely to join in on the next refrain.

○ Serves 4 (1 full cup)

> 1 (10¾-ounce) can Healthy Request Cream of Chicken Soup
> 1 cup skim milk
> ½ cup (one 2.5-ounce jar) sliced mushrooms, undrained
> 1 cup finely chopped celery
> ½ cup finely chopped onion
> 1 cup uncooked instant rice
> 16 ounces skinned and boned uncooked chicken breast,
>   cut into 32 pieces

Spray a slow cooker container with butter-flavored cooking spray. In prepared container, combine chicken soup, skim milk, and undrained mushrooms. Stir in celery, onion, and uncooked rice. Add chicken pieces. Mix well to combine. Cover and cook on LOW for 4 to 6 hours. Mix well before serving.

Each serving equals:

HE: 3 Protein • 1 Vegetable • ¾ Bread • ¼ Skim Milk •
½ Slider • 5 Optional Calories

281 Calories • 5 gm Fat • 30 gm Protein •
29 gm Carbohydrate • 496 mg Sodium •
111 mg Calcium • 2 gm Fiber

DIABETIC: 3 Meat • 1½ Starch/Carbohydrate • 1 Vegetable

Special Baked Chicken

Imagine how wonderful it will be to find a little "surprise" inside your beef rolls—in the form of chicken! This luscious and creamy dish is truly a meat-lover's dream, yet it's still low in fat. Now that's "special"!

○ Serves 4

1 (2.5-ounce) package Carl Buddig 90% lean pressed beef
16 ounces skinned and boned uncooked chicken breast, cut into 4
    pieces
1 (10¾-ounce) can Healthy Request Cream of Mushroom Soup
2 tablespoons Land O Lakes no-fat sour cream
3 tablespoons all-purpose flour
1 teaspoon dried parsley flakes

Spray a slow cooker container with butter-flavored cooking spray. Divide pressed beef into 4 even bundles. Wrap chicken pieces inside beef bundles. Place chicken bundles in prepared container. In a medium bowl, combine mushroom soup, sour cream, flour, and parsley flakes. Pour soup mixture evenly over chicken bundles. Cover and cook on LOW for 8 hours. When serving, evenly spoon sauce over chicken bundles.

Each serving equals:

HE: 3⅔ Protein • ¼ Bread • ½ Slider • 9 Optional Calories

205 Calories • 5 gm Fat • 28 gm Protein •
12 gm Carbohydrate • 613 mg Sodium • 87 mg Calcium •
0 gm Fiber

DIABETIC: 3½ Meat • 1 Starch/Carbohydrate

Chicken Teriyaki

Just one bite can transport you to the Orient, where this tasty chicken classic is a popular dish among locals and visitors! The sauce ingredients smell as good as they taste, and if you've never tried to eat with chopsticks, this dish might inspire you. ❂ Serves 6 (²/₃ cup)

> 2 cups (one 16-ounce can) Healthy Request Chicken Broth
> 2 tablespoons Brown Sugar Twin
> 2 tablespoons reduced-sodium soy sauce
> ½ teaspoon ground ginger
> 1 teaspoon Worcestershire sauce
> 1 cup uncooked instant rice
> 1 cup (one 8-ounce can) pineapple chunks, packed in fruit juice,
>   drained
> 16 ounces skinned and boned uncooked chicken breast, cut into 18
>   pieces

Spray a slow cooker container with butter-flavored cooking spray. In prepared container, combine chicken broth, Brown Sugar Twin, soy sauce, ginger, and Worcestershire sauce. Add uncooked rice, pineapple chunks, and chicken. Mix well to combine. Cover and cook on LOW for 4 hours. Mix well before serving.

Each serving equals:

HE: 2 Protein • ½ Bread • ⅓ Fruit • 7 Optional Calories

142 Calories • 2 gm Fat • 17 gm Protein •
14 gm Carbohydrate • 366 mg Sodium • 23 mg Calcium •
1 gm Fiber

DIABETIC: 2 Meat • 1 Starch

Saucy Italian Chicken

This might be the easiest entree in this entire book, but it doesn't taste like it! The secret is in the seasoning, so make sure your spice bottle hasn't been sitting in the sun (or the cabinet) for years.

● Serves 4

> *16 ounces skinned and boned uncooked chicken breast, cut into 4*
> *pieces*
> *1 cup (one 8-ounce can) Hunt's Tomato Sauce*
> *1 teaspoon Italian Seasoning*
> *1 tablespoon pourable Splenda or Sugar Twin*
> *1 teaspoon dried onion flakes*

Spray a slow cooker container with butter-flavored cooking spray. Evenly arrange chicken pieces in prepared container. In a medium bowl, combine tomato sauce, Italian seasoning, Splenda, and onion flakes. Spoon sauce mixture evenly over chicken pieces. Cover and cook on LOW for 6 to 8 hours. When serving, evenly spoon sauce over chicken.

Each serving equals:

HE: 3 Protein • 1 Vegetable • 1 Optional Calorie

143 Calories • 3 gm Fat • 24 gm Protein •
5 gm Carbohydrate • 425 mg Sodium • 20 mg Calcium •
1 gm Fiber

DIABETIC: 3 Meat • 1 Vegetable

Chicken Salsa

Southwestern-style food is great for stimulating your palate and transporting your taste buds out of a rut and into spicy heaven! Instead of piling the kids into the car and heading to your favorite Mexican restaurant tonight, turn your kitchen into olé City when you stir this one up.

◑ Serves 6 (scant 1 cup)

1 (10¾-ounce) can Healthy Request Cream of Chicken Soup
1½ cups chunky salsa (mild, medium, or hot)
1 cup + 2 tablespoons shredded Kraft reduced-fat Cheddar cheese
6 (6-inch) corn tortillas, torn into large pieces
2 full cups (12 ounces) diced cooked chicken breast
1 teaspoon dried parsley flakes

Spray a slow cooker container with olive oil–flavored cooking spray. In prepared container, combine chicken soup and salsa. Add Cheddar cheese and tortilla pieces. Mix well to combine. Stir in chicken and parsley flakes. Cover and cook on LOW for 6 to 8 hours. Mix well before serving.

HINT: If you don't have leftovers, purchase a chunk of cooked chicken breast from your local deli.

Each serving equals:

HE: 3 Protein • 1 Bread • ½ Vegetable • ¼ Slider •
10 Optional Calories

263 Calories • 7 gm Fat • 25 gm Protein •
25 gm Carbohydrate • 752 mg Sodium •
159 mg Calcium • 1 gm Fiber

DIABETIC: 3 Meat • 1½ Starch/Carbohydrate • ½ Vegetable

Chicken Supreme

When your family asks "What's for dinner?" and you reply, "Chicken Supreme," they don't even have to wonder about the ingredients. Any dish whose name says it's "tops" better be prepared to back up that statement—and be spectacular! This one truly is.　　○　Serves 4

16 ounces skinned and boned uncooked chicken breast, cut into 4
　　pieces
1 (10¾-ounce) can Healthy Request Cream of Chicken Soup
½ cup (one 2.5-ounce jar) sliced mushrooms, drained
1 cup chopped celery
½ cup chopped onion
1 teaspoon dried parsley flakes
⅛ teaspoon black pepper

Spray a slow cooker container with butter-flavored cooking spray. Evenly arrange chicken pieces in prepared container. In a medium bowl, combine chicken soup and mushrooms. Add celery, onion, parsley flakes, and black pepper. Mix well to combine. Spoon sauce mixture evenly over chicken pieces. Cover and cook on LOW for 6 to 8 hours. When serving, evenly spoon sauce over chicken.

Each serving equals:

HE: 3 Protein • 1 Vegetable • ½ Slider •
5 Optional Calories

---

180 Calories • 4 gm Fat • 25 gm Protein •
11 gm Carbohydrate • 459 mg Sodium • 30 mg Calcium •
1 gm Fiber

DIABETIC: 3 Meat • 1 Vegetable • ½ Starch/Carbohydrate

Cola Chicken

Remember that old motto about necessity being the mother of invention? It's often true, but another version might say, "Proximity has something to do with it, too!" I opened the refrigerator and saw the ketchup bottle and diet Coke can sitting side by side, and a little buzzer in my head went off, saying "What if . . . ?" Here's the answer!

● Serves 4

    4 (4-ounce) skinned and boned chicken breasts
    ¼ cup reduced-sodium ketchup
    ¼ cup diet Coke
    1 teaspoon dried onion flakes
    1 teaspoon dried parsley flakes

Spray a slow cooker container with butter-flavored cooking spray. Evenly arrange chicken pieces in prepared container. In a medium bowl, combine ketchup, diet Coke, onion flakes, and parsley flakes. Mix well. Pour sauce mixture evenly over chicken pieces. Cover and cook on LOW for 4 to 6 hours. When serving, evenly spoon sauce over chicken pieces.

Each serving equals:

HE: 3 Protein • ¼ Slider

---

135 Calories • 3 gm Fat • 23 gm Protein •
4 gm Carbohydrate • 59 mg Sodium • 16 mg Calcium •
0 gm Fiber

DIABETIC: 3 Meat

Chicken with Sunshine Sauce

For years, people have said, "If only they could bottle sunshine to get us through the long gray winters!" I can't promise you all the benefits of sun—the vitamin D, the tan, the warm rays of heat—but you'll feel as if the sun had smiled on you when you enjoy this sweet and tasty dish that sparkles with culinary heat.   ☻   Serves 4

> 16 ounces skinned and boned uncooked chicken breast, cut into
>   4 pieces
> 2 tablespoons unsweetened orange juice
> 1 tablespoon Brown Sugar Twin
> ½ teaspoon apple pie spice
> 1 teaspoon dried onion flakes
> 1 teaspoon dried parsley flakes
> ¼ cup orange marmalade spreadable fruit

Spray a slow cooker container with butter-flavored cooking spray. Evenly arrange chicken pieces in prepared container. In a medium bowl, combine orange juice, Brown Sugar Twin, and apple pie spice. Stir in onion flakes, parsley flakes, and spreadable fruit. Evenly spoon mixture over chicken. Cover and cook on LOW for 6 to 8 hours. When serving, evenly spoon sauce over chicken pieces.

HINT: Good served with rice.

Each serving equals:

HE: 3 Protein • 1 Fruit • 5 Optional Calories

163 Calories • 3 gm Fat • 23 gm Protein •
11 gm Carbohydrate • 57 mg Sodium • 20 mg Calcium •
0 gm Fiber

DIABETIC: 3 Meat • 1 Fruit

Barbequed Chicken Breast

Maybe it's raining so there's no way to light up the grill. Maybe there is snow outside and no sense in trying to cook on your icy patio. Or maybe you're just a barbecue lover who thinks it would be lovely to come home to a pot of chicken that's been playing footsie for hours with a savory sauce! Enjoy!   ☻   Serves 6

> 6 (4-ounce) skinned and boned uncooked chicken breast pieces
> ½ cup Healthy Choice Barbeque Sauce
> ½ cup finely chopped onion
> ¼ cup finely chopped green bell pepper
> 1 teaspoon dried parsley flakes

Spray a slow cooker container with butter-flavored cooking spray. Arrange chicken pieces in prepared container. In a medium bowl, combine barbeque sauce, onion, green pepper, and parsley flakes. Evenly pour mixture over chicken. Cover and cook on LOW for 6 to 8 hours. When serving, evenly spoon sauce over chicken pieces.

Each serving equals:

HE: 3 Protein • ¼ Vegetable • ¼ Slider •
13 Optional Calories

131 Calories • 3 gm Fat • 23 gm Protein •
3 gm Carbohydrate • 120 mg Sodium • 19 mg Calcium •
0 gm Fiber

DIABETIC: 3 Meat

Barbecued Chicken

Perhaps you're a purist who'd rather make barbecue sauce from scratch than pour it from a bottle, or maybe you just don't have any on hand. Whatever the reason, this recipe for barbecue-in-a-pot is downright delicious! ◐ Serves 4

16 ounces skinned and boned uncooked chicken breast, cut into 4 pieces

1 cup (one 8-ounce can) Hunt's Tomato Sauce

2 tablespoons Brown Sugar Twin

1 tablespoon Worcestershire sauce

1 tablespoon white vinegar

2 tablespoons prepared yellow mustard

¼ cup finely chopped onion

¼ cup finely chopped celery

2 teaspoons dried parsley flakes

⅛ teaspoon black pepper

Spray a slow cooker container with butter-flavored cooking spray. Evenly arrange chicken pieces in prepared container. In a large bowl, combine tomato sauce, Brown Sugar Twin, Worcestershire sauce, vinegar, and mustard. Add onion, celery, parsley flakes, and black pepper. Mix well to combine. Spoon sauce mixture evenly over chicken pieces. Cover and cook on LOW for 6 to 8 hours. When serving, evenly spoon sauce over chicken.

Each serving equals:

HE: 3 Protein • 1¼ Vegetable • 3 Optional Calories

151 Calories • 3 gm Fat • 24 gm Protein •
7 gm Carbohydrate • 576 mg Sodium • 44 mg Calcium •
1 gm Fiber

DIABETIC: 3 Meat • 1 Vegetable

Terrific Turkey Hash

Turkey is a wonderful choice for the slow cooker—it's sturdy so the long cooking time doesn't bother it a bit, it's easy to dry it out when cooking it in traditional ways, and it's happy to share space in the pot with whatever veggies you choose to offer your family tonight.

● Serves 6 (1⅓ cups)

> 3 cups diced cooked turkey breast
> 1 cup finely chopped celery
> ½ cup finely chopped onion
> 9 cups shredded loose-packed frozen potatoes
> 1 (12-ounce) jar Heinz Fat Free Chicken Gravy
> 1 teaspoon dried parsley flakes
> ⅛ teaspoon black pepper

Spray a slow cooker container with butter-flavored cooking spray. In prepared container, combine turkey, celery, onion, and potatoes. Add gravy, parsley flakes, and black pepper. Mix well to combine. Cover and cook on LOW for 6 to 8 hours. Mix well before serving.

HINTS: 1. If you don't have leftovers, purchase a chunk of cooked turkey breast from your local deli.
2. Mr. Dell's frozen shredded potatoes are a good choice, or raw shredded potatoes may be used in place of frozen potatoes.

Each serving equals:

HE: 2½ Protein • 1 Bread • ½ Vegetable • ¼ Slider • 5 Optional Calories

235 Calories • 3 gm Fat • 25 gm Protein • 27 gm Carbohydrate • 385 mg Sodium • 33 mg Calcium • 4 gm Fiber

DIABETIC: 2½ Meat • 1 Starch • ½ Vegetable

Tasty Turkey Tetrazzini

This has been one of my favorite kitchen classics since I started creating recipes all those years ago. Now I've reinvented it for the slow cooker, and I'm delighted to report that nothing has been lost to this easier preparation. It's appealing to kids of all ages, so make it when your grandkids come for the day or when it's just the two of you for dinner.

Serves 6 (1 cup)

1 (10¾-ounce) can Healthy Request Cream of Chicken Soup
1 cup hot water
½ cup (one 2.5-ounce jar) sliced mushrooms, undrained
¼ cup (one 2-ounce jar) chopped pimiento, undrained
2 full cups diced cooked turkey breast
1 cup + 2 tablespoons shredded Kraft reduced-fat Cheddar cheese
¼ cup chopped onion
1 teaspoon dried parsley flakes
2 cups broken uncooked spaghetti

Spray a slow cooker container with butter-flavored cooking spray. In prepared container, combine chicken soup, water, undrained mushrooms, and undrained pimiento. Stir in turkey, Cheddar cheese, onion, and parsley flakes. Add uncooked spaghetti. Mix well to combine. Cover and cook on LOW for 4 to 6 hours. Mix well before serving.

HINT: If you don't have leftovers, purchase a chunk of cooked turkey breast from your local deli.

Each serving equals:

HE: 3 Protein • 1 Bread • ¼ Vegetable • ¼ Slider • 10 Optional Calories

254 Calories • 6 gm Fat • 26 gm Protein • 24 gm Carbohydrate • 463 mg Sodium • 157 mg Calcium • 1 gm Fiber

DIABETIC: 3 Meat • 1½ Starch/Carbohydrate

Easy Jambalaya

If you enjoy a delectable "jumble" of ingredients that is as superbly spicy as it is simple to fix, here's the dish for you! Even if New Orleans isn't on your travel itinerary this year, you can still "let the good times roll!"

● Serves 6 (1 cup)

> 16 ounces extra lean ground turkey or beef
> 3 cups sliced raw potatoes
> ¾ cup chopped onion
> ¾ cup chopped green bell pepper
> 6 ounces (one 8-ounce can) red kidney beans, rinsed and drained
> 1 teaspoon dried parsley flakes
> 2 to 3 drops Tabasco sauce
> 1 (10¾-ounce) can Healthy Request Tomato Soup

In a large skillet sprayed with butter-flavored cooking spray, brown meat. Spoon browned meat into a slow cooker container sprayed with butter-flavored cooking spray. Layer potatoes, onion, green pepper, and kidney beans over top. Stir parsley flakes and Tabasco sauce into tomato soup. Evenly spoon tomato soup mixture over top. Cover and cook on LOW for 6 to 8 hours. Mix well before serving.

Each serving equals:

HE: 2½ Protein • ½ Bread • ½ Vegetable • ¼ Slider •
10 Optional Calories

---

235 Calories • 7 gm Fat • 17 gm Protein •
26 gm Carbohydrate • 265 mg Sodium • 11 mg Calcium •
4 gm Fiber

DIABETIC: 2½ Meat • 1 Starch • ½ Vegetable

Pot of Pizza

Pizza in a slow cooker? Well, not exactly, but you'll be pleasantly surprised how well this recipe brings that family favorite to mind! Instead of waiting for delivery, you can just arrive home and dig in.

● Serves 6 (1 cup)

> 8 ounces extra lean ground turkey or beef
> ½ cup chopped onion
> ½ cup chopped green bell pepper
> ½ cup (one 2.5-ounce jar) sliced mushrooms, drained
> 1¾ cups (one 15-ounce can) Hunt's Tomato Sauce
> 1 teaspoon Italian Seasoning
> 1 teaspoon pourable Splenda or Sugar Twin
> 3 cups cooked noodles, rinsed and drained
> ¼ cup grated Kraft fat-free Parmesan cheese
> ¾ cup shredded Kraft reduced-fat Cheddar cheese
> ¾ cup shredded Kraft reduced-fat mozzarella cheese

In a large skillet sprayed with olive oil–flavored cooking spray, brown meat, onion, and green pepper. Stir in mushrooms, tomato sauce, Italian seasoning, and Splenda. Pour mixture into a slow cooker container sprayed with butter-flavored cooking spray. Spread noodles over meat mixture. Sprinkle Parmesan cheese over noodles. Layer Cheddar and mozzarella cheeses evenly over top. Cover and cook on LOW for 6 to 8 hours. Mix well before serving.

HINT: 2⅔ cups uncooked noodles usually cooks to about 3 cups.

Each serving equals:

HE: 2½ Protein • 1⅔ Vegetable • 1 Bread

305 Calories • 9 gm Fat • 21 gm Protein •
35 gm Carbohydrate • 866 mg Sodium •
209 mg Calcium • 4 gm Fiber

DIABETIC: 2 Meat • 1½ Vegetable • 1½ Starch

Easy Pot Spaghetti

There's just something so homey and relaxing about a spaghetti meal, isn't there? Kids of all ages love those strings of tender pasta served in an utterly delicious classic tomato sauce. ❂ Serves 4 (1 cup)

> *8 ounces extra lean ground turkey or beef*
> *½ cup chopped onion*
> *¼ teaspoon dried minced garlic*
> *1¾ cups (one 15-ounce can) Hunt's Tomato Sauce*
> *1½ cups reduced-sodium tomato juice*
> *1 cup (one 4-ounce can) sliced mushrooms, drained*
> *1 teaspoon Italian Seasoning*
> *1⅓ cups broken uncooked spaghetti*
> *¼ cup grated Kraft fat-free Parmesan cheese*

In a large skillet sprayed with olive oil–flavored cooking spray, brown meat. In a slow cooker container sprayed with olive oil–flavored cooking spray, combine browned meat, onion, garlic, tomato sauce, tomato juice, mushrooms, and Italian seasoning. Add uncooked spaghetti and Parmesan cheese. Mix well to combine. Cover and cook on LOW for 4 hours. Mix well before serving.

Each serving equals:

HE: 3¼ Vegetable • 1¾ Protein • 1 Bread

241 Calories • 5 gm Fat • 16 gm Protein •
33 gm Carbohydrate • 901 mg Sodium • 42 mg Calcium •
4 gm Fiber

DIABETIC: 3 Vegetable • 2 Meat • 1 Starch

Grande Celery Loose Meat Sandwiches

Here's one of those Midwestern marvels, the loose meat sandwich, now "translated" in a way that people everywhere can enjoy! This version is extra tangy and crunchy, which just adds to the fun and flavor.

❤ Serves 6

16 ounces extra lean ground turkey or beef
1 (10¾-ounce) can Healthy Request Cream of Celery Soup
1¾ cups finely chopped celery
¼ cup chunky salsa (mild, medium, or hot)
1 teaspoon chili seasoning
6 small hamburger buns

In a large skillet sprayed with butter-flavored cooking spray, brown meat. Spray a slow cooker container with olive oil–flavored cooking spray. In prepared container, combine browned meat, celery soup, celery, salsa, and chili seasoning. Cover and cook on LOW for 6 to 8 hours. When serving, spoon about ⅓ cup meat mixture between each bun.

Each serving equals:

HE: 2 Protein • 1 Bread • ⅔ Vegetable • ¼ Slider • 8 Optional Calories

215 Calories • 7 gm Fat • 17 gm Protein • 21 gm Carbohydrate • 549 mg Sodium • 79 mg Calcium • 2 gm Fiber

DIABETIC: 2 Meat • 1½ Vegetable

Layered Tijuana Casserole

Considering how much Cliff and I savor South-of-the-Border cooking, you might wonder why we don't spend all our free time in Mexico! (Free time? What free time?) With recipes like this tasty, spicy combo, we can save on fuel and driving time—and just tap our toes to the beat of the maracas. ☯ Serves 6

> 8 ounces extra lean ground turkey or beef
> ¾ cup chopped onion
> ½ teaspoon dried minced garlic
> 4 (6-inch) corn tortillas ☆
> 1¼ cups chunky salsa (mild, medium, or hot) ☆
> 1 cup (one 8-ounce can) Hunt's Tomato Sauce ☆
> 10 ounces (one 16-ounce can) pinto beans, rinsed
>   and drained ☆
> Scant 1 cup shredded Kraft reduced-fat
>   Cheddar cheese ☆
> 1 cup frozen whole-kernel corn, thawed ☆
> ⅓ cup sliced ripe olives ☆

In a large skillet sprayed with olive oil–flavored cooking spray, brown meat and onion. Stir in garlic. Place 1 tortilla in slow cooker container. Spoon half of meat mixture over tortilla. Layer ½ cup salsa, ½ cup tomato sauce, and ¼ cup Cheddar cheese over top. Place another tortilla over cheese. Layer half of pinto beans, ¼ cup Cheddar cheese, ½ cup corn, and half of olives over top. Repeat all layers. Cover and cook on LOW for 6 to 7 hours.

HINT: Thaw corn by placing in a colander and rinsing under hot
        water for one minute.

Each serving equals:

HE: 2⅔ Protein • 1 Bread • 1 Vegetable • ¼ Fat

264 Calories • 8 gm Fat • 16 gm Protein •
32 gm Carbohydrate • 906 mg Sodium •
161 mg Calcium • 4 gm Fiber

DIABETIC: 2 Meat • 1½ Starch • 1 Vegetable • ½ Fat

Slow Cooker Party Meatballs

If you love to entertain but juggling all those different stovetop pots and pans is exhausting, slow cooker recipes like this one are a cook's best friend! What's even better, you can serve these delectable appetizers right from the slow cooker pot. ☻ Serves 6 (3 each)

16 ounces extra lean ground turkey or beef

1 cup quick oats

¾ cup finely chopped onion

⅛ teaspoon black pepper

2 teaspoons dried parsley flakes

6 tablespoons water ☆

1 (10¾-ounce) can Healthy Request Tomato Soup

2 tablespoons Brown Sugar Twin

Spray a slow cooker container with butter-flavored cooking spray. In a large bowl, combine meat, oats, onion, black pepper, parsley flakes, and ¼ cup water. Mix well to combine. Form into 18 (1-inch) meatballs. Gently arrange meatballs in prepared slow cooker container. In a small bowl, combine tomato soup, Brown Sugar Twin, and remaining 2 tablespoons water. Spoon sauce mixture evenly over meatballs. Cover and cook on LOW for 4 to 6 hours.

Each serving equals:

HE: 2 Protein • ⅔ Bread • ¼ Vegetable • ¼ Slider • 12 Optional Calories

207 Calories • 7 gm Fat • 17 gm Protein • 19 gm Carbohydrate • 263 mg Sodium • 16 mg Calcium • 2 gm Fiber

DIABETIC: 2 Meat • 1 Starch

Burger Heaven Casserole

When I saw the name "Burger Heaven" on a restaurant while visiting New York City, I thought, "Now there's a place I'd like to visit, at least in culinary terms!" Here's my take on what that divine locale might taste like. ☺ Serves 6 (1 full cup)

16 ounces extra lean ground turkey or beef
2 cups diced raw potatoes
1½ cups thinly sliced carrots
1 cup chopped celery
½ cup diced onion
1 cup frozen peas, thawed
1 cup frozen whole-kernel corn, thawed
1 (10¾-ounce) can Healthy Request Tomato Soup
½ cup water
1 teaspoon dried parsley flakes

In a large skillet sprayed with butter-flavored cooking spray, brown meat. In a slow cooker container sprayed with butter-flavored cooking spray, combine browned meat, potatoes, carrots, celery, onion, peas, and corn. Stir in tomato soup, water, and parsley flakes. Cover and cook on LOW for 6 to 8 hours. Mix well before serving.

HINT: Thaw peas and corn by placing them in a colander and rinsing them under hot water for one minute.

Each serving equals:

HE: 2 Protein • 1 Bread • 1 Vegetable • ¼ Slider • 10 Optional Calories

243 Calories • 7 gm Fat • 17 gm Protein • 28 gm Carbohydrate • 333 mg Sodium • 33 mg Calcium • 4 gm Fiber

DIABETIC: 2 Meat • 1½ Starch • 1 Vegetable

Mexican Meatballs

Why should healthy food be bland and uninteresting when there are so many easy and delicious ways to prepare it with sparkle and sizzle? This has a sweetly smoky barbecue flavor, but instead of spending hours scrubbing the grill, cleanup will be a breeze.

○ Serves 6 (4 each)

> *16 ounces extra lean ground turkey or beef*
> *21 small fat-free saltine crackers, made into*
> *fine crumbs*
> *½ cup frozen whole-kernel corn, thawed*
> *½ cup finely chopped green bell pepper*
> *½ cup finely chopped onion*
> *2 teaspoons chili seasoning*
> *1¾ cups (one 15-ounce can) Hunt's Tomato*
> *Sauce ☆*
> *1 tablespoon Brown Sugar Twin*
> *1 teaspoon dried parsley flakes*

In a large bowl, combine meat, cracker crumbs, corn, green pepper, onion, chili seasoning, and ¼ cup tomato sauce. Mix well to combine. Form into 24 (1-inch) balls. Evenly arrange meatballs in a large skillet sprayed with olive oil–flavored cooking spray and brown for 2 to 3 minutes. Place meatballs in a slow cooker container sprayed with olive oil–flavored cooking spray. Stir Brown Sugar Twin and parsley flakes into remaining tomato sauce. Evenly spoon sauce over meatballs. Cover and cook on LOW for 4 to 6 hours. When serving, evenly spoon sauce over meatballs.

HINTS: 1. A self-seal sandwich bag works great for crushing crackers.
2. Thaw corn by placing it in a colander and rinsing it under hot water for 30 seconds.

Each serving equals:

HE: 2 Protein • 1½ Vegetable • ⅔ Bread •
1 Optional Calorie

194 Calories • 6 gm Fat • 16 gm Protein •
19 gm Carbohydrate • 640 mg Sodium • 19 mg Calcium •
2 gm Fiber

DIABETIC: 2 Meat • 1 Vegetable • 1 Starch

Slow Cooker Meat Loaf

Every diner and truckstop features this American standby, so I knew I needed to find a way to make it using a slow cooker. It's a little untraditional, I admit it, but the comforting feeling is there in every bite!

● Serves 8

24 ounces extra lean ground turkey or beef

1 cup finely chopped onion

4 slices reduced-calorie white bread, torn into small pieces

2 teaspoons prepared yellow mustard

1 tablespoon pourable Splenda or Sugar Twin

1 teaspoon dried parsley flakes

1 cup (one 8-ounce can) Hunt's Tomato Sauce ☆

Spray a slow cooker container with butter-flavored cooking spray. In a large bowl, combine meat, onion, bread pieces, mustard, and ½ cup tomato sauce. Mix well to combine. Form into a large ball. Place in prepared slow cooker container. Stir Splenda and parsley flakes into remaining ½ cup tomato sauce and spoon mixture evenly over meat loaf. Cover and cook on LOW for 6 to 8 hours. Divide into 8 servings. When serving, evenly spoon sauce over top.

Each serving equals:

HE: 2¼ Protein • ¾ Vegetable • ¼ Bread

167 Calories • 7 gm Fat • 17 gm Protein • 9 gm Carbohydrate • 340 mg Sodium • 18 mg Calcium • 1 gm Fiber

DIABETIC: 2 Meat • ½ Vegetable • ½ Starch

Hamburger Casserole

Remember those old cookbooks that every young bride received at her wedding shower—*1,001 Ways to Cook Hamburger*—or something like that? Well, having lots of tasty ways to prepare America's most popular and handy meat ingredient makes good sense, especially if you're on a budget or your kids turn up their noses at fish.

◔ Serves 6 (1½ cups)

> 3 cups diced raw potatoes
> 2 cups sliced carrots
> 1½ cups frozen peas, thawed
> 1 cup chopped onion
> 1½ cups sliced celery
> 16 ounces extra lean ground turkey or beef
> 1 (10¾-ounce) can Healthy Request Tomato Soup
> ¾ cup hot water
> 2 teaspoons dried parsley flakes

Spray a slow cooker container with butter-flavored cooking spray. Layer potatoes, carrots, peas, onion, and celery in prepared container. In a large skillet sprayed with butter-flavored cooking spray, brown meat. Layer browned meat evenly over celery. In same skillet, combine tomato soup, water, and parsley flakes. Evenly spoon soup mixture over meat. Cover and cook on LOW for 6 to 8 hours. Mix well before serving.

HINT: Thaw peas by placing them in a colander and rinsing them under hot water for one minute.

Each serving equals:

> HE: 2 Protein • 1½ Vegetable • 1 Bread • ¼ Slider • 10 Optional Calories
>
> ---
>
> 255 Calories • 7 gm Fat • 18 gm Protein • 30 gm Carbohydrate • 365 mg Sodium • 47 mg Calcium • 5 gm Fiber
>
> ---
>
> DIABETIC: 2 Meat • 1½ Starch • 1 Vegetable

New World "Stuffed" Cabbage

Real stuffed cabbage takes lots of effort from the chef, because the filling has to be rolled up in individual cabbage leaves. If you have the time and inclination, great—but most of us would just as soon enjoy the flavor without all that work. Here's a way to do it and smile with every bite. ☻ Serves 6 (1 full cup)

> 16 ounces extra lean ground turkey or beef
> 1³⁄₄ cups (one 15-ounce can) Hunt's Tomato Sauce
> 2 teaspoons prepared yellow mustard
> 2 tablespoons pourable Splenda or Sugar Twin
> ¹⁄₈ teaspoon black pepper
> 6 cups shredded cabbage
> 1 cup chopped onion
> 1 cup uncooked instant rice

In a large skillet sprayed with butter-flavored cooking spray, brown meat. Spray a slow cooker container with butter-flavored cooking spray. In prepared container, combine browned meat, tomato sauce, mustard, Splenda, and black pepper. Add cabbage, onion, and uncooked rice. Mix well to combine. Cover and cook on LOW for 8 hours. Mix well before serving.

Each serving equals:

HE: 2¹⁄₂ Vegetable • 2 Protein • ¹⁄₂ Bread •
2 Optional Calories

---

223 Calories • 7 gm Fat • 17 gm Protein •
23 gm Carbohydrate • 543 mg Sodium • 63 mg Calcium •
4 gm Fiber

DIABETIC: 2¹⁄₂ Vegetable • 2 Meat • ¹⁄₂ Starch

Scandinavian Meatballs

It's interesting how just a bit of spice can help your taste buds cross international borders on a journey of culinary discovery. The nutmeg here is what makes the difference in these tangy, hearty meatballs—and if your hair starts turning a bit blonder, well, that's gotta be magic!

● Serves 6 (4 each)

16 ounces extra lean ground turkey or beef

1 cup instant potato flakes

1¾ cups (one 14½-ounce can) Swanson Beef Broth ☆

1 (10¾-ounce) can Healthy Request Cream of Mushroom Soup

2 teaspoons dried onion flakes

2 teaspoons dried parsley flakes

½ teaspoon ground nutmeg

In a large bowl, combine meat, potato flakes, and ½ cup beef broth. Form into 24 (1-inch) meatballs. Place meatballs in a large skillet sprayed with butter-flavored cooking spray and brown on all sides. Spray a slow cooker container with butter-flavored cooking spray. Evenly arrange browned meatballs in prepared container. In a medium bowl, combine mushroom soup, the remaining 1¼ cups beef broth, onion flakes, parsley flakes, and nutmeg. Evenly spoon soup mixture over meatballs. Cover and cook on LOW for 6 to 8 hours. When serving evenly spoon sauce over meatballs.

HINT: Wonderful served with cooked noodles.

Each serving equals:

HE: 2 Protein • ½ Bread • ¼ Slider • 13 Optional Calories

163 Calories • 7 gm Fat • 15 gm Protein •
10 gm Carbohydrate • 507 mg Sodium • 44 mg Calcium •
0 gm Fiber

DIABETIC: 2 Meat • ½ Starch

Ravioli Casserole

Did you ever find yourself practically hypnotized by an infomercial that encouraged you to buy your own pasta-making machine? Did you actually buy one that is gathering dust in your garage? Most of us just aren't going to take the time to make real ravioli from scratch, and that's okay. But now we don't have to deny ourselves the pleasure of that kind of pasta pleasure anymore. ☻ Serves 6 (1⅓ cups)

16 ounces extra lean ground turkey or beef
¾ cup chopped onion
1¾ cups (one 15-ounce can) Hunt's Tomato Sauce
1¾ cups (one 14½-ounce can) stewed tomatoes,
* undrained*
1½ teaspoons Italian Seasoning
3 cups uncooked rotini pasta
1 (10-ounce) package frozen chopped spinach, thawed, and
* thoroughly drained*
¼ cup grated Kraft fat-free Parmesan cheese
½ cup + 1 tablespoon shredded Kraft reduced-fat
* mozzarella cheese*

In a large skillet sprayed with olive oil–flavored cooking spray, brown meat and onion. Spray a slow cooker container with olive oil–flavored cooking spray. In prepared container, combine tomato sauce, undrained stewed tomatoes, Italian seasoning, and browned meat mixture. Stir in uncooked rotini pasta. Cover and cook on LOW for 4 hours. Add spinach, Parmesan cheese, and mozzarella cheese. Mix well to combine. Re-cover and continue cooking for 20 to 30 minutes or until cheese melts. Mix well before serving.

HINT: Thaw spinach by placing it in a colander and rinsing it under
    hot water for one minute.

Each serving equals:

Taco Macaroni Pot

Tacos can be fun to eat, but if you serve them the truly traditional way, you've got all those dishes of garnishes to prepare, plus you have to keep the crispy shells from breaking into pieces in your hands. Aaargh! I figured, if I can fill my tummy with the flavor of those tacos but cut down on the work, we'd all be happier!

⚫ Serves 6 (1 full cup)

> *16 ounces extra lean ground turkey or beef*
> *½ cup chopped onion*
> *1¾ cups (one 15-ounce can) Hunt's Tomato Sauce*
> *1 cup water*
> *½ cup chunky salsa (mild, medium, or hot)*
> *2 cups uncooked elbow macaroni*
> *2 teaspoons taco seasoning*
> *¾ cup shredded Kraft reduced-fat Cheddar cheese*

In a large skillet sprayed with olive oil–flavored cooking spray, brown meat and onion. Spray a slow cooker container with olive oil–flavored cooking spray. In prepared container, combine meat mixture, tomato sauce, water, and salsa. Stir in uncooked macaroni and taco seasoning. Cover and cook on LOW for 4 hours. Add Cheddar cheese. Mix well to combine. Re-cover and continue cooking on LOW for 10 to 15 minutes or until cheese melts. Mix well before serving.

Each serving equals:

HE: 2⅔ Protein • 1½ Vegetable • 1 Bread

261 Calories • 9 gm Fat • 21 gm Protein •
24 gm Carbohydrate • 723 mg Sodium •
110 mg Calcium • 2 gm Fiber

DIABETIC: 2½ Meat • 1½ Vegetable • 1 Starch

Sweet and Sour Meat and Rice

There's a luscious feel and taste of the tropics when you stir some sweet ingredients into a traditional meat dish. Maybe it's all that extra sunshine that tickles your taste buds and invites them to dance . . . or maybe, just maybe, it's a recipe that offers a melange of flavors in every bite. ❂ Serves 6 (1 full cup)

16 ounces extra lean ground turkey or beef

1 cup (one 8-ounce can) crushed pineapple, packed in fruit juice, undrained

1¾ cups (one 15-ounce can) Hunt's Tomato Sauce

2 tablespoons Brown Sugar Twin

1 tablespoon reduced-sodium soy sauce

1½ cups chopped green bell pepper

1 cup chopped onion

2 teaspoons dried parsley flakes

1⅓ cups uncooked instant rice

In a large skillet sprayed with butter-flavored cooking spray, brown meat. Spray a slow cooker container with butter-flavored cooking spray. In prepared container, combine undrained pineapple, tomato sauce, Brown Sugar Twin, and soy sauce. Stir in green pepper, onion, and parsley flakes. Add browned meat and uncooked rice. Mix well to combine. Cover and cook on LOW for 6 hours. Mix well before serving.

Each serving equals:

HE: 2 Protein • 2 Vegetable • ⅔ Bread • ⅓ Fruit •
2 Optional Calories

239 Calories • 7 gm Fat • 16 gm Protein •
28 gm Carbohydrate • 587 mg Sodium • 31 mg Calcium •
3 gm Fiber

DIABETIC: 2 Meat • 2 Vegetable • 1 Starch

Italian Meat Loaf

Because we're a nation of immigrants, even if some of our families came here generations ago, our cuisine is made up of recipes from all over the globe. Instead of eating only what our ancestors enjoyed, we tend to try the best of every ethnic group's food. Here's my take on good old meat loaf, with some *Italiano* pizzazz mixed in!   ❤   Serves 6

> *16 ounces extra lean ground turkey or beef*
> *½ cup chopped onion*
> *½ cup chopped green bell pepper*
> *½ cup + 1 tablespoon shredded Kraft reduced-fat mozzarella cheese*
> *½ cup + 1 tablespoon dried fine bread crumbs*
> *1½ teaspoons Italian Seasoning* ☆
> *1 cup (one 8-ounce can) Hunt's Tomato Sauce* ☆
> *1 tablespoon pourable Splenda or Sugar Twin*

Spray a slow cooker container with olive oil–flavored cooking spray. In a large bowl, combine meat, onion, green pepper, mozzarella cheese, bread crumbs, 1 teaspoon Italian seasoning, and ⅓ cup tomato sauce. Mix well to combine. Pat meat mixture into a slow cooker container. In a small bowl, combine remaining ⅔ cup tomato sauce, the remaining ½ teaspoon Italian seasoning, and Splenda. Evenly spoon sauce mixture over top. Cover and cook on LOW for 8 to 10 hours. Cut into 6 wedges and carefully remove from container. When serving, evenly spoon sauce over top.

Each serving equals:

HE: 2½ Protein • 1 Vegetable • ½ Bread •
1 Optional Calorie

---

205 Calories • 9 gm Fat • 18 gm Protein •
13 gm Carbohydrate • 480 mg Sodium •
102 mg Calcium • 1 gm Fiber

DIABETIC: 2½ Meat • 1 Vegetable • 1 Starch

Sloppy Joes

Here's another familiar dish that is just ideal for slow cooker preparation. This recipe makes enough for a crowd, so serve it whenever the sofas overflow with friends or your teenagers invite everyone home after a game! ♥ Serves 12

2½ pounds extra lean ground turkey or beef

1¾ cups (one 15-ounce can) Hunt's Tomato Sauce

2 tablespoons cider vinegar

2 tablespoons Worcestershire sauce

¼ cup prepared yellow mustard

¼ cup pourable Splenda or Sugar Twin

1 tablespoon chili seasoning

2 teaspoons dried parsley flakes

1½ cups finely chopped onion

1 cup finely chopped green bell pepper

12 small hamburger buns

In a large skillet sprayed with butter-flavored cooking spray, brown meat. Spray a slow cooker container with butter-flavored cooking spray. In prepared container, combine tomato sauce, vinegar, and Worcestershire sauce. Stir in mustard, Splenda, chili seasoning, and parsley flakes. Add browned meat, onion, and green pepper. Mix well to combine. Cover and cook on LOW for 6 to 8 hours. When serving, spoon about ⅓ cup meat mixture between each bun.

Each serving equals:

HE: 2½ Protein • 2 Vegetable • 1 Bread •
2 Optional Calories

232 Calories • 8 gm Fat • 20 gm Protein •
20 gm Carbohydrate • 565 mg Sodium • 22 mg Calcium •
2 gm Fiber

DIABETIC: 2½ Meat • 1 Vegetable • 1 Starch

BBQ Meatballs

If you've never used Brown Sugar Twin before, I think you will be impressed by just how well this handy product transforms a tomato-y sauce into a smoky-sweet, just-off-the-grill combination that is hard to beat! When you keep the menu interesting night after night, you're much more likely to stick with your healthy lifestyle.

◑   Serves 6 (4 each)

> 16 ounces extra lean ground turkey or beef
> ½ cup + 1 tablespoon dried fine bread crumbs
> ¼ cup sweet pickle relish
> 1 tablespoon Brown Sugar Twin
> 1¾ cups (one 15-ounce can) Hunt's Tomato Sauce ☆
> 2 tablespoons Worcestershire sauce
> 2 tablespoons cider vinegar
> 2 tablespoons pourable Splenda or Sugar Twin
> 1 teaspoon prepared yellow mustard
> 1 cup finely chopped onion

Spray a slow cooker container with butter-flavored cooking spray. In a large bowl, combine meat, bread crumbs, pickle relish, Brown Sugar Twin, and ¼ cup tomato sauce. Mix gently to combine. Form into 24 (1-inch) meatballs. Carefully arrange meatballs in prepared container. In a medium bowl, combine remaining 1½ cups tomato sauce, Worcestershire sauce, vinegar, Splenda, and mustard. Stir in onion. Evenly spoon sauce over meatballs. Cover and cook on LOW for 6 to 8 hours. Mix well before serving.

Each serving equals:

HE: 2 Protein • 1½ Vegetable • ½ Bread •
13 Optional Calories

207 Calories • 7 gm Fat • 16 gm Protein •
20 gm Carbohydrate • 742 mg Sodium • 49 mg Calcium •
2 gm Fiber

DIABETIC: 2 Meat • 1½ Vegetable • ½ Starch

Macaroni Jackpot

If you want to feel like a winner tonight, but there's no casino within driving distance, let me tip the odds in your favor and suggest this creamy macaroni and beef delight! Because it's a thrifty as well as tasty choice, you'll be saving your money in more ways than one!

● Serves 6 (1⅓ cups)

> 16 ounces extra lean ground turkey or beef
> ¾ cup chopped onion
> ½ cup (one 2.5-ounce jar) sliced mushrooms, undrained
> 1 (10¾-ounce) can Healthy Request Cream of Mushroom Soup
> 1¾ cups (one 14½-ounce can) stewed tomatoes, chopped and undrained
> 2 cups uncooked elbow macaroni
> 1 teaspoon dried parsley flakes

In a large skillet sprayed with butter-flavored cooking spray, brown meat and onion. Spray a slow cooker container with butter-flavored cooking spray. In prepared container, combine browned meat mixture, undrained mushrooms, mushroom soup, and undrained stewed tomatoes. Add uncooked macaroni and parsley flakes. Mix well to combine. Cover and cook on LOW for 6 to 8 hours. Mix well before serving.

Each serving equals:

> HE: 2 Protein • 1 Bread • 1 Vegetable • ¼ Slider • 8 Optional Calories
>
> ---
>
> 235 Calories • 7 gm Fat • 17 gm Protein • 26 gm Carbohydrate • 475 mg Sodium • 74 mg Calcium • 2 gm Fiber
>
> ---
>
> DIABETIC: 2 Meat • 1½ Starch • 1 Vegetable

Steak Teriyaki

No one seems to like steak better than the Japanese, who are world-famous for their super-rich, super-expensive cuts of prime beef. Well, you don't have to spend a fortune on fancy cuts—just sauce it as they do in the steakhouse restaurants and then don't be surprised if your family shouts *"Domo arigato"*—"thanks" in Japanese!

○ Serves 6

⅓ cup reduced-sodium soy sauce

1 tablespoon pourable Splenda or Sugar Twin

1 teaspoon dried minced garlic

½ teaspoon ground ginger

1 teaspoon dried parsley flakes

16 ounces lean round steak, cut into 36 pieces

3 cups hot cooked rice

Spray a slow cooker container with butter-flavored cooking spray. In prepared container, combine soy sauce, Splenda, garlic, ginger, and parsley flakes. Stir in steak pieces. Cover and cook on LOW for 6 to 8 hours. For each serving, place ½ cup rice on a plate and spoon about ¼ cup steak mixture over top.

HINT: 2 cups uncooked instant rice usually cooks to about 3 cups.

Each serving equals:

HE: 2 Protein • 1 Bread • 1 Optional Calorie

245 Calories • 5 gm Fat • 30 gm Protein •
20 gm Carbohydrate • 477 mg Sodium • 11 mg Calcium •
1 gm Fiber

DIABETIC: 2 Meat • 1 Starch

Steak and Vegetable Casserole

Remember how I promised that slow cooking turns meat so scrumptiously tender you probably won't need a knife to cut it? Here's a great example of that in a dish that uses chunks of round steak combined with lots of tasty, healthy vegetables.   ☻   Serves 6 (1⅓ cups)

> 1 cup sliced onion
> 16 ounces lean round steak,
>   cut into 24 pieces
> 3 cups peeled and diced raw potatoes
> 2 cups frozen cut green beans, thawed
> 2 cups frozen sliced carrots, thawed
> 1 cup (one 8-ounce can) tomatoes, coarsely chopped and
>   drained
> 1 (10¾-ounce) can Healthy Request Tomato Soup
> 1 teaspoon Worcestershire sauce
> 2 teaspoons dried parsley flakes
> ½ teaspoon dried minced garlic
> ⅛ teaspoon black pepper

Spray a slow cooker container with butter-flavored cooking spray. Place onion in bottom of prepared container. Arrange steak pieces over onion. Layer potatoes, green beans, and carrots over steak. In a medium bowl, combine tomatoes, tomato soup, Worcestershire sauce, parsley flakes, garlic, and black pepper. Pour tomato mixture over vegetables. Cover and cook on LOW for 8 to 9 hours. Mix well before serving.

HINT: Thaw green beans and carrots by placing them in a colander and rinsing them under hot water for one minute.

Each serving equals:

HE: 2 Protein • 2 Vegetable • ½ Bread • ¼ Slider •
10 Optional Calories

---

261 Calories • 5 gm Fat • 24 gm Protein •
30 gm Carbohydrate • 328 mg Sodium •
53 mg Calcium • 5 gm Fiber

DIABETIC: 2 Meat • 1½ Vegetable • 1 Starch

Easy German Steak

You might never have thought of serving steaks with a sauerkraut-based sauce, but it's a surprisingly good way to enjoy this man-pleasing favorite! While you might not find this exact dish on the menu in your favorite German restaurant, it delivers the hearty satisfaction you've come to expect from that nation's meat dishes.   ☻   Serves 4

> 2 cups (one 16-ounce can) sauerkraut, well drained
> ½ cup chopped onion
> 2 cups reduced-sodium tomato juice
> 1 tablespoon Brown Sugar Twin
> 1 teaspoon dried parsley flakes
> 4 (4-ounce) lean tenderized round or cube steaks

Spray a slow cooker container with butter-flavored cooking spray. In prepared container, combine sauerkraut, onion, tomato juice, Brown Sugar Twin, and parsley flakes. Evenly arrange steak pieces over vegetable mixture. Cover and cook on LOW for 6 to 8 hours. When serving, place 1 piece of meat on a plate and spoon about 1 cup sauerkraut mixture over top.

Each serving equals:

HE: 3 Protein • 2¼ Vegetable • 1 Optional Calorie

222 Calories • 6 gm Fat • 32 gm Protein • 10 gm Carbohydrate • 440 mg Sodium • 52 mg Calcium • 2 gm Fiber

DIABETIC: 3 Meat • 2 Vegetable

Super Swiss Steak

Sometimes I like to think of my slow cooker as a great big and deep skillet that can make dinner without my help! Swiss steak has always been one of my family's favorite meals, and this version can be ready to serve moments after we pull into the driveway.   ●   Serves 4

> 3 tablespoons all-purpose flour
> 4 (4-ounce) lean tenderized minute or cube steaks
> 1 (10¾-ounce) can Healthy Request Tomato Soup
> 1 cup (one 8-ounce can) stewed tomatoes, chopped and undrained
> 1 teaspoon Worcestershire sauce
> 2 teaspoons dried parsley flakes
> ⅛ teaspoon black pepper
> ½ cup shredded carrots
> ½ cup chopped onion

Spray a slow cooker container with butter-flavored cooking spray. Place flour in a shallow saucer and coat steak pieces on both sides in flour. Evenly arrange coated steak pieces in prepared container. In a medium bowl, combine tomato soup and undrained tomatoes. Stir in Worcestershire sauce, parsley flakes, black pepper, and any remaining flour. Add carrots and onion. Mix well to combine. Evenly spoon mixture over steak. Cover and cook on LOW for 6 to 8 hours. When serving, evenly spoon sauce over meat.

Each serving equals:

HE: 3 Protein • 1 Vegetable • ¼ Bread • ½ Slider •
5 Optional Calories

---

274 Calories • 6 gm Fat • 33 gm Protein •
22 gm Carbohydrate • 476 mg Sodium • 36 mg Calcium •
2 gm Fiber

DIABETIC: 3 Meat • 1 Vegetable • 1 Starch

Creamy Swiss Steak Pot

Using healthy cream soups to make luscious sauces is one of my best techniques for keeping "the customer satisfied." By customer, of course, I mean your son the picky eater who shies away from what's "good for him" or your daughter, who longs for rich food at the same time she's concerned about keeping her figure. Isn't it great to please everyone and still please yourself?   ☀   Serves 4

1 cup sliced onion

3 tablespoons all-purpose flour

1 teaspoon dried parsley flakes

1/8 teaspoon black pepper

4 (4-ounce) lean tenderized minute or cube steaks

1 cup chopped celery

1 cup (one 8-ounce can) tomatoes, undrained

1 (10¾-ounce) can Healthy Request Cream of Mushroom Soup

Spray a slow cooker container with butter-flavored cooking spray. Place sliced onion in bottom of prepared container. In a medium sauce dish, combine flour, parsley flakes, and black pepper. Coat steaks on both sides. Arrange coated meat evenly over onion. Top with celery. In a small bowl, combine undrained tomatoes, mushroom soup, and any remaining flour. Spoon mixture evenly over vegetables. Cover and cook on LOW for 8 hours. When serving, evenly spoon vegetables and sauce over meat.

Each serving equals:

HE: 3 Protein • 1½ Vegetable • ¼ Bread • ½ Slider • 1 Optional Calorie

262 Calories • 6 gm Fat • 33 gm Protein • 19 gm Carbohydrate • 471 mg Sodium • 101 mg Calcium • 2 gm Fiber

DIABETIC: 3 Meat • 1½ Vegetable • 1 Starch

Smothered Oriental Steak

We can learn a lot from the cooking styles of Asian countries, where certain medical concerns occur in a much lower percentage of the population. We can start by eating less meat and more veggies but never sacrificing great flavor to feel satisfied. ❤ Serves 6 (¾ cup)

16 ounces lean round steak, cut into 36 pieces

3 tablespoons all-purpose flour

1 teaspoon dried parsley flakes

2 cups (one 16-ounce can) tomatoes, coarsely chopped and undrained

2 tablespoons reduced-sodium soy sauce

1 cup sliced onion

1 cup (one 4-ounce can) sliced mushrooms, drained

1 cup (one 8-ounce can) sliced water chestnuts, drained

Spray a slow cooker container with olive oil–flavored cooking spray. In prepared container, combine steak pieces, flour, and parsley flakes. Add undrained tomatoes and soy sauce. Mix well to combine. Stir in onion, mushrooms, and water chestnuts. Cover and cook on LOW for 6 to 8 hours. Mix well before serving.

HINT: Great served over rice, potatoes, or pasta.

Each serving equals:

HE: 2 Protein • 1⅓ Vegetable • ½ Bread

188 Calories • 4 gm Fat • 23 gm Protein • 15 gm Carbohydrate • 455 mg Sodium • 26 mg Calcium • 4 gm Fiber

DIABETIC: 2 Meat • 1½ Vegetable • 1 Starch

Home-Style Pot Roast

Whether your mom or grandmom made pot roast worth writing home about, or no one in your house even tried, now you've got a recipe to start your own tradition—a dish worth passing along to your kids and grandkids that tastes like love! ❂ Serves 6

1½ cups coarsely chopped celery
1½ cups coarsely chopped carrots
1 cup coarsely chopped onion
½ cup (one 2.5-ounce jar) sliced mushrooms, drained
3 cups chopped raw potatoes
1 (24-ounce) lean boneless beef roast
1 teaspoon dried parsley flakes
1 (12-ounce) jar Heinz Fat Free Beef Gravy

Spray a slow cooker container with butter-flavored cooking spray. In prepared container, combine celery, carrots, onion, mushrooms, and potatoes. Place beef roast on top of vegetables. Stir parsley flakes into gravy. Pour gravy mixture evenly over top. Cover and cook on LOW for 8 hours. Remove roast and cut into 6 pieces. Mix vegetable mixture well. For each serving, place 1 piece of meat on a plate and spoon 1 cup vegetable mixture next to it.

Each serving equals:

HE: 3 Protein • 1½ Vegetable • ½ Bread • ¼ Slider • 5 Optional Calories

251 Calories • 7 gm Fat • 27 gm Protein • 20 gm Carbohydrate • 645 mg Sodium • 32 mg Calcium • 3 gm Fiber

DIABETIC: 3 Meat • 1½ Vegetable • 1 Starch

Italian Pot Roast

If your husband could dine on pot roast five nights a week (I've met some of those men at my speaking engagements over the years!), you'll need more recipes! I like this one for its Old-World hearty goodness and the wonderful, savory nature of its gravy.　　●　Serves 6

1 cup chopped onion

1½ cups chopped celery

1½ cups chopped carrots

3 cups diced raw potatoes

1 (24-ounce) lean boneless beef roast

1 (12-ounce) jar Heinz Fat Free Beef Gravy

1 cup (one 8-ounce can) tomatoes, coarsely chopped and undrained

1 cup (one 4-ounce can) sliced mushrooms, drained

1½ teaspoons Italian seasoning

Spray a slow cooker container with butter-flavored cooking spray. In prepared container, combine onion, celery, carrots, and potatoes. Arrange roast over vegetables. In a small bowl, combine beef gravy, undrained tomatoes, mushrooms, and Italian seasoning. Spoon mixture evenly over roast. Cover and cook on LOW for 8 hours. Remove roast and cut into 6 pieces. For each serving, place 1 piece of meat on a plate and spoon 1 cup vegetable mixture on top.

Each serving equals:

HE: 3 Protein • 2 Vegetable • ½ Bread • ¼ Slider • 5 Optional Calories

279 Calories • 7 gm Fat • 29 gm Protein • 25 gm Carbohydrate • 627 mg Sodium • 47 mg Calcium • 4 gm Fiber

DIABETIC: 3 Meat • 1½ Vegetable • 1 Starch

Beef Barbecue Sandwiches

Are you a fan of tailgate parties before, during, and after your favorite football team plays? Well, here's a recipe that you can prepare in advance and take along. It serves a carload of hungry cheerleaders, official or not! ☻ Serves 12

> 1 (3 pound) uncooked lean beef roast
> 1 cup (one 8-ounce can) Hunt's Tomato Sauce
> 1 tablespoon Brown Sugar Twin
> 1 teaspoon prepared yellow mustard
> ¾ cup finely chopped onion
> ¼ cup finely chopped green bell pepper
> 12 small hamburger buns

Spray a slow cooker container with butter-flavored cooking spray. Place beef roast in prepared container. In a large bowl, combine tomato sauce, Brown Sugar Twin, and mustard. Stir in onion and green pepper. Spoon mixture evenly over roast. Cover and cook on LOW for 8 hours. Remove roast and finely shred. Stir shredded roast into sauce mixture. Re-cover and cook on HIGH for 30 minutes. When serving, spoon about ½ cup meat mixture between each bun.

Each serving equals:

HE: 3 Protein • 1 Bread • ½ Vegetable

245 Calories • 9 gm Fat • 24 gm Protein •
17 gm Carbohydrate • 377 mg Sodium • 20 mg Calcium •
1 gm Fiber

DIABETIC: 3 Meat • 1 Starch

Shredded Italian Beef

Anytime you've got lots of mouths to feed but not much time or help, your slow cooker can serve as your kitchen assistant! Meat-lovers will simply sigh in satisfaction at each and every mouthful of this delectable sandwich filling.   ●   Serves 12

6 full cups finely shredded cooked lean roast beef

1 cup chopped onion

½ cup (one 2.5-ounce jar) sliced mushrooms, drained

1 (12-ounce) jar Heinz Fat Free Beef

2 teaspoons Italian Seasoning

12 small hamburger buns

In a slow cooker container, combine beef, onion, and mushrooms. Add beef gravy and Italian seasoning. Mix well to combine. Cover and cook on LOW for 6 to 8 hours. When serving, spoon about ½ cup meat mixture between each bun.

Each serving equals:

HE: 3 Protein • 1 Bread • ¼ Vegetable •
13 Optional Calories

248 Calories • 8 gm Fat • 27 gm Protein •
17 gm Carbohydrate • 607 mg Sodium • 11 gm Calcium •
1 gm Fiber

DIABETIC: 3 Meat • 1 Starch

Grande BBQ Sandwiches

This reminded me of the rich and tangy beef served at barbecue restaurants all across Texas and into Oklahoma. There's no more satisfying lunch when you're on the road, but even when you're stuck in the house in the middle of an Iowa blizzard, you can enjoy a taste of freedom and fun with this recipe. ☺ Serves 6

> 1 cup (one 8-ounce can) Hunt's Tomato Sauce
> ½ cup chunky salsa (mild, medium, or hot)
> ½ cup finely chopped onion
> 2 tablespoons Brown Sugar Twin
> 1 teaspoon dried parsley flakes
> 3 full cups finely diced cooked lean roast beef
> 6 small hamburger buns

Spray a slow cooker container with butter-flavored cooking spray. In prepared container, combine tomato sauce, salsa, onion, Brown Sugar Twin, and parsley flakes. Stir in roast beef. Cover and cook on LOW for 4 to 6 hours. When serving, spoon about ½ cup meat mixture between each bun.

HINTS: 1. If you don't have leftovers, purchase a chunk of lean cooked roast beef from your local deli or use Healthy Choice Deli slices.
2. Also good served over warm corn bread.

Each serving equals:

HE: 3 Protein • 1 Bread • 1 Vegetable • 1 Optional Calorie

260 Calories • 8 gm Fat • 27 gm Protein •
20 gm Carbohydrate • 761 mg Sodium • 17 mg Calcium •
2 gm Fiber

DIABETIC: 3 Meat • 1 Starch • 1 Vegetable

Beef Pot Hash

Slow cooker recipes like this one are just about perfect when you're not sure what time everyone is getting home. Once it's ready, it's ready and willing to wait until the car full of ravenous soccer players pulls into the driveway. ☻ Serves 6 (1 cup)

3 full cups diced lean cooked roast beef

1½ cups finely chopped onion

6 cups shredded loose-packed frozen potatoes

1 (12-ounce) jar Heinz Fat Free Beef Gravy

1 teaspoon Worcestershire sauce

2 teaspoons dried parsley flakes

⅛ teaspoon black pepper

Spray a slow cooker container with butter-flavored cooking spray. In prepared container, combine roast beef, onion, and potatoes. Stir in gravy, Worcestershire sauce, parsley flakes, and black pepper. Cover and cook on LOW for 6 to 8 hours. Mix well before serving.

HINTS: 1. If you don't have leftovers, purchase a chunk of lean cooked roast beef from your local deli.
2. Mr. Dell's frozen shredded potatoes are a good choice or raw shredded potatoes may be used in place of frozen potatoes.

Each serving equals:

HE: 3 Protein • ⅔ Bread • ½ Vegetable • ¼ Slider • 5 Optional Calories

263 Calories • 7 gm Fat • 28 gm Protein • 22 gm Carbohydrate • 595 mg Sodium • 24 mg Calcium • 3 gm Fiber

DIABETIC: 3 Meat • 1 Starch • ½ Vegetable

Beef and Creamy Pasta

I chose rotini for this recipe because it holds its shape well over the hours of long, slow cooking. If you decide to experiment with other kinds of pasta, be aware that some do better when cooked this way than others. Did you ever see the pasta called *radiatore*? It's shaped like little radiators—wonder who thought of that?   ❂   Serves 6 (1 cup)

> 16 ounces lean round steak, cut into 36 pieces
> 1 (10¾-ounce) can Healthy Request Cream of Mushroom Soup
> 1 cup (one 4-ounce can) sliced mushrooms, undrained
> ¼ cup (one 2-ounce jar) chopped pimiento, undrained
> ½ cup hot water
> ½ cup finely chopped onion
> 2 teaspoons dried parsley flakes
> 2½ cups uncooked rotini pasta

Spray a slow cooker container with butter-flavored cooking spray. In prepared container, combine steak pieces, mushroom soup, undrained mushrooms, undrained pimiento, and water. Stir in onion, parsley flakes, and uncooked rotini pasta. Cover and cook on LOW for 6 to 8 hours. Mix well before serving.

Each serving equals:

HE: 2 Protein • 1 Bread • ½ Vegetable • ¼ Slider •
8 Optional Calories

229 Calories • 5 gm Fat • 30 gm Protein •
16 gm Carbohydrate • 344 mg Sodium • 54 mg Calcium •
2 gm Fiber

DIABETIC: 2 Meat • 1 Starch • ½ Vegetable

Beef Rouladens

If you've ever tried to prepare a dish like these rolled-up "packets" of beef and veggies, you know that they don't always stay nicely rolled up when you prepare them the traditional way. But the slow cooker is great for this kind of cooking, because nobody has to shift the rolls until the very end, and so they hold their shape. ☻ Serves 4

1/4 cup Hormel Bacon Bits
3/4 cup diced celery
1/4 cup finely chopped onion
16 ounces lean round steak, cut into 4 pieces
1 (12-ounce) jar Heinz Fat Free Beef Gravy
1 teaspoon dried parsley flakes

Spray a slow cooker container with butter-flavored cooking spray. In a medium bowl, combine bacon bits, celery, and onion. Spoon about 1/3 cup mixture on each piece of steak. Roll up each piece and secure ends with toothpicks. Place beef rolls in prepared container. In same medium bowl, combine beef gravy and parsley flakes. Evenly spoon gravy mixture over top. Cover and cook on LOW for 6 to 8 hours. When serving, place 1 beef roll on a plate and spoon 1/2 cup sauce over top.

Each serving equals:

HE: 3 Protein • 1/2 Vegetable • 3/4 Slider •
2 Optional Calories

222 Calories • 6 gm Fat • 35 gm Protein •
7 gm Carbohydrate • 805 mg Sodium • 15 mg Calcium •
1 gm Fiber

DIABETIC: 3 Meat • 1 Starch/Carbohydrate • 1/2 Vegetable

Green Beans and Pork

This is such a simple list of ingredients, you may wonder what the excitement is all about. But the missing ingredients on this short list is TIME. When you blend these few items in a pot and close the lid for hours, you get an amazingly scrumptious meal that brings each and every element to life!   ☻   Serves 6 (1 cup)

4 cups frozen cut green beans, thawed
½ cup chopped onion
¼ cup (one 2-ounce jar) chopped pimiento, drained
1 teaspoon lemon pepper
16 ounces lean pork tenderloin, cut into 36 pieces

Spray a slow cooker container with butter-flavored cooking spray. In prepared container, combine green beans and onion. Stir in pimiento and lemon pepper. Add pork pieces. Mix well to combine. Cover and cook on LOW for 8 hours. Mix well before serving.

HINT: Thaw green beans by placing them in a colander and rinsing them under hot water for one minute.

Each serving equals:

HE: 2 Protein • 1½ Vegetable

131 Calories • 3 gm Fat • 18 gm Protein •
8 gm Carbohydrate • 36 mg Sodium • 42 mg Calcium •
3 gm Fiber

DIABETIC: 2 Meat • 1½ Vegetable

Bavarian Pork Pot Roast

If you've ever traveled to Germany or eastern Europe, you know that one tradition of their cooking is using fruit or fruit juice to deepen and sweeten meat dishes like this savory pork roast. The best apples for this recipe are sturdy ones—try Rome or Gala or even Granny Smith.

❤ Serves 6

1 (32-ounce) lean boneless pork loin roast
1¾ cups (one 14½-ounce can) Frank's Bavarian-style sauerkraut, drained
1¾ cups chopped carrots
1 cup finely chopped onion
2½ cups cored, peeled, and quartered cooking apples
½ cup unsweetened apple juice
2 teaspoons dried parsley flakes

Spray a slow cooker container with butter-flavored cooking spray. Place pork roast in prepared container. In a medium bowl, combine sauerkraut, carrots, onion, and apples. Evenly arrange sauerkraut mixture over top of roast. In same medium bowl, combine apple juice and parsley flakes. Pour apple juice mixture evenly over top. Cover and cook on LOW for 6 to 8 hours. Evenly cut roast into 6 pieces. When serving, place 1 piece of meat on a plate and spoon about ⅔ cup sauerkraut mixture over top.

HINT: If you can't find Bavarian sauerkraut, use regular sauerkraut, ½ teaspoon caraway seeds, and 1 teaspoon Brown Sugar Twin.

Each serving equals:

HE: 4 Protein • 1½ Vegetable • 1 Fruit

274 Calories • 6 gm Fat • 34 gm Protein •
21 gm Carbohydrate • 473 mg Sodium • 25 mg Calcium •
4 gm Fiber

DIABETIC: 4 Meat • 1½ Vegetable • 1 Fruit

Pork and Sweet Potato Casserole

Sweet potatoes have so many nutrients, and yet too many people reserve them for eating only around Thanksgiving. Here's a terrific and satisfying main dish that brings out their best qualities. (By the way, whether the sign at the market says sweet potatoes or yams, you can buy them—they're basically the same in this country.)

❂ Serves 6 (1 full cup)

> 1½ pounds lean pork tenderloin, cut into 36 pieces
> 3 full cups peeled and sliced raw sweet potatoes
> ½ cup chopped onion
> ½ cup chopped green bell pepper
> 2 cups (one 16-ounce can) tomatoes, chopped and drained
> 1 tablespoon Brown Sugar Twin
> 1 teaspoon dried parsley flakes
> ⅛ teaspoon black pepper

Spray a slow cooker container with butter-flavored cooking spray. In prepared container, combine pork pieces, sweet potatoes, onion, and green pepper. In a medium bowl, combine tomatoes, Brown Sugar Twin, parsley flakes, and black pepper. Pour tomato mixture over pork mixture. Cover and cook on LOW for 8 to 10 hours. Mix well before serving.

Each serving equals:

HE: 3 Protein • 1 Bread • 1 Vegetable • 1 Optional Calorie

232 Calories • 4 gm Fat • 26 gm Protein •
23 gm Carbohydrate • 241 mg Sodium • 44 mg Calcium •
3 gm Fiber

DIABETIC: 3 Meat • 1 Starch • 1 Vegetable

Roast Pork with Peach Chutney

If you've never tasted roast pork except from your Chinese restaurant, you've got a treat in store! This recipe produces a hearty and tasty dish that celebrates the special flavors of this good-for-you meat.

◐ Serves 6

> 1 (32-ounce) lean boneless pork loin roast
> 2 cups (one 16-ounce can) sliced peaches, packed in fruit juice, drained
> 2 tablespoons cider vinegar
> 2 teaspoons prepared yellow mustard
> 2 tablespoons pourable Splenda or Sugar Twin
> ¼ cup raisins
> ¾ cup finely chopped onion

Spray a slow cooker container with butter-flavored cooking spray. Place pork roast in prepared container. Finely chop peach slices. In a medium bowl, combine vinegar, mustard, and Splenda. Stir in chopped peaches, raisins, and onion. Spoon fruit mixture evenly over roast. Cover and cook on LOW for 6 to 8 hours. When serving, cut roast into 6 pieces and top each piece with ⅓ cup fruit mixture.

Each serving equals:

HE: 4 Protein • 1 Fruit • ¼ Vegetable • 2 Optional Calories

250 Calories • 6 gm Fat • 33 gm Protein •
16 gm Carbohydrate • 91 mg Sodium • 19 mg Calcium •
2 gm Fiber

DIABETIC: 4 Meat • 1 Fruit

Bavarian Sauerkraut and Ham

Are you as big a fan of caraway seeds as some of my readers? If you always buy the rye bread with seeds, this is your kind of recipe! It doesn't take a lot of protein to make you feel as if you're getting a real meal, as long as other delicious elements contribute to the recipe's culinary magic.   ♥   Serves 4 (1½ cups)

> 1¾ cups (one 14½-ounce can) Frank's Bavarian-style sauerkraut, well
> drained
> 1 cup chopped celery
> ¾ cup finely chopped onion
> ½ cup water
> 1½ cups diced Dubuque 97% fat-free ham or any extra-lean ham
> 2 cups diced unpeeled raw potatoes

Spray a slow cooker container with butter-flavored cooking spray. In prepared container, combine sauerkraut, celery, onion, and water. Add ham and potatoes. Mix well to combine. Cover and cook on LOW for 6 to 8 hours. Mix well before serving.

HINT: If you can't find Bavarian sauerkraut, use regular sauerkraut, ½ teaspoon caraway seeds and 1 teaspoon Brown Sugar Twin.

Each serving equals:

HE: 1¾ Vegetable • 1½ Protein • 1 Bread

182 Calories • 2 gm Fat • 14 gm Protein •
27 gm Carbohydrate • 934 mg Sodium • 21 mg Calcium •
4 gm Fiber

DIABETIC: 1½ Vegetable • 1½ Meat • 1 Starch

Creole Crock Jambalaya

What I have always enjoyed about jambalaya (besides its musical name!) is the way all the flavors combine to please my palate. This version, which draws its inspiration from the combination of food traditions found in and around New Orleans, is especially savory.

☻ Serves 6 (¾ cup)

> 2 full cups diced Dubuque 97% fat-free ham or any extra-lean ham
> ¾ cup chopped green bell pepper
> ½ cup chopped onion
> 1¾ cups (one 14½-ounce can) stewed tomatoes, undrained
> 1 tablespoon dried parsley flakes
> ½ teaspoon dried minced garlic
> 2 teaspoons Worcestershire sauce
> ⅛ teaspoon black pepper
> 6 ounces frozen shrimp, thawed

Spray a slow cooker container with butter-flavored cooking spray. In prepared container, combine ham, green pepper, onion, undrained stewed tomatoes, parsley flakes, garlic, Worcestershire, and black pepper. Cover and cook on LOW for 6 hours. Add shrimp. Mix well to combine. Re-cover and cook on HIGH for 1 hour.

HINT: Good served with rice, noodles, or corn bread.

Each serving equals:

HE: 2⅓ Protein • 1 Vegetable

127 Calories • 3 gm Fat • 16 gm Protein •
9 gm Carbohydrate • 706 mg Sodium • 48 mg Calcium •
1 gm Fiber

DIABETIC: 2 Meat • 1 Vegetable

Pinto Bean Supper

If your doctor has encouraged you to eat more fiber, join the club! Beans provide a wonderful amount of fiber in this dish, but you're also getting the delectable flavor of ham mixed in. I try to keep lots of canned beans on the shelf, since they're so nourishing and don't require overnight soaking to be used in a recipe.   ◐   Serves 6 (1 full cup)

> 20 ounces (two 16-ounce cans) pinto beans, rinsed and drained
> 1 full cup diced Dubuque 97% fat-free ham or any extra-lean ham
> 2 cups (one 16-ounce can) tomatoes, coarsely chopped and undrained
> ½ cup diced onion
> ¾ cup diced celery
> ¾ cup finely chopped carrots
> 1 teaspoon chili seasoning
> 1 cup (one 8-ounce can) Hunt's Tomato Sauce

Spray a slow cooker container with butter-flavored cooking spray. In prepared container, combine pinto beans, ham, undrained tomatoes, onion, celery, and carrots. Stir in chili seasoning and tomato sauce. Cover and cook on LOW for 6 to 8 hours. Mix well before serving.

Each serving equals:

HE: 2⅔ Protein • 2 Vegetable

158 Calories • 2 gm Fat • 11 gm Protein • 24 gm Carbohydrate • 934 mg Sodium • 74 mg Calcium • 7 gm Fiber

DIABETIC: 1½ Meat • 1½ Vegetable • 1 Starch

Sunrise Casserole

Years ago, I remember a song that urged us to get out of our beds and let the sunshine fill our heads. This recipe is my answer to that encouragement—a terrific brunch entree that would also be a fine Sunday supper.   ☻   Serves 8

1½ cups Bisquick Reduced Fat Baking Mix
⅔ cup Carnation Nonfat Dry Milk Powder
⅔ cup water
¼ cup Land O Lakes no-fat sour cream
4 eggs or equivalent in egg substitute
1 teaspoon dried parsley flakes
½ cup chopped onion
½ cup (one 2.5-ounce jar) sliced mushrooms, drained
¼ cup grated Kraft fat-free Parmesan cheese
1½ cups diced Dubuque 97% fat-free ham or any extra-lean ham
¾ cup shredded Kraft reduced-fat Cheddar cheese

Spray a slow cooker container with butter-flavored cooking spray. In a large bowl, combine baking mix, dry milk powder, water, sour cream, and eggs. Stir in parsley flakes, onion, mushrooms, and Parmesan cheese. Add ham and Cheddar cheese. Mix well to combine. Pour mixture into prepared container. Cover and cook on LOW for 5 to 6 hours. Cut into 8 wedges.

Each serving equals:

HE: 2 Protein • 1 Bread • ¼ Skim Milk • ¼ Vegetable • 8 Optional Calories

214 Calories • 6 gm Fat • 16 gm Protein •
24 gm Carbohydrate • 685 mg Sodium •
193 mg Calcium • 1 gm Fiber

DIABETIC: 2 Meat • 1½ Starch/Carbohydrate

Ham and Potatoes au Gratin

If you're a fan of happy couples in food as well as romance, you know that ham and cheese belong together anytime day or night! Stir in some potatoes, and you've got a meal as perfect as the circle formed by a wedding ring. Enjoy! ☻ Serves 6 (1 cup)

2 full cups diced Dubuque 97% fat-free ham or any extra-lean ham

4 cups diced raw potatoes

1 cup chopped onion

3/4 cup shredded Kraft reduced-fat Cheddar cheese

1 (10¾-ounce) can Healthy Request Cream of Celery Soup

1/8 teaspoon black pepper

1 teaspoon dried parsley flakes

1 teaspoon prepared yellow mustard

Spray a slow cooker container with butter-flavored cooking spray. In prepared container, combine ham, potatoes, and onion. Sprinkle Cheddar cheese evenly over top. In a small bowl, combine celery soup, black pepper, parsley flakes, and mustard. Add soup mixture to potato mixture. Mix well to combine. Cover and cook on LOW for 8 hours. Mix well before serving.

Each serving equals:

HE: 2 Protein • ⅔ Bread • ⅓ Vegetable • ¼ Slider • 8 Optional Calories

181 Calories • 5 gm Fat • 15 gm Protein • 19 gm Carbohydrate • 973 mg Sodium • 165 mg Calcium • 3 gm Fiber

DIABETIC: 2 Meat • 1 Starch

Divine Ham Tetrazzini

Instead of serving up the same old turkey tetrazzini again, surprise your family with this innovative and heavenly version featuring ham! It's amazingly filling, easy to fix, and with a slow cooker, your cleanup takes only minutes. ☻ Serves 6 (1 full cup)

1 (10¾-ounce) can Healthy Request Cream of Mushroom Soup

1 cup (one 4-ounce can) sliced mushrooms, undrained

¼ cup (one 2-ounce jar) chopped pimiento, undrained

¾ cup water

2 full cups diced Dubuque 97% fat-free ham or any extra-lean ham

¾ cup shredded Kraft reduced-fat Cheddar cheese

½ cup chopped onion

3 cups hot cooked spaghetti, rinsed and drained

Spray a slow cooker container with butter-flavored cooking spray. In prepared container, combine mushroom soup, undrained mushrooms, undrained pimiento, and water. Add ham, Cheddar cheese, and onion. Mix well to combine. Cover and cook on LOW for 6 to 8 hours. Just before serving, stir in cooked spaghetti. Re-cover and continue cooking on LOW for 15 minutes. Mix well before serving.

HINT: 2½ cups broken uncooked spaghetti usually cooks to about 3 cups.

Each serving equals:

HE: 2 Protein • 1 Bread • ½ Vegetable • ¼ Slider • 8 Optional Calories

229 Calories • 5 gm Fat • 18 gm Protein • 28 gm Carbohydrate • 888 mg Sodium • 145 mg Calcium • 2 gm Fiber

DIABETIC: 2 Meat • 1½ Starch/Carbohydrate • ½ Vegetable

Ultimate Corn-Ham Bake

I think this would be a great choice for supper after a day spent cheering on your kids at soccer or painting the garage! It's creamy and rich, it's full of favorite flavors, and oh yes, it's ready when you are.

○ Serves 6 (⅔ cup)

> 3 cups frozen whole-kernel corn, thawed
> 1½ cups chopped Dubuque 97% fat-free ham or any extra-lean ham
> ½ cup finely chopped onion
> ½ cup finely chopped green bell pepper
> ½ cup (one 2.5-ounce jar) sliced mushrooms, undrained
> 1 (10¾-ounce) can Healthy Request Cream of Mushroom Soup
> ⅛ teaspoon black pepper
> ½ cup + 1 tablespoon shredded Kraft reduced-fat Cheddar cheese

Spray a slow cooker container with butter-flavored cooking spray. In prepared container, combine corn, ham, onion, and green pepper. Stir in undrained mushrooms, mushroom soup, and black pepper. Add Cheddar cheese. Mix well to combine. Cover and cook on LOW for 4 to 6 hours. Mix well before serving.

HINT: Thaw corn by placing it in a colander and rinsing it under hot water for one minute.

Each serving equals:

HE: 1½ Protein • 1 Bread • ½ Vegetable • ¼ Slider • 8 Optional Calories

---

197 Calories • 5 gm Fat • 13 gm Protein • 25 gm Carbohydrate • 704 mg Sodium • 120 mg Calcium • 3 gm Fiber

---

DIABETIC: 1½ Meat • 1½ Starch/Carbohydrate

Pasta Supper Casserole

Here's what I call a "not-so-slow" cooker recipe—one that takes only four hours to reach its point of perfection. Maybe you were planning to make dinner as usual for the family and you needed to go out for a few hours. In just a few minutes, you can get dinner ready, go do what you must, and return knowing that you're all set. Phew, what a relief!

Serves 6 (1 cup)

1 (10¾-ounce) can Healthy Request Cream of Mushroom Soup
1⅓ cups hot water
1 teaspoon prepared yellow mustard
¼ cup (one 2-ounce jar) chopped pimiento, undrained
1 tablespoon dried parsley flakes
⅛ teaspoon black pepper
2 full cups diced Dubuque 97% fat-free ham or any extra-lean ham
1 cup chopped celery
½ cup chopped onion
2 cups uncooked rotini pasta

Spray a slow cooker container with butter-flavored cooking spray. In prepared container, combine mushroom soup, water, mustard, undrained pimiento, parsley flakes, and black pepper. Add ham, celery, and onion. Mix well to combine. Stir in uncooked macaroni. Cover and cook on LOW for 4 hours. Mix well before serving.

Each serving equals:

HE: 1⅓ Protein • 1 Bread • ½ Vegetable • ¼ Slider •
8 Optional Calories

187 Calories • 3 gm Fat • 13 gm Protein •
27 gm Carbohydrate • 708 mg Sodium • 60 mg Calcium •
2 gm Fiber

DIABETIC: 1½ Meat • 1½ Starch

Italian Hot Dog Spaghetti

My grandsons adore hot dogs and they also like spaghetti, so when Grandma cooked up this kid-pleasing combo, they cheered and held up their plates to be served! Why shouldn't food be fun for all? With a recipe like this one, it can be. ● Serves 6 (1⅓ cups)

2 full cups broken uncooked spaghetti
1 (16 ounce) package Healthy Choice 97% fat-free frankfurters, each
cut into ½-inch pieces
1½ cups diced unpeeled zucchini
1 cup shredded carrots
1 cup (one 8-ounce can) Hunt's Tomato Sauce
2 cups hot water
1½ teaspoons Italian seasoning
2 teaspoons pourable Splenda or Sugar Twin

Spray a slow cooker container with olive oil–flavored cooking spray. In prepared container, combine uncooked spaghetti, frankfurters, zucchini, and carrots. In a medium bowl, combine tomato sauce, water, Italian seasoning, and Splenda. Pour sauce mixture over spaghetti mixture. Cover and cook on LOW for 4 to 6 hours. Mix well before serving.

HINT: Break uncooked spaghetti into small pieces.

Each serving equals:

HE: 1¾ Protein • 1½ Vegetable • 1 Bread •
3 Optional Calories

186 Calories • 2 gm Fat • 14 gm Protein •
28 gm Carbohydrate • 922 mg Sodium • 19 mg Calcium •
2 gm Fiber

DIABETIC: 2 Meat • 1½ Starch • 1 Vegetable

Fall Franks and Sauerkraut

Imagine coming in chilled to the bone after a day spent raking leaves and rooting for the high school football team—and knowing that you've got this comforting dish ready to serve! Even if you think these ingredients sound mismatched and funny, give this sweet-and-yummy recipe a try. And save a few of those cheers for me.

☻ Serves 4 (1 cup)

1¾ cups (one 14½-ounce can) Frank's Bavarian-style sauerkraut, drained
¼ cup finely chopped onion
1½ cups cored, unpeeled, and chopped cooking apples
½ cup unsweetened apple juice
8 ounces Healthy Choice 97% fat-free frankfurters, diced

Spray a slow cooker container with butter-flavored cooking spray. In prepared container, combine sauerkraut, onion, and apples. Stir in apple juice. Add frankfurters. Mix well to combine. Cover and cook on LOW for 6 to 8 hours. Mix well before serving.

HINT: If you can't find Bavarian sauerkraut, use regular sauerkraut, ½ teaspoon caraway seeds, and 1 teaspoon Brown Sugar Twin.

Each serving equals:

HE: 1⅓ Protein • 1 Fruit • 1 Vegetable

153 Calories • 1 gm Fat • 10 gm Protein •
26 gm Carbohydrate • 971 mg Sodium • 7 mg Calcium •
3 gm Fiber

DIABETIC: 1 Meat • 1 Fruit • 1 Vegetable

Milwaukee Kielbasa and Bean Bake

Sausage used to be a real no-no for anyone hoping to lose weight or lower cholesterol, but I'm happy to report that the folks at Healthy Choice decided that it wasn't fair to make us go through life sausage-free! Their clever revision of this classic Polish meat is amazingly tasty and especially good in this recipe. The beer provides an intriguing dash of flavor but absolutely no alcohol, so feel free to serve this to both kids and adults. ☻ Serves 6 (scant 1 cup)

> 20 ounces (two 16-ounce cans) butter or lima beans, rinsed and drained
> 8 ounces Healthy Choice 97% lean Polish Kielbasa sausage, sliced into ½-inch pieces
> 1 cup chopped onion
> 1 cup (one 8-ounce can) Hunt's Tomato Sauce
> ½ cup lite beer or non-alcoholic beer
> 2 tablespoons Brown Sugar Twin
> 1 teaspoon prepared yellow mustard
> ½ teaspoon dried minced garlic

Spray a slow cooker container with butter-flavored cooking spray. In prepared container, combine beans, kielbasa, and onion. Add tomato sauce, beer, Brown Sugar Twin, mustard, and garlic. Mix well to combine. Cover and cook on LOW for 6 to 8 hours. Mix well before serving.

Each serving equals:

HE: 2½ Protein • 1 Vegetable • 12 Optional Calories

221 Calories • 5 gm Fat • 13 gm Protein • 31 gm Carbohydrate • 997 mg Sodium • 49 mg Calcium • 6 gm Fiber

DIABETIC: 2 Meat • 1½ Starch • 1 Vegetable

Potato Pepperoni Pizza Pot

I thought, one late evening before I fell asleep, what if I crossed pizza with potatoes and let it cook for hours? When I woke up the next morning, the recipe was already forming in my head. Is it a dish of pizza-flavored potatoes, or is it a potato pizza in a pot? You'll have to decide. Whatever you call it, it's really, really good.

○ Serves 6 (1 cup)

> 9 cups shredded loose-packed frozen potatoes
> ½ cup finely chopped onion
> ½ cup (one 2.5-ounce jar) sliced mushrooms, drained
> ¾ cup shredded Kraft reduced-fat mozzarella cheese
> ¾ cup shredded Kraft reduced-fat Cheddar cheese
> 2 (3.5-ounce) packages Hormel reduced-fat pepperoni
> 1½ teaspoons Italian seasoning
> 1 cup (one 8-ounce can) Hunt's Tomato Sauce

Spray a slow cooker container with olive oil–flavored cooking spray. In prepared container, combine potatoes, onion, and mushrooms. Add mozzarella cheese, Cheddar cheese, and pepperoni. Mix well to combine. Stir Italian seasoning into tomato sauce. Evenly spoon sauce mixture over top. Cover and cook on LOW for 6 to 8 hours. Mix gently before serving.

HINT: Mr. Dell's frozen shredded potatoes are a good choice, or raw shredded potatoes may be used in place of frozen potatoes.

Each serving equals:

HE: 2½ Protein • 1 Bread • 1 Vegetable

281 Calories • 9 gm Fat • 22 gm Protein •
28 gm Carbohydrate • 964 mg Sodium •
324 mg Calcium • 4 gm Fiber

DIABETIC: 2½ Meat • 1½ Starch • 1 Vegetable

Cabbage Sausage Dinner

You used to have to supervise any cooked cabbage dish as it bubbled away on the stove, but your slow cooker has other plans for you now! Cut, chop, stir, and set the timer, then spend your free time making family scrapbooks or telling your grandkids about the "good old days."

☻ Serves 6 (1 full cup)

6 cups coarsely chopped cabbage

3 cups diced unpeeled raw potatoes

1 cup chopped onion

2 cups frozen cut green beans, thawed

1¾ cups (one 15-ounce can) Swanson Beef Broth

16 ounces Healthy Choice 97% lean Polish Kielbasa sausage, cut into
*   18 pieces*

Spray a slow cooker container with butter-flavored cooking spray. In prepared container, combine cabbage, potatoes, onion, and green beans. Pour beef broth evenly over vegetables. Arrange sausage pieces evenly over top. Cover and cook on LOW for 8 to 10 hours. Mix well before serving.

HINT: Thaw green beans by placing them in a colander and rinsing them under hot water for one minute.

Each serving equals:

HE: 2 Vegetable • 1¾ Protein • ½ Bread •
8 Optional Calories

191 Calories • 3 gm Fat • 13 gm Protein •
28 gm Carbohydrate • 911 mg Sodium • 96 mg Calcium •
4 gm Fiber

DIABETIC: 2 Vegetable • 2 Meat • 1 Starch

Crocked Corned Beef and Cabbage

I'm very proud of my Irish heritage on my father's side, and I've always enjoyed the dishes that are such a special part of that ethnic tradition. Over the years, I've created a variety of corned beef and cabbage dishes, but now I've got one that will cook just right while you're off at the parade.   ☻   Serves 6 (1½ cups)

1½ cups sliced carrots
1 cup chopped onion
7 cups coarsely chopped cabbage
6 (2.5-ounce) packages Carl Buddig lean corned beef, coarsely
    shredded
1½ cups water
1 teaspoon dried parsley flakes
⅛ teaspoon black pepper

Spray a slow cooker container with butter-flavored cooking spray. In prepared container, combine carrots, onion, cabbage, and corned beef. In a small bowl, combine water, parsley flakes, and black pepper. Evenly pour water mixture over top. Cover and cook on LOW for 6 to 8 hours. Mix well before serving.

Each serving equals:

HE: 2½ Protein • 2 Vegetable

157 Calories • 5 gm Fat • 16 gm Protein •
12 gm Carbohydrate • 982 mg Sodium • 76 mg Calcium •
4 gm Fiber

DIABETIC: 3 Meat • 2 Vegetable

My Best Beverages, Sauces, Dips, and Desserts

This section is what I refer to as my "marvelous miscellany"—a bundle of recipes that makes more of your slow cooker than you ever expected! I remember using mine way back when to serve steaming hot apple cider for a Halloween party my kids had. I don't think I ever employed it to make pasta sauce or party dips, and I'm pretty sure I never imagined stirring up a delectable turkey dressing that cooked for hours when the bird was in the oven. (But now you can!)

It's the desserts in this section that will truly take you back—those kinds of slow-cooked puddings that took hours to prepare on your Grandma's wood-burning stove, and those irresistible compotes and cobblers that would fill the house with the most amazing aromas of stewed fruits. I almost felt my grandmother looking over my shoulder as I was testing some of these wonderfully cozy and comforting dishes. My memories of her standing and stirring with a big wooden spoon are as vivid today as they were many years ago. She and my mother surely inspired the creation of these recipes—the spirit and warmth that they carry I joyfully share with you!

With an extensive selection of everything from beverages to breakfast dishes, party foods to the prettiest baked beauties, you're likely to set your slow cooker on the counter the day you bring it home from the store—and never, ever put it away! Whether you're serving up mugs of creamy hot chocolate after a sledding party (Pot of Cocoa) or setting out snacks for an NBA All-Star Game fan fest (Reuben Party Dip, Spicy Franks) or dazzling your family with a luscious dessert any evening at all (Apple Pie Bread Pudding or Raspberry Dessert Strata), you're sure to find the perfect "potful" in here somewhere!

My Best Beverages, Sauces, Dips, and Desserts

Pot of Cocoa

I thought of calling this "Cocoa for a Crowd" because that's what it definitely is! I think it would be absolutely delicious to go holiday caroling for a few hours, then return home to enjoy this pot of pleasure, along with some sweets. ☻ Serves 10 (½ cup)

3⅓ cups Carnation Nonfat Dry Milk Powder
½ cup unsweetened cocoa
¾ cup pourable Splenda or Sugar Twin
6 cups water
1 teaspoon vanilla extract

In a slow cooker container, combine dry milk powder, cocoa, and Splenda. Stir in water and vanilla extract. Cover and cook on LOW for 3 to 4 hours. Mix well with a wire whisk before serving.

Each serving equals:

HE: 1 Skim Milk • 19 Optional Calories

92 Calories • 0 gm Fat • 9 mg Protein •
14 gm Carbohydrate • 127 mg Sodium •
308 mg Calcium • 0 gm Fiber

DIABETIC: 1 Skim Milk

Variations: Spiced Cocoa—add 1½ teaspoons apple pie spice before adding water.

Mocha Cocoa—add 2 tablespoons dry instant coffee crystals before adding water.

Apricot-Apple Cider

If you like this recipe as much as I suspect you will, I bet you'll decide to keep a potful warm whenever company is coming! Once you lift the lid, it will fill your kitchen with a sweet aroma that is truly intoxicating.

◑ Serves 8 (¾ cup)

> 2 cups (one 16-ounce can) apricots, packed in fruit juice, undrained
> 2 cups unsweetened apple juice
> 2 cups water
> ¼ cup pourable Splenda or Sugar Twin
> 1½ tablespoons lemon juice
> 2 teaspoons apple pie spice

In a blender container, combine undrained apricots and apple juice. Cover and process on BLEND for 30 seconds or until mixture is smooth. Pour mixture into a slow cooker container. Stir in water, Splenda, lemon juice, and apple pie spice. Cover and cook on HIGH for 4 hours. Mix well before serving.

Each serving equals:

HE: 1 Fruit • 3 Optional Calories

60 Calories • 0 gm Fat • 0 gm Protein •
15 gm Carbohydrate • 5 mg Sodium • 19 mg Calcium •
1 gm Fiber

DIABETIC: 1 Fruit

Pot Luck Oatmeal

Sure, I could stir up a pot of oatmeal for breakfast, or even use the instant packet kind. But here's an unforgettable treat that will delight everyone sitting at your breakfast table—a dish so scrumptious that it's worth getting out of bed for, even on a cold, cold morning when there's snow to be shoveled!   ☻   Serves 4 (1 cup)

1½ cups (one 12-fluid-ounce can) Carnation Evaporated Skim Milk

½ cup water

2 tablespoons pourable Splenda or Sugar Twin

2 tablespoons Brown Sugar Twin

½ teaspoon apple pie spice

¼ cup Log Cabin or Cary's Sugar Free Maple Syrup

1 cup quick oats

1 cup cored, peeled and chopped cooking apples

¼ cup raisins

¼ cup chopped walnuts

Spray a slow cooker container with butter-flavored cooking spray. Pour evaporated skim milk and water into prepared container. Stir in Splenda, Brown Sugar Twin, apple pie spice, and maple syrup. Add oats, apples, raisins, and walnuts. Mix well to combine. Cover and cook on LOW for 8 hours. Mix well before serving.

HINTS: 1. Start cooking just before going to bed and it will be ready in the morning.

2. Enjoy as is or with skim milk.

Each serving equals:

HE: 1 Fruit • 1 Bread • ¾ Skim Milk • ½ Fat • ¼ Protein • 16 Optional Calories

234 Calories • 6 gm Fat • 10 gm Protein • 35 gm Carbohydrate • 160 mg Sodium • 268 mg Calcium • 3 gm Fiber

DIABETIC: 1 Fruit • 1 Starch • 1 Fat • ½ Skim Milk

Fresh Tomato Basil Sauce

Whether you've got vines overflowing with ripe red tomatoes or you've simply succumbed to a few baskets of the farmer's best at your local market, you're ready to stir up a spectacularly good pasta sauce. If you've got the tomatoes, make a couple of batches, and give it as a gift to close friends. ☻ Serves 6 (full ¾ cup)

5 cups peeled and finely chopped fresh tomatoes
½ cup finely chopped onion
1 cup (one 8-ounce can) Hunt's Tomato Sauce
2 tablespoons pourable Splenda or Sugar Twin
2 teaspoons dried basil leaves

Spray a slow cooker container with olive oil–flavored cooking spray. In prepared container, combine chopped tomatoes and onion. Stir in tomato sauce, Splenda, and basil. Cover and cook on LOW for 6 to 8 hours. Mix well before serving.

Each serving equals:

HE: 2½ Vegetable • 2 Optional Calories

---

52 Calories • 0 gm Fat • 2 gm Protein •
11 gm Carbohydrate • 261 mg Sodium • 24 mg Calcium •
3 gm Fiber

DIABETIC: 2 Vegetable

Simple Spaghetti Sauce

It's true that in the United States, we can get tomatoes most of the year, but they're often not that flavorful—especially not for a fresh sauce like the one I shared earlier. The rest of the year, you can still make your own delicious sauce using handy canned ingredients. The result will surprise you in its savory splendor.   ☻   Serves 6 (¾ cup)

1¾ cups (one 15-ounce can) Hunt's Tomato Sauce
1¾ cups (one 14½-ounce can) stewed tomatoes, finely chopped and
    undrained
¾ cup reduced-sodium tomato juice
¼ cup water
½ cup finely chopped onion
1 cup (one 4-ounce can) sliced mushrooms, undrained
1 tablespoon pourable Splenda or Sugar Twin
2 tablespoons grated Kraft fat-free Parmesan cheese
1½ teaspoons Italian seasoning
⅛ teaspoon black pepper

Spray a slow cooker container with olive oil–flavored cooking spray. In prepared container, combine tomato sauce, undrained tomatoes, tomato juice, and water. Stir in onion and undrained mushrooms. Add Splenda, Parmesan cheese, Italian seasoning, and black pepper. Mix well to combine. Cover and cook on LOW for 6 to 8 hours. Mix well before serving.

Each serving equals:

HE: 2½ Vegetable • 6 Optional Calories

72 Calories • 0 gm Fat • 3 gm Protein •
15 gm Carbohydrate • 762 mg Sodium • 45 mg Calcium •
3 gm Fiber

DIABETIC: 2½ Vegetable

Pot of Sage Dressing

Does your family call it dressing or stuffing, that irresistible bread-based herb-flavored treat that is too often relegated to holidays alone? Whatever it's called, it's a great side dish year round, and here's a simple recipe that delivers a tasty result.   ☻   Serves 8 (¾ cup)

2 cups finely chopped celery

1 cup finely chopped onion

1 cup (one 4-ounce can) sliced mushrooms, drained

16 slices reduced-calorie bread, torn into small pieces

2 cups (one 16-ounce can) Healthy Request Chicken Broth

2 teaspoons dried sage

½ teaspoon dried poultry seasoning

1 teaspoon dried parsley flakes

⅛ teaspoon black pepper

Spray a slow cooker container with butter-flavored cooking spray. In prepared container, combine celery, onion, mushrooms, and bread pieces. In a small bowl, combine chicken broth, sage, poultry seasoning, parsley flakes, and black pepper. Pour broth mixture evenly over bread mixture. Mix well to combine. Cover and cook on LOW for 6 to 8 hours. Mix well before serving.

Each serving equals:

HE: 1 Bread • 1 Vegetable • 4 Optional Calories

121 Calories • 1 gm Fat • 6 gm Protein •
22 gm Carbohydrate • 459 mg Sodium • 56 mg Calcium •
5 gm Fiber

DIABETIC: 1 Starch • 1 Vegetable

Reuben Party Dip

If you adore that overstuffed deli treat known as a Reuben sandwich, I've got something truly seductive for your next special event! Served hot from the pot or even lukewarm, this dip will dazzle anyone lucky enough to taste it. ☻ Serves 8 (⅓ cup)

2 cups (one 16-ounce can) sauerkraut, drained
¼ cup Kraft Fat Free Thousand Island Dressing
2 tablespoons Kraft fat-free mayonnaise
2 (2.5-ounce) packages Carl Buddig lean corned beef, shredded
11 (¾-ounce) slices Kraft reduced-fat Swiss cheese, shredded

In a slow cooker container sprayed with butter-flavored cooking spray, combine sauerkraut, Thousand Island dressing, and mayonnaise. Add corned beef and Swiss cheese. Mix well to combine. Cover and cook on LOW for 2 hours. Mix well before serving.

HINT: Good served on cocktail rye bread.

Each serving equals:

HE: 2 Protein • ½ Vegetable • 15 Optional Calories

143 Calories • 7 gm Fat • 12 gm Protein •
8 gm Carbohydrate • 989 mg Sodium • 261 mg Calcium •
0 gm Fiber

DIABETIC: 1½ Meat • ½ Vegetable

Tom's Bean Dip

My son Tom put kidney beans on his "no" list at a young age, but that doesn't mean he abstains from all beans, I promise you. He and Angie lived for a while in the Southwest and developed a real taste for chips with tangy dip. Tommy, this one's for you!

☺ Serves 8 (½ cup)

20 ounces (two 16-ounce cans) pinto beans, rinsed and drained

1 cup chunky salsa (mild, medium, or hot)

1 cup + 2 tablespoons shredded Kraft reduced-fat Cheddar cheese

1 cup Land O Lakes no-fat sour cream

Spray a slow cooker container with olive oil–flavored cooking spray. In a medium bowl, mash pinto beans with a potato masher or fork. Stir in salsa. Add bean mixture to prepared container. Add Cheddar cheese and sour cream. Mix well to combine. Cover and cook on LOW for 2 hours. Mix well before serving.

HINT: Great with fat-free Nacho Chips.

Each serving equals:

HE: 2 Protein • ¼ Vegetable • ¼ Slider •
10 Optional Calories

135 Calories • 3 gm Fat • 8 gm Protein •
19 gm Carbohydrate • 532 mg Sodium •
175 mg Calcium • 3 gm Fiber

DIABETIC: 1½ Meat • 1 Starch/Carbohydrate

Wimp's Chile Con Queso

I'm an equal opportunity cook when it comes to spicing my food—I think you should stir in whatever level of heat that makes you happy! Cliff likes smoke coming out his ears; my kids definitely prefer some sizzle on the tongue; and I like it mild, so I guess I'm the wimp in question. But this recipe will work for all of us.

☺ Serves 8 (½ cup)

> 1 (16-ounce) package Velveeta Light processed cheese, cubed
> 2 cups thick and chunky salsa (mild, medium, or hot)
> 1 teaspoon dried parsley flakes
> ¼ cup (one 2-ounce jar) chopped pimiento, undrained

Spray a slow cooker container with butter-flavored cooking spray. In prepared container, combine Velveeta cheese and salsa. Add parsley flakes and undrained pimiento. Mix well to combine. Cover and cook on LOW for 2 to 3 hours. Mix well before serving.

HINT: Good with corn chips, crackers, or spooned over a hot baked potato.

Each serving equals:

HE: 2 Protein • ½ Vegetable

120 Calories • 4 gm Fat • 14 gm Protein • 7 gm Carbohydrate • 305 mg Sodium • 389 mg Calcium • 0 gm Fiber

DIABETIC: 2 Meat • ½ Vegetable

Mexican Grande Dip

Isn't it a relief to have great-tasting party food that doesn't have to also be high in fat? There isn't a teen in town who wouldn't delight in a dollop of this meaty, spicy dip—and we're all teens when it comes to snacking, aren't we? ☻ Serves 8 (½ cup)

16 ounces extra lean ground turkey or beef

1 cup chopped onion

1 cup chopped green bell pepper

1 cup chunky salsa (mild, medium, or hot)

1 (10¾-ounce) can Healthy Request Cream of Mushroom Soup

2 teaspoons taco seasoning

1½ cups cubed Velveeta Light processed cheese

In a large skillet sprayed with olive oil–flavored cooking spray, brown meat, onion, and green pepper. In a slow cooker container sprayed with olive oil–flavored cooking spray, combine salsa, mushroom soup, and taco seasoning. Stir in browned meat mixture. Add Velveeta cheese. Mix well to combine. Cover and cook on LOW for 3 to 4 hours. Mix well before serving.

Each serving equals:

HE: 2½ Protein • ¾ Vegetable • ¼ Slider •
1 Optional Calorie

150 Calories • 6 gm Fat • 15 gm Protein •
9 gm Carbohydrate • 353 mg Sodium • 145 mg Calcium •
1 gm Fiber

DIABETIC: 2½ Meat • ½ Vegetable •
½ Starch/Carbohydrate

Let's Party! Bean Dip

Is there a reason why so many of our favorite festive foods come from South of the Border? Maybe it's the sunshine or the lively music of Mexico, or maybe it's just that insistence on intense flavors in Mexican cuisine. Here's a recipe that sends out invitations with every taste—turn up the volume on the CD player, and let's dance!

☻ Serves 8 (½ cup)

> 8 ounces extra lean ground turkey or beef
> 1 cup chopped onion
> 1 cup (one 8-ounce can) Hunt's Tomato Sauce
> 1 cup chunky salsa (mild, medium, or hot)
> 1½ teaspoons chili seasoning
> ½ cup sliced ripe olives
> 10 ounces (one 16-ounce can) pinto beans, rinsed and drained ☆
> ¾ cup shredded Kraft reduced-fat Cheddar cheese

In a large skillet sprayed with olive oil–flavored cooking spray, brown meat and onion. In a slow cooker container sprayed with olive oil–flavored cooking spray, combine browned meat mixture, tomato sauce, salsa, chili seasoning, and olives. Mash half of pinto beans with a potato masher. Stir both mashed and remaining unmashed beans into meat mixture. Cover and cook on HIGH for 2 hours. Just before serving, stir Cheddar cheese into hot mixture.

Each serving equals:

HE: 1¾ Protein • 1 Vegetable • ¼ Fat •
8 Optional Calories

---

137 Calories • 5 gm Fat • 10 gm Protein •
13 gm Carbohydrate • 622 mg Sodium •
101 mg Calcium • 3 gm Fiber

DIABETIC: 1½ Meat • 1 Vegetable • ½ Starch • ½ Fat

Hot Spinach Cheese Dip

There's a famous hot dip made of cream cheese and flavored with cheese that was first popular back in the 1950s, but it didn't stay warm very long, and it was very high in calories and fat. Well, here's a dip for the new century and for all of us who care as much about good health as great taste. It's still scrumptious, but now it's sinless, too!

⏺ Serves 8 (¼ cup)

1 (8-ounce) package Philadelphia fat-free cream cheese
1 (10-ounce) package frozen chopped spinach, thawed and well
    drained
1 cup finely chopped onion
½ teaspoon dried minced garlic
1½ cups shredded Kraft reduced-fat Cheddar cheese

Spray a slow cooker container with butter-flavored cooking spray. In prepared container, stir cream cheese with a spoon until soft. Stir in spinach and onion. Add garlic and Cheddar cheese. Mix well to combine. Cover and cook on HIGH for 1 hour. Mix well before serving.

HINTS: 1. Thaw spinach by placing it in a colander and rinsing it under hot water for one minute.
2. Good with crackers and chips. Also good spooned over a hot baked potato.

Each serving equals:

HE: 1½ Protein • ½ Vegetable

95 Calories • 3 gm Fat • 11 gm Protein •
6 gm Carbohydrate • 341 mg Sodium • 264 mg Calcium •
1 gm Fiber

DIABETIC: 1 Meat • ½ Vegetable

Spicy Franks

Whenever I speak to large groups, many people tell me what a relief it is to use my recipes because they never really learned how to mix ingredients for flavorful sauces—and so they get bored with the same old meats and poultry dishes. I'm happy to share the results of a recent experiment with a blend of varied flavors. This dish is spicy without being, as the song goes, "too darn hot." ☻ Serves 8 (¼ cup)

  1 cup (one 8-ounce can) Hunt's Tomato Sauce
  2 tablespoons pourable Splenda or Sugar Twin
  2 tablespoons Brown Sugar Twin
  1 tablespoon cider vinegar
  1 tablespoon reduced-sodium soy sauce
  1 tablespoon Dijon Country mustard
  1 (16 ounce) package Healthy Choice 97% fat-free frankfurters, cut
      into 1-inch pieces

Spray a slow cooker container with butter-flavored cooking spray. In prepared container, combine tomato sauce, Splenda, Brown Sugar Twin, vinegar, soy sauce, and mustard. Stir in frankfurter pieces. Cover and cook on HIGH for 2 hours. Mix well before serving.

Each serving equals:

HE: 1⅓ Protein • ½ Vegetable • 3 Optional Calories

69 Calories • 1 gm Fat • 8 gm Protein •
7 gm Carbohydrate • 867 mg Sodium • 4 mg Calcium •
0 gm Fiber

DIABETIC: 1 Meat • ½ Vegetable

Glazed Cocktail Franks

These make-your-own party snacks are as much fun to nibble on as they were to create! The golden glaze looks so beautiful and festive, you don't need a roomful of guests to serve these delights. But I'm a believer in celebrating whenever you can!   ☻   Serves 8 (3 pieces)

½ cup apricot spreadable fruit

¼ cup prepared yellow mustard

2 teaspoons dried parsley flakes

2 teaspoons dried onion flakes

1 (16-ounce) package Healthy Choice 97% fat-free frankfurters, each cut into 2-inch piece

Spray a slow cooker container with butter-flavored cooking spray. In prepared container, combine spreadable fruit, mustard, parsley flakes, and onion flakes. Stir in frankfurter pieces. Cover and cook on LOW for 2 hours. Mix well before serving. When serving, evenly spoon sauce over frankfurter pieces.

Each serving equals:

HE: 1⅓ Protein • 1 Fruit

105 Calories • 1 gm Fat • 8 gm Protein •
16 gm Carbohydrate • 676 mg Sodium • 8 mg Calcium •
0 gm Fiber

DIABETIC: 1 Meat • 1 Fruit

Cinnamon Applesauce

Even if you've never considered making applesauce from scratch, this recipe may be just the enticement you need. Why not make it a family project, starting with apple picking at a nearby orchard? As long as the apples hold out, you've got a wonderful way to top your cereal or pancakes.   ◐   Serves 8 (¼ cup)

> 6 cups cored, peeled and chopped cooking apples
> 2 tablespoons lemon juice
> ½ cup pourable Splenda or Sugar Twin
> 2 tablespoons Brown Sugar Twin
> 1 teaspoon ground cinnamon

Spray a slow cooker container with butter-flavored cooking spray. In prepared container, combine apples, lemon juice, Splenda, and Brown Sugar Twin. Stir in cinnamon. Cover and cook on LOW for 8 hours. Mash well with a potato masher.

HINTS: 1. Granny Smith apples work great.
         2. Good warm or cold.

Each serving equals:

HE: 1½ Fruit • 8 Optional Calories

104 Calories • 0 gm Fat • 0 gm Protein •
26 gm Carbohydrate • 7 mg Sodium • 13 mg Calcium •
3 gm Fiber

DIABETIC: 1½ Fruit

Grandma's Rhubarb Sauce

This is one grandma who has been stirring up rhubarb recipes even before her oldest grandchild was a glimmer in her eye! But until now, I never employed my slow cooker to create this truly delectable topping—and I am so glad I did!   ☻   Serves 8 (scant ½ cup)

½ cup water
1 cup pourable Splenda or Sugar Twin
1 (4-serving) package JELL-O sugar-free strawberry gelatin
8 cups chopped fresh or frozen rhubarb, thawed

In a slow cooker container, combine water, Splenda, and dry gelatin. Stir in rhubarb. Cover and cook on LOW for 8 hours. Mix well before serving.

Each serving equals:

HE: 2 Vegetable • 17 Optional Calories

24 Calories • 0 gm Fat • 1 gm Protein •
5 gm Carbohydrate • 7 mg Sodium • 105 mg Calcium •
2 gm Fiber

DIABETIC: 1 Vegetable

Peach Melba Patchwork Sauce

My daughter, Becky, has adored peach "anything" since she was a little girl, and so I had her in mind when I was creating this beautifully tinted and flavored fruity sauce. Her husband, John, says it's terrific on top of any flavor ice cream, but particularly vanilla.

○ Serves 6 (¾ cup)

> *3 cups frozen unsweetened sliced peaches, partially thawed, chopped, and undrained*
> *1½ cups frozen unsweetened raspberries, thawed and undrained*
> *½ cup pourable Splenda or Sugar Twin*

Spray a slow cooker container with butter-flavored cooking spray. Add peaches, raspberries, and Splenda to prepared container. Mix well to combine. Cover and cook on HIGH for 2 hours. Mix gently before serving.

Each serving equals:

HE: 1 Fruit • 8 Optional Calories

56 Calories • 0 gm Fat • 1 gm Protein •
13 gm Carbohydrate • 0 mg Sodium • 11 mg Calcium •
4 gm Fiber

DIABETIC: 1 Fruit

Hawaiian Rhubarb Pineapple Compote

This is such a super method for making fruit compote, I could almost publish a cookbooklet of just stewed fruit recipes! The taste of the tropics is so strong and special in this blend, I felt a whisper of a summer breeze as I spooned it up.   ☻   Serves 6 (½ cup)

3 cups (three 8-ounce cans) pineapple tidbits, packed in fruit juice, drained, and ½ cup liquid reserved

6 to 8 drops red food coloring

¼ cup pourable Splenda or Sugar Twin

½ teaspoon coconut extract

3 cups chopped fresh or frozen rhubarb, thawed

2 tablespoons flaked coconut

Spray a slow cooker container with butter-flavored cooking spray. In prepared container, combine pineapple, reserved liquid, red food coloring, Splenda, and coconut extract. Stir in rhubarb. Cover and cook on LOW for 6 to 8 hours. When serving, top each with 1 teaspoon coconut. Good warm or cold.

HINT: If you can't find pineapple tidbits, coarsely chop chunk pineapple.

Each serving equals:

HE: 1 Fruit • 1 Vegetable • 9 Optional Calories

---

60 Calories • 0 gm Fat • 1 gm Protein •
14 gm Carbohydrate • 7 mg Sodium • 71 mg Calcium •
 2 gm Fiber

DIABETIC: 1 Fruit

Cranberry Orange Relish

There used to be a great Ben and Jerry's sorbet flavor that combined these two fruits to dazzling effect, but it seems to have been discontinued, alas. Don't mourn a moment longer, though, now that you can cook up a relish to serve warm or cold that weaves the wonderful magic of these two once more. ◐ Serves 6 (½ cup)

½ cup unsweetened orange juice
¼ cup water
1 cup pourable Splenda or Sugar Twin
3 cups chopped fresh or frozen cranberries
1 cup (one 11-ounce can) mandarin oranges, rinsed and drained

In a slow cooker container, combine orange juice, water, and Splenda. Stir in cranberries and mandarin oranges. Cover and cook on LOW for 6 to 8 hours. Mix well before serving.

Each serving equals:

HE: 1 Fruit • 16 Optional Calories

48 Calories • 0 gm Fat • 0 gm Protein •
12 gm Carbohydrate • 3 mg Sodium • 10 mg Calcium •
2 gm Fiber

DIABETIC: 1 Fruit

Pumpkin Custard Pudding

Even the word "custard" sounds lush and smooth, doesn't it? And when you add pumpkin to the mix, you've got a dream of a dessert sure to please family and friends from 5 to 95! It's pretty to look at and luscious to lick off a spoon.   ☻   Serves 6 (¾ cup)

> 2 cups (one 15-ounce can) pumpkin
>
> 1½ cups (one 12-fluid-ounce can) Carnation Evaporated Skim Milk
>
> 2 teaspoons vanilla extract
>
> 2½ teaspoons pumpkin pie spice
>
> ½ cup pourable Splenda or Sugar Twin
>
> ½ cup + 1 tablespoon Bisquick Reduced Fat Baking Mix
>
> 2 tablespoons reduced-calorie margarine
>
> 2 eggs or equivalent in egg substitute

Spray a slow cooker container with butter-flavored cooking spray. In a large bowl, combine pumpkin, evaporated skim milk, vanilla extract, and pumpkin pie spice. Add Splenda, baking mix, margarine, and eggs. Using an electric mixer, mix on HIGH until mixture is smooth. Pour into prepared container and cook on LOW for 6 to 8 hours. Mix gently before serving.

Each serving equals:

HE: ⅔ Vegetable • ½ Skim Milk • ½ Bread • ½ Fat • ⅓ Protein • 8 Optional Calories

---

156 Calories • 4 gm Fat • 8 gm Protein • 22 gm Carbohydrate • 280 mg Sodium • 208 mg Calcium • 3 gm Fiber

---

DIABETIC: 1 Starch/Carbohydrate • ½ Skim Milk • ½ Fat

Old-fashioned Rice Pudding

One of the nicest aspects of using a slow cooker is the chance to enjoy recipes that don't require "instant" readiness! Sure, I can make quick rice pudding (and I often do, since my Cliff and I both like it), but oh, how sweet it is to cook it long and slow and smooth and rich. The good old days are here again! ☽ Serves 6 (²/₃ cup)

3 cups cold cooked rice

1½ cups (one 12-fluid-ounce can) Carnation Evaporated Skim Milk

½ cup water

½ cup pourable Splenda or Sugar Twin

1 tablespoon vanilla extract

2 tablespoons reduced-calorie margarine

1½ teaspoons ground cinnamon

¾ cup raisins

Spray a slow cooker container with butter-flavored cooking spray. In prepared container, combine rice, evaporated skim milk, water, and Splenda. Stir in vanilla extract, margarine, and cinnamon. Add raisins. Mix well to combine. Cover and cook on LOW for 2 to 3 hours. Mix well before serving.

HINT: 2 cups uncooked instant rice usually cooks to about 3 cups.

Each serving equals:

HE: 1 Bread • 1 Fruit • ½ Skim Milk • ½ Fat • 8 Optional Calories

174 Calories • 2 gm Fat • 5 gm Protein • 34 gm Carbohydrate • 132 mg Sodium • 175 mg Calcium • 2 gm Fiber

DIABETIC: 1 Starch • 1 Fruit • ½ Skim Milk

Baked Fruit Cocktail Rice Pudding

Fruit cocktail was everyone's favorite back in the 1950s, but in recent years it's less commonly used as more canned fruits have become available. But it's still as good as it always was—the taste of childhood stirred into a gloriously rich rice pudding.   ☻   Serves 6 (²/₃ cup)

1 (4-serving) package JELL-O sugar-free vanilla cook-and-serve
    pudding mix
1½ cups (one 12-fluid-ounce can) Carnation evaporated skim milk
2 cups (one 16-ounce can) fruit cocktail, packed in fruit juice,
    undrained
1 teaspoon vanilla extract
1⅓ cups uncooked instant rice
¼ cup chopped walnuts

Spray a slow cooker container with butter-flavored cooking spray. In prepared container, combine dry pudding mix and evaporated skim milk. Stir in undrained fruit cocktail and vanilla extract. Add uncooked rice and walnuts. Mix well to combine. Cover and cook on HIGH for 2 to 3 hours. Mix well before serving.

Each serving equals:

HE: ²/₃ Bread • ²/₃ Fruit • ½ Skim Milk • ⅓ Fat •
¼ Slider • 3 Optional Calories

191 Calories • 3 gm Fat • 6 gm Protein •
35 gm Carbohydrate • 162 mg Sodium • 176 Calcium •
1 gm Fiber

DIABETIC: 1 Starch • 1 Fruit • ½ Skim Milk • ½ Fat

Paradise Fruit Cobbler

Paradise has always meant to me a little piece of heaven we're allowed to experience here on earth. A few times on vacation, I felt as if I'd discovered that special place, and I hope you have, too. Here's the taste of that happy feeling in a sweet and crusty dessert that doesn't cost you a single frequent flyer mile! ☻ Serves 6 (1 cup)

1 (7.5-ounce) package Pillsbury refrigerated buttermilk biscuits
1 cup (one 8-ounce can) crushed pineapple, packed in fruit juice, undrained
2 cups (one 16-ounce can) apricot halves, packed in fruit juice, undrained
1/4 cup pourable Splenda or Sugar Twin
2 tablespoons flaked coconut

Bake biscuits according to package directions. Place biscuits on a wire rack and allow to cool completely. When cooled, cut each biscuit into 3 pieces. Spray a slow cooker container with butter-flavored cooking spray. In prepared container, combine undrained pineapple, undrained apricots, and Splenda. Stir in biscuit pieces. Evenly sprinkle coconut over top. Cover and cook on LOW for 2 hours. Mix gently before serving.

Each serving equals:

HE: 1¼ Bread • 1 Fruit • 9 Optional Calories

150 Calories • 2 gm Fat • 3 gm Protein •
30 gm Carbohydrate • 311 mg Sodium • 16 mg Calcium •
3 gm Fiber

DIABETIC: 1½ Starch/Carbohydrate • 1 Fruit

Apple Pie Bread Pudding

If you love bread pudding as much as I do, but wouldn't mind a bit if it smelled and tasted like Mom's apple pie, have I got a recipe for you! I wanted to test this an extra time or two just because it tasted so good (and because I love bread pudding)! ◑ Serves 6 (¾ cup)

> 12 slices reduced-calorie white bread, torn into medium-size pieces
> 3½ cups cored, peeled, and chopped cooking apples
> 1 cup unsweetened apple juice
> ½ cup Diet Mountain Dew
> ½ cup pourable Splenda or Sugar Twin
> 1½ teaspoons apple pie spice

Spray a slow cooker container with butter-flavored cooking spray. In prepared container, combine bread pieces and apples. In a small bowl, combine apple juice, Diet Mountain Dew, Splenda, and apple pie spice. Drizzle juice mixture evenly over bread mixture. Mix gently to combine. Cover and cook on LOW for 6 hours. Mix well before serving.

Each serving equals:

HE: 1½ Fruit • 1 Bread • 8 Optional Calories

157 Calories • 1 gm Fat • 5 gm Protein •
32 gm Carbohydrate • 233 mg Sodium • 42 mg Calcium •
2 gm Fiber

DIABETIC: 1½ Fruit • 1 Starch

Apple-Mincemeat Bread Pudding

Don't worry, there's no "meat" in this mincemeat recipe, just a crunchy-sweet melange of fruit and nuts that is a fantastic complement to the creamy lusciousness of the pudding. It's a five-star winner!

○ Serves 6 (1 cup)

> 1 (4-serving) package JELL-O sugar-free vanilla cook-and-serve
>   pudding mix
> ½ cup unsweetened apple juice
> 2½ cups water
> 1½ teaspoons apple pie spice
> 1½ cups cored, peeled, and chopped cooking apples
> ¼ cup raisins
> ¼ cup chopped walnuts
> 12 slices reduced-calorie Italian or French bread, toasted and cut into
>   1-inch cubes

Spray a slow cooker container with butter-flavored cooking spray. In a large bowl, combine dry pudding mix, apple juice, water, and apple pie spice. Stir in apples, raisins, and walnuts. Add bread. Mix gently to combine. Spoon mixture into prepared container. Cover and cook on HIGH for 2 hours. Let set for 5 minutes before serving.

Each serving equals:

HE: 1 Bread • 1 Fruit • ⅓ Fat • ¼ Slider •
3 Optional Calories

180 Calories • 4 gm Fat • 6 gm Protein •
30 gm Carbohydrate • 309 mg Sodium • 44 mg Calcium •
2 gm Fiber

DIABETIC: 1 Starch • 1 Fruit • ½ Fat

Pineapple Bread Pudding

Yes, I've included more bread pudding recipes than usual in this cookbook, but the slow cooker is the ideal appliance for my favorite dessert! If you could nibble pineapple from morning to night, this is the one you should try first.   ☻   Serves 6 (⅔ cup)

> 2 cups (two 8-ounce cans) crushed pineapple, packed in fruit juice, undrained
>
> 1 cup water
>
> 1 (4-serving) package JELL-O sugar-free vanilla cook-and-serve pudding mix
>
> 1 cup (one 8-ounce can) pineapple tidbits, packed in fruit juice, undrained
>
> 1 teaspoon ground cinnamon
>
> 12 slices reduced-calorie bread, toasted and cut into cubes

Spray a slow cooker container with butter-flavored cooking spray. In a large bowl, combine undrained crushed pineapple, water, and dry pudding mix. Stir in undrained pineapple tidbits and cinnamon. Pour mixture into prepared container. Add bread cubes. Mix well to combine. Cover and cook on LOW for 6 to 8 hours. Mix well before serving.

HINT: If you can't find pineapple tidbits, coarsely chop chunk pineapple.

Each serving equals:

HE: 1 Bread • 1 Fruit • 13 Optional Calories

---

154 Calories • 1 gm Fat • 5 gm Protein •
31 gm Carbohydrate • 308 mg Sodium • 58 mg Calcium •
2 gm Fiber

DIABETIC: 1 Starch • 1 Fruit

Pot of Peaches Kugel Dessert

If you're not familiar with the term "kugel," it's an Eastern European noodle pudding dish that is most commonly served on festive Jewish holidays. The most traditional version generally includes raisins as the primary fruit, but I thought that peaches—ripe, ripe ones—would be exceptionally good served this way. ☻ Serves 6 (²/₃ cup)

²/₃ cup Carnation Nonfat Dry Milk Powder

1 cup water

¹/₂ cup pourable Splenda or Sugar Twin

1 teaspoon vanilla extract

3 cups cooked noodles, rinsed and drained

3 cups peeled and chopped fresh peaches

3 tablespoons chopped pecans

Spray a slow cooker container with butter-flavored cooking spray. In prepared container, combine dry milk powder, water, Splenda, and vanilla extract. Stir in noodles. Add peaches and pecans. Cover and cook on HIGH for 2 hours. Mix well before serving.

HINT: 2²/₃ cups uncooked noodles usually cooks to about 3 cups.

Each serving equals:

HE: 1 Bread • 1 Fruit • ¹/₂ Fat • ¹/₃ Skim Milk

191 Calories • 3 gm Fat • 7 gm Protein •
34 gm Carbohydrate • 47 mg Sodium • 115 mg Calcium •
3 gm Fiber

DIABETIC: 1¹/₂ Starch/Carbohydrate • 1 Fruit • ¹/₂ Fat

Raspberry Dessert Strata

Here's another "bread-based" dessert delight that simply oozes irresistible ingredients—beautiful fresh berries, crunchy nuts, sweet chocolate bits, layered with a vanilla custard that will win your heart in no time!　　○　Serves 8 (1 cup)

12 slices reduced-calorie white bread, cut into 1-inch cubes ☆

½ cup mini chocolate chips ☆

3 cups fresh raspberries ☆

¼ cup slivered almonds ☆

2 (4-serving) packages JELL-O sugar-free vanilla cook-and-serve pudding mix

⅔ cup Carnation Nonfat Dry Milk Powder

3 cups water

1½ teaspoons almond extract

Spray a slow cooker container with butter-flavored cooking spray. Layer half of bread cubes, half of chocolate chips, half of raspberries, and half of almonds in prepared container. Repeat layer. In a large bowl, combine dry pudding mixes and dry milk powder. Stir in water and almond extract. Evenly pour mixture over top. Cover and cook on HIGH for 2 hours or until set. Let set for 5 minutes before serving.

Each serving equals:

HE: ¾ Bread • ½ Fruit • ¼ Skim Milk • ¼ Fat •
½ Slider • 15 Optional Calories

193 Calories • 5 gm Fat • 7 gm Protein •
30 gm Carbohydrate • 320 mg Sodium •
122 mg Calcium • 4 gm Fiber

DIABETIC: 1½ Starch/Carbohydrate • 1 Fat • ½ Fruit

Peanut Butter and Hot Fudge Pleasure Pot

If ever a dessert sounded too good to be true, it might be this one! I mean, I'm offering you peanut butter and hot fudge, served up warm and rich and creamy-good. Mm-mmm. Imagine a melted peanut butter cup, and you've got a hint of what pleasure is contained in this dish!

⏺ Serves 6 (scant ½ cup)

> 1 cup + 2 tablespoons Bisquick Reduced Fat Baking Mix
>
> 1 cup pourable Splenda or Sugar Twin ☆
>
> ¼ cup skim milk
>
> 2 teaspoons vegetable oil
>
> 2 teaspoons vanilla extract
>
> ¼ cup Peter Pan reduced-fat chunky peanut butter
>
> 3 tablespoons unsweetened cocoa
>
> 2 cups boiling water

Spray a slow cooker container with butter-flavored cooking spray. In a medium bowl, combine baking mix and ¼ cup Splenda. Add skim milk, vegetable oil, and vanilla extract. Mix well until mixture is smooth. Stir in peanut butter. Pour batter into prepared container. In a small bowl, combine remaining ¾ cup Splenda and cocoa. Gradually stir in boiling water. Carefully pour mixture over batter in slow cooker. DO NOT stir. Cover and cook on HIGH for 2 hours. Evenly spoon into 6 dessert dishes.

HINTS: 1. This is supposed to be an oohey gooey mess!
2. Good served warm with sugar- and fat-free vanilla ice cream.

Each serving equals:

HE: 1 Bread • 1 Fat • ⅔ Protein • ¼ Slider •
7 Optional Calories

175 Calories • 7 gm Fat • 5 gm Protein •
23 gm Carbohydrate • 317 mg Sodium • 39 mg Calcium •
2 gm Fiber

DIABETIC: 1 Starch/Carbohydrate • 1 Fat • ½ Meat

Peanut Butter Apple Crumble

I've saved some of the very best for last, especially for all you members of the Peanut Butter Lovers' Club! If you've ever dipped an apple slice into an open jar of chunky peanut butter, you know what a great couple they make. This cozy-warm dessert celebrates the two in a duet you will surely love. ☻   Serves 6 (⅔ cup)

> 4½ cups cored, peeled, and sliced cooking apples
> ½ cup quick oats
> 6 tablespoons Bisquick Reduced Fat Baking Mix
> ⅓ cup pourable Splenda or Sugar Twin
> 1 teaspoon apple pie spice
> 6 tablespoons Peter Pan reduced-fat chunky peanut butter

Spray a slow cooker container with butter-flavored cooking spray. Evenly arrange apple slices in prepared container. In a medium bowl, combine oats, baking mix, Splenda, and apple pie spice. Add peanut butter. Mix with a fork until mixture is crumbly. Sprinkle crumb mixture evenly over apples. Cover and cook on LOW for 6 to 8 hours. Mix well before serving.

Each serving equals:

HE: 1½ Fruit • 1 Protein • 1 Fat • ⅔ Bread •
5 Optional Calories

190 Calories • 6 gm Fat • 5 gm Protein •
29 gm Carbohydrate • 162 mg Sodium • 17 mg Calcium •
4 gm Fiber

DIABETIC: 1½ Fruit • ½ Meat • ½ Fat •
½ Starch/Carbohydrate

Slow-Cookin', Good Eatin' Menus

Irealize that most of you probably don't own more than one slow cooker, but I thought that once you paged through the recipes in this book, you might decide to pick up another one (or even two)! And of course some of these dishes can be made in advance and reheated in your microwave while another is bubbling in the slow cooker. Because so many of my readers have told me they appreciate my suggestions for menus, I decided to include a batch here.

"No Time to Cook?" Sunday Supper
Creamy Baked Potato Soup
Country Sweet-Sour Cabbage
Terrific Turkey Hash
Apple Pie Bread Pudding

"Everybody's Busy!" Not-So-Frantic Family Dinner
Mexican Chicken Stew
Southwestern Corn Scallop
Savory Green Beans
Old-Fashioned Rice Pudding

"Too Hot to Turn on the Oven" Sultry Summer Soiree
Zucchini Souffle Pot
Easy Jambalaya
Sensational Baked Beans
Pot of Peaches Dessert

"Something Smells Wonderful!" Lazy Weekend Brunch
>Grandma's Custard Corn Pudding
>Ham and Potatoes Au Gratin
>Peach Melba Patchwork Cobbler
>Pot of Cocoa

"A Chicken in Every Pot" Election Eve Party
>Hot Spinach Cheese Dip
>Spicy Apricot-Glazed Chicken
>Peanut Butter Apple Crumble
>Apricot-Apple Cider

"Blowing the Lid Off" Graduation Day Delight
>Remarkable Reuben Dip
>Barbecued Chicken
>Sloppy Joes
>Raspberry Dessert Strata

Making Healthy Exchanges Work for You

You're now ready to begin a wonderful journey to better health. In the preceding pages, you've discovered the remarkable variety of good food available to you when you begin eating the Healthy Exchanges way. You've stocked your pantry and learned many of my food preparation secrets that will point you on the way to delicious success.

But before I let you go, I'd like to share a few tips that I've learned while traveling toward healthier eating habits. It took me a long time to learn how to eat *smarter*. In fact, I'm still working on it. But I am getting better. For years, I could *inhale* a five-course meal in five minutes flat—and still make room for a second helping of dessert!

Now I follow certain signposts on the road that help me stay on the right path. I hope these ideas will help point you in the right direction as well.

1. **Eat slowly** so your brain has time to catch up with your tummy. Cut and chew each bite slowly. Try putting your fork down between bites. Stop eating as soon as you feel full. Crumple your napkin and throw it on top of your plate so you don't continue to eat when you are no longer hungry.

2. **Smaller plates** may help you feel more satisfied by your food portions *and* limit the amount you can put on the plate.

3. **Watch portion size**. If you are *truly* hungry, you can always add more food to your plate once you've finished your initial serving. But remember to count the additional food accordingly.

4. **Always eat at your dining-room or kitchen table**. You deserve better than nibbling from an open refrigerator or over the sink. Make an attractive place setting, even if you're eating alone. Feed your eyes as well as your stomach. By always eating at a table, you will become much more aware of your true food intake. For some reason, many of us conveniently "forget" the food we swallow while standing over the stove or munching in the car or on the run.

5. **Avoid doing anything else while you are eating**. If you read the paper or watch television while you eat, it's easy to consume too much food without realizing it, because you are concentrating on something else besides what you're eating. Then, when you look down at your plate and see that it's empty, you wonder where all the food went and why you still feel hungry.

Day by day, as you travel the path to good health, it will become easier to make the right choices, to eat *smarter*. But don't ever fool yourself into thinking that you'll be able to put your eating habits on cruise control and forget about them. Making a commitment to eat good healthy food and sticking to it takes some effort. But with all the good-tasting recipes in this Healthy Exchanges cookbook, just think how well you're going to eat—and enjoy it—from now on!

Healthy Lean Bon Appetit!

Index

I want to hear from you . . .

Besides my family, the love of my life is creating "common folk" healthy recipes and solving everyday cooking questions in *The Healthy Exchanges Way*. Everyone who uses my recipes is considered part of the Healthy Exchanges Family, so please write to me if you have any questions, comments, or suggestions. I will do my best to answer. With your support, I'll continue to stir up even more recipes and cooking tips for the Family in the years to come.

Write to: JoAnna M. Lund
c/o Healthy Exchanges, Inc.
P.O. Box 80
DeWitt, IA 52742-0080

If you prefer, you can fax me at 1-563-659-2126 or contact me via e-mail by writing to HealthyJo@aol.com. Or visit my Healthy Exchanges Internet website at: http://www.healthyexchanges.com.

Healthy Exchanges recipes are a great way to begin—
but if your goal is living healthy for a lifetime,

You Need HELP!

JoAnna M. Lund's
Healthy Exchanges Lifetime Plan

"I lost 130 pounds and reclaimed my health by following a Four Part
Plan that emphasizes not only Healthy Eating, but also Moderate
Exercise, Lifestyle Changes and Goal-Setting, and most important of
all, Positive Attitude."

- If you've lost weight before but failed to keep it off . . .
- If you've got diabetes, high blood pressure, high cholesterol, or
  heart disease—and you need to reinvent your lifestyle . . .
- If you want to raise a healthy family and encourage good lifelong
  habits in your kids . . .

HELP is on the way!

- **The Support You Need** • **The Motivation You Want** •
  A Program That Works•

HELP: Healthy Exchanges Lifetime Plan is available
at your favorite bookstore.

Ever since I began stirring up Healthy Exchanges recipes, I wanted every dish to be rich in flavor and lively in taste. As part of my pursuit of satisfying eating and healthy living for a lifetime, I decided to create my own line of spices.

JO'S SPICES

. . . A Healthy Way to Spice Up Your Life™

JO's Spices are salt-, sugar-, wheat-, and MSG-free, and you can substitute them in any of the recipes calling for traditional spice mixes. If you're interested in hearing more about my special blends, please call Healthy Exchanges at 1-563-659-8234 for more information or to order. If you prefer, write to JO's Spices, c/o Healthy Exchanges, P.O. Box 80, DeWitt, IA 52742-0080.

Now That You've Seen
A Potful of Recipes, Why Not Order *The Healthy Exchanges Food Newsletter?*

If you enjoyed the recipes in this cookbook and would like to cook up even more of these "common folk" healthy dishes, you may want to subscribe to *The Healthy Exchanges Food Newsletter*.

This monthly 12-page newsletter contains 30-plus new recipes *every month,* in such columns as:

- Reader Exchange
- Reader Requests
- Recipe Makeover
- Micro Corner
- Dinner for Two

- Crock Pot Luck
- Meatless Main Dishes
- Rise & Shine
- Our Small World

- Brown Bagging It
- Snack Attack
- Side Dishes
- Main Dishes
- Desserts

In addition to all the recipes, other regular features include:

- The Editor's Motivational Corner
- Dining Out Question & Answer
- Cooking Question & Answer
- New Product Alert
- Success Profiles of Winners in the Losing Game
- Exercise Advice from a Cardiac Rehab Specialist
- Nutrition Advice from a Registered Dietitian
- Positive Thought for the Month

Just as in this cookbook, all *Healthy Exchanges Food Newsletter* recipes are calculated in three distinct ways: 1) Weight Loss Choices, 2) Calories with Fat and Fiber Grams, and 3) Diabetic Exchanges.

The cost for a one-year (12-issue) subscription is $22.50. To order, simply complete the form and mail to us **or** call our toll-free number and pay with your VISA or MasterCard.

_____ Yes, I want to subscribe to *The Healthy Exchanges Food Newsletter*

$22.50 Yearly Subscription Cost . . . . $_____

_____ Foreign orders please add $6.00 for money exchange and extra postage . . . . $_____

_____ I'm not sure, so please send me a sample copy at $2.50 . . . . $_____

Please make check payable to HEALTHY EXCHANGES or pay by VISA / MasterCard

CARD NUMBER: _____   EXPIRATION DATE: _____

SIGNATURE: _____

Signature required for all credit card orders.

Or Order Toll-Free, using your credit card, at 1-800-766-8961

NAME: _____   _____

ADDRESS: _____

CITY: _____   STATE: _____   ZIP: _____

TELEPHONE: (____) _____

If additional orders for the newsletter are to be sent to an address other than the one listed above, please use a separate sheet and attach to this form.

MAIL TO: **HEALTHY EXCHANGES**
P.O. BOX 80
DeWitt, IA 52742-0080

1-800-766-8961 For Customer Orders
1-563-659-8234 For Customer Service

Thank you for your order, and for choosing to become a part of the Healthy Exchanges Family!